To Kenneth, Jesus loves you and [handwritten inscription]

JOY COMES IN THE MORNING

A DAILY DEVOTIONAL GUIDE

JOAN CLAYTON

PublishAmerica
Baltimore

Softcover 9781630007881
PUBLISHED BY PUBLISHAMERICA, LLLP
www.publishamerica.com
Baltimore

Printed in the United States of America

ACKNOWLEDGEMENTS

Jesus is my Rock…a Rock that cannot be moved.
He is a Rock that holds me steady.
He is a place of safety…
a shield that stands off enemies.
He is my Fortress, my Light.
He is all I need, my all in all.
Yes, Jesus is my Rock.

He can be your Rock too!

DEDICATION

A Servant's Prayer

"Dear God,

Help me to live just for today. Yesterday is gone and tomorrow I cannot see. Let me be quick to express my love to others. Help me to memorize my husband's face and may I never take his love for granted.

Guide me to find happiness in simple pleasures, the soft sound of snow crunching underneath my feet, the cooing of a dove, the welcome dripping of rain against my window-pane.

Help me to minister Your love to a lost and dying world. Remove my pride and selfishness. May others see Your love manifested through me.

Teach me to number my days. May I make each moment count, for time is fleeting. Grant me deeper truths of Your heavenly Kingdom.

Bless my wonderful son Lane, who has given me so much love and help in writing this book.

In that wonderful name of Jesus. Amen."

JANUARY

January 1 Read Matthew 5:3-12

EMBRACE THE NEW YEAR WITH HOPE

Bible Thought: "...for the joy of the LORD is your strength (Nehemiah 8:10).

The New Year is an opportunity to expect the best, to look for the good, to see every trial as a challenge, and to grow in faith and courage. We are on a journey and the way we live this life determines our destiny.

Psalm 37 gives a wonderful blueprint for a successful year:

1. Do not fret. Stress is a killer. Think, *will this situation be important 100 years from now?* Let's do our best and God will do the rest.
2. Rest in God. How many burdens can one carry? Give them to him. He can carry them all.
3. Delight in the Lord. "He will give you the desires of your heart." (Verse 4)
4. Commit your way to the Lord. He is a "lamp unto your feet and a light unto your pathway" (Psalm 119:105).
5. Rest and be still. Patiently wait for guidance. Impatience brings anxiety.
6. Refrain from anger. Anger steals joy.

We have a brand New Year upon us. It has not been lived before. Make each day a masterpiece. Live it to the fullest. You have a chance to begin again in spite of past mistakes or regrets from last year.

Start anew and resolve to leave precious memories in the lives of others. Be joyful, grateful and cheerful.

Dear God, thank You for another year. May each day glorify You. In Jesus' name. Amen.

January 2 Read Psalm 34:1-10

A PRAYER FOR YOU IN THE NEW YEAR

Bible Thought: "The righteous cry, and the LORD heareth, and delivereth them out of all their troubles" (Psalm 34:17).

May you have courage to meet life's challenges, to hold on to God's promises and to refuse and reject the enemy's attacks on your God-given purpose.

May you walk in God's way with overcoming victory, forgetting the past and straining toward the future, looking with expectant hope of God's wonderful blessings.

I pray God's protection and favor upon you as you pursue God's plan for your life. May your days be filled with strong faith, an overcoming faith that defeats failure, trials and obstacles. When storms of life seem to be prevailing, I pray you will be able to say, "Blow, wind blow, but I will still be standing when the storm is over, because the Greater One lives in me."

I pray you are far from oppression and fear does not come near you, "God has not given you the spirit of fear but of power, and of love and of a sound mind" (2 Timothy 1:7).

I pray you will walk upon the "high places of the earth, for he has made your feet like hind's feet," and you will not stumble. (Psalm 18:33)

May all of your days be filled with the love of God.

Dear precious Lord, thank You for our time to live and may we break the chain of evil in our generation. May we never cease to pray for others. Help us to count their interest above our own. Blessed be the name of our wonderful Savior. His name is Jesus. Amen.

January 3 Read Jeremiah 29:11-15

GOD'S PLAN FOR YOU

Bible Thought: "There are many devices in a man's heart; nevertheless the counsel of the LORD, that shall stand" (Proverbs 19:21).

I firmly believe God has a purpose for every person born on this earth. I also believe the highest form of selfishness and immaturity is to say, "I wish I had never been born." To be given a chance at life is the highest form of love. To me, this earthly journey is a training ground...a time to learn to forgive, to laugh, to love, to bless and to encourage people. All of us have been given "x" amount of time to "lose our lives to find them." (Luke 17:33). The only thing we get to keep is what we have given away.

If the Lord had given me a choice to be born or not, I would exuberantly say, "Yes Lord. I will go to earth. I will take the risk. I will love. I may not be loved in return, but I will risk rejection and pain. It hurts to love and I cannot thank You enough for enduring such shame and pain for me."

Yes, God has a plan for each one of us. Let us seek forgiveness and overlook offenses. Trust in His plan. Let's fight the good fight of faith and complete the journey.

Thank the Lord for your time on earth and His plan for you.

Dear loving Savior, thank You for loving us, forgiving us and for Jesus who died for us. May we glorify His name in word, thought and deed while following Your plan for our lives. In that beautiful name... Jesus. Amen.

January 4 Read 2 Chronicles 7:14

PRAY WITHOUT CEASING

Bible Thought: "Confess your faults one to another, and pray one for another, that ye may be healed. The effective fervent prayer of a righteous man availeth much" (James 5:16).

Those who pray have a steadfast hope and trust in God's faithfulness despite problems and challenges. God responds when He is approached in true repentance and humility. Let us seek forgiveness for our nation and ourselves.

Prayer overcomes. People who pray hold this nation together. The mountain moving faith of prayer warriors accomplishes much.

I like to think when we pray for others a wall of love surrounds them. These walls are made with sincere care and concern. These "prayer walls" keep positive affirmations coming while giving a support system that embraces healing and well being. In times of crisis we realize how desperately we need prayers for our nation and for each other.

Praying for others requires sacrifice. It is motivated by love and is one of the highest pinnacles of unselfishness. Let us humbly fall to our knees, praying to God with honor, truth and respect.

We can light this nation. Prayer can change America. We serve a mighty God. He hears the prayers of His people.

Let your light shine with flames of faith.

Dear wonderful Lord, we humbly bow before You. Cleanse us with Your precious blood and light our fire again. In that beautiful name of Jesus. Amen.

January 5 Read Psalm 43

I AM DETERMINED

Bible Thought: "For the Lord GOD will help me; therefore shall I not be confounded: therefore have I set my face like a flint, and I know that I shall not be ashamed" (Isaiah 50:7).

I am determined:
- to seek the Lord with all my heart
- to look forward to the coming of Jesus
- to live each moment as if it were my very last
- to love and praise my Savior until my dying breath
- to tell everyone I see about the love and forgiveness of Jesus
- to find something good in every situation and in every person
- to leave this world a better place than it was when I came into it
- to forgive and release all hurts, injustices and pain inflicted upon me by others
- to live just for today, packing all the living, learning and loving into it that I can
- to strain toward the mark, pressing on and taking every opportunity to grow into a mature Christian
- to choose the words carefully that I say today, realizing that life and death are in the power of the tongue that causes many wounds

Dear heavenly Father, I come to You with praise and thanksgiving. Because of Your Son I have life and have it abundantly. Thank You for sending Him to a sinful dark world to die for all of us. I will honor You all of my days and live with You forever. In Jesus' beautiful wonderful name. Amen.

January 6 Read Romans 8:35-39

GOD'S LOVE IS FOREVER

Bible Thought: "The LORD hath appeared of old unto me, saying Yea, I have loved thee with an everlasting love: therefore with loving-kindness have I drawn thee" (Jeremiah 31:3).

The holidays are over. Tearful goodbyes are said. The house is strangely quiet. Yet my loved ones are never far away in my heart or prayers for there is no distance with those you love.

We are God's children and He feels the same way about us. He knows the inner recesses of our being. He delights in us. He joys over us with singing. We are precious in His sight. We are unique, the only pattern and He loves us just like we are. We don't have to be someone we aren't, keeping up a false front, trying to impress people or seek approval. You are you and I am me in God's love.

God will never leave or forsake and He will never allow our feet to stumble. You and I can soar with Him in heavenly places, living in the "secret place and dwelling under the shadow of the Almighty," who is our refuge, fortress and redeemer.

God gave His only Son to die for you and me. His love is forever.

Let us rejoice and shout it from the rooftops!

Dear God, we thank You for Your everlasting love and we praise You today for Jesus, our Savior. In His precious name. Amen.

January 7 Read Psalm 91

JOY IN SALVATION

Bible Thought: "O clap your hands, all ye people; shout unto God with the voice of triumph" (Psalm 47:1).

I witnessed an unforgettable event in childhood. It happened at a summer revival in a little church my grandmother attended. An elderly lady had one married son and his wife. The lady's son, daughter-in-love, and husband rarely came to church. The lady attended church regularly by herself and always sat near the front.

One night as the congregation sang "Just As I Am" at the end of the service the lady's son, his wife and the lady's husband came walking down the aisle to receive Jesus. The lady didn't even know they were there. When she saw them she literally shouted, running and crying all the way. She ran to her loved ones with hugs, kisses and tears. As I remember the whole congregation cried too. She had experienced the joy of her family's salvation and her cup had run over.

I recently witnessed another event that brought joy of salvation. A woman came forth from the baptismal waters crying with tears of happiness. She burst into sobs that were heard all over the building. She had just realized the depth of her commitment. She arose a new creature, on her "way to that fair land" with shouts of gratitude.

I am like that lady. If you hear me shouting, it's the joy of my salvation!

Dear precious Lord, thank You for the joy that dwells within us knowing we are on our way to live with You forever. In that wonderful, beautiful, marvelous name of our Savior. Jesus. Amen.

January 8 Read Psalm 31:1-3

JEHOVAH HIDES ME

Bible Thought: "But the LORD *is* my defense; and my God *is* the rock of my refuge" (Psalm 94:22).

My husband ordered a huge rock that had to be delivered and set with a crane. "It goes right there," he said. Then he designed small crossties around it and placed attractive shrubs on either side. We both enjoy the landscape.

This huge beautiful rock reminds me of a song we used to sing in our prayer group. "Jehovah hides me under the rock." I love that song and I love my rock. It is a symbol that causes me to remember Jesus is my Rock. He is not only the "Rock of my salvation," but also my Rock of life. He is my Rock in every trial or situation.

In my early morning quiet time this morning, my mind lingered back to all the things God has done for me. He never once left me. He makes "All things for good for those who love Him and are called according to His purpose" (Romans 8:28).

Are you in the midst of trails today? Remember God is your Refuge, your Fortress and your Rock.

Jehovah hides you under the Rock!

Dear wonderful Lord, thank You for hiding us under the "Rock" of Your protection and safety. We are still standing when the storm is over because of You, our steady "Rock". Thank You for Jesus and blessed be His name. Amen.

January 9 Read 1 Kings 19:9-12

UNEXPECTED GUIDANCE

Bible Thought: "Be still, and know that I am God; I will be exalted among the heathen, I will be exalted in the earth" (Psalm 46:10).

I had uneasiness about picking up scattered old boards of my husband's corral. I was at peace as long as I worked close to him, but as I looked at the mess that needed to be picked up before he could finish his fencing I ignored the feeling of apprehension.

I picked up a long, rotten, musty, weathered old board. I screamed and jumped back. There underneath the board lay a coiled rattlesnake. My husband came running with the shovel and killed it.

I realized then the source of my previous anxiety. There had been a warning, a check in my spirit.

Elijah heard the still small voice of God in the quiet of his restlessness. I need to do that too.

Are you seeking God's guidance? Get alone with God. Be still before the Lord and listen humbly before Him.

Wait quietly for His guidance because it may come when you least expect it.

Dear precious Lord, thank You for Your guidance. Help us to be still and listen. May we be sensitive to Your voice. In that wonderful of Jesus. Amen.

January 10 Read Psalm 91:1-8

IN THE PRESENCE OF ENEMIES

Bible Thought: "Ye are of God, little children, and have overcome them: because greater is he that is in you, than he that is in the world" (1 John 4:4).

A family of cats chose to live under our spreading evergreen bush. A tall yucca tree grew in the middle. A mother sparrow chose the top of that spiny dagger yucca tree to build her nest. She carefully intertwined her home between the dagger leaves of the tree.

I watched in amazement as the cats tried desperately to capture the mother bird and her babies, but they could climb just so far only to be gouged by the sharp arrows.Many times you and I are in the presence of our enemies. The enemy constantly tries to shoot those darts and daggers at us but we have a shield of faith and we dwell in our "Strong Tower." His name is Jesus.

The mother bird and all of us have a mission in life. We will not be distracted or discouraged.

I shed a tear when I saw the mother bird's children leave the nest for the last time, but since God watches over the sparrow and her children, I know he watches over my children and me.

Dear God, we are all your children and we thank You for surrounding us with your loving care. In Jesus' beautiful name. Amen.

January 11 Read 1 Kings 19:10-18

LIVE LIFE ON THE WINNING SIDE

Bible Thought: "I press toward the mark for the prize of the high calling of God in Christ Jesus" (Philippians 3:14).

We are winning! It may seem the enemy is gaining ground but every day I see honest hard working people who love the Lord. Despite all the bad news and controversy we are winning.

The enemy thrives on problems but he is no match for our God. Throughout the Bible God's people faced tremendous challenges. Ezra and his workers were a team of winners who realized a life of faith would not be easy but they never wavered nor compromised.

Elijah thought he was the only one left who loved God but God reminded him of the seven thousand who remained in love and obedience.

Jeremiah preached the same message for many years and never gave up. In times of opposition he just keep moving.

Why are we winning? Those who oppose us oppose God and God always triumphs. That makes us winners. We may be only one person in the world, but we may also be the world to one person.

We will fight the good fight of faith and when the battle is over and our life's work on earth is done, we will win the prize, wearing a crown of glory.

I just love to win. Don't you?

Dear precious Lord, thank You for equipping us with heavenly armor to win life's battles. With You, "No weapon formed against us prospers." In that name of all names. His name is Jesus. Amen.

January 12 Read Psalm 133

GOD'S FAMILY

Bible Thought: "A devout man and one that feared God with all his house, which gave much alms to the people, and prayed to God always" (Acts 10:2).

The family is God's idea. His plan cannot be improved upon. Spending time with family brings much joy.

Think of seeing your grownup children when they have been away a long time. Your happiness can hardly be contained. It is the same in God's family. Time spent in God's presence brings blessings untold. Meeting with God's family brings encouragement and builds relationships with one another.

The journey of life is temporary at best. Eternity is forever. The gift of salvation is a free gift, a treasure of love from a loving God. All He asks in return is our love and faithfulness to Him and to our earthly families.

Be in God's family. Give Him a home in your heart. It's the greatest gift of your entire life. You will

See Jesus today in a little child's face.

See His love in a mother's embrace.

See Jesus today beside a hospital bed.

See His love when the homeless are fed.

See Jesus today in a dew-kissed rose,

See the nature in everything that grows.

See the only way to joy and happiness.

Dear precious Lord, we thank You today for our earthly family. What a day it will be when we are reunited in heaven. We will be with You and our heavenly family forever and ever. It's all because of Jesus. Blessed be His beautiful name and it's in that name we pray. Amen.

January 13 Read Psalm 122

LESSONS FROM A CHURCH PEW

Bible Thought: "LORD, I have loved the habitation of thy house, and the place where thine honour dwelleth" (Psalm 27:8)

Memories of faith filled people living simply godly lives blessed my childhood. Maybe that's why I bought an old church pew. I put it in my patio that overlooks my flower garden. It's a perfect place to spend quiet moments. Somehow I can still hear beloved hymns and I wonder how many people sat on this same bench, asking Jesus to come into their hearts. My church pew is perfect for meditation and I delight in God's presence.

As I pondered I realized a life living for Jesus leaves no regrets. So I must guard my faith. It is my lifeline. I must put God first. I want to face each trial with hope and faith in my heart.

My desire is to share with others the joy and hope of a godly blessed life.

Please never stop praying because the answer is on the way. God knows your heart and He listens.

I learned many things while meditating in the quiet of my garden.

I love the view from my church pew. You may not have a personal pew but praying anywhere will do.

Dear precious Lord, You are always in the garden of our hearts. You make everything beautiful. Thank You for our beautiful Savior. In His wonderful name…Jesus. Amen.

January 14 Read Philippians 4:6-9

STABILITY IN GOD'S WORD

Bible Thought: "Heaven and earth will pass away but my words will not pass away" (Matthew 24:35).

The Bible has an answer for every problem that confronts mankind. Wouldn't it be grand if everyone could recognize this Holy Book has the key to life? When biblical principles are supplied success appears.

In this modern-day world of bio chemicals and nuclear threats, there is no security apart from God. Without God's Word, people are tossed to and fro in confusion, not knowing what to do or what to believe.

Dictators have tried to destroy it. Communism has tried to annihilate it. Atheists have denied it and opponents have tried to discount it.

In spite of all the corruption we see, there is hope. His name is Jesus. Daily Bible reading provides strength, comfort, peace, joy and direction for our lives. Let's open the Bible. It is filled with hidden treasures. Believe and receive. It provides the standard of behavior and any deviation from its principles results in devastation.

The Bible is the only stability of our existence.

Dear God, thank You for the Bible. Guide us to hide it in our hearts forever. In Jesus' wonderful name. Amen.

January 15 Read Psalm 100

NO FINER GIFT

Bible Thought: "And now abideth faith, hope, charity, these three; but the greatest of these is charity" (1 Corinthians 13:13).

The gift of love is available to all of us and there is no finer gift. One by one, I have lost a grandparent, an aunt, an uncle and my parents. The brevity of time has brought me to the realization of the most important things in life.

I must be sure to tell loved ones what they mean to me. I want to see their needs are met, to be sure thy are cared for to make their days brighter. They once sacrificed for me and I'm sure that took a lot of patience.

As much as I loved my family there is an even greater love. His name is Jesus. It's because of His love the greatest sacrifice known to mankind occurred. When I think of the agony, suffering and shame Jesus endured for me, I can hardly bear it. When I see TV clips, passion plays, or movies portraying Jesus I burst into tears. However, they cannot make it as real as it really happened.

What a Savior! Can you fathom the depths of His love? Can you imagine the pain of it all? Can you hear the jeering soldiers as they inflict unbearable wounds?

Jesus' love is stronger than death and no finer gift could be given.

If you have not accepted that love, the time is now. Jesus is waiting at the door of your heart.

Dear precious Lord, words are not enough to tell You of our love. Thank You for Jesus who willingly gave His life to save all of us. We want to love You with every breath. In Jesus' beautiful name. Amen.

January 16 Read Philippians 4:4-8

REJOICE IN THE LORD

Bible Thought: "Be glad in the LORD, O ye righteous: for praise is comely for the upright" (Psalm 32:11).

We live in tumultuous times. In every turn the world seems to give only bad news but I have "Good News." For those who love the Lord, the best is yet to be. We should be the happiest people on earth.

God "makes our feet like hind feet and we walk on the high places." (Habakkuk 3:19) The "joy of the Lord is our strength." (Nehemiah 8:10) "We are the head and not the tail." (Deuteronomy 28:44). "God supplies all we need according to His riches in glory." (Philippians 4:19)..."let the weak say, *I am strong.*" (Joel 3:10) He is our "High Tower" and we run to Him. (Proverbs 18:10)

Should I say more? These are just a few of His promises. Our job is to be joyful. Happiness is temporal. Joy lasts forever.

Let's be the kind of people that others want what we have, in good times or bad. God never loses His children.

We know where we're going and our joy can cause someone else to want to go with us.

Sing today. Be joyful. We have been redeemed.

Rejoice with me today and every day.

Dear Lord, thank You for the joy in our hearts. May we be joyful with others as we share our faith. In the name above all names. His name is Jesus.

January 17 Read 2 Timothy 4:7-8

LAST TIME OR FIRST TIME

Bible Thought: "To everything there is a season, and a time to every purpose under the heaven (Ecclesiastes 3:1).

My heart ached when we moved Aunt Floy to a rest home.

"This will be the last night she will spend in her own home," I moaned. "I guess there's a last time for everything."

"Or a first time," my husband added. "She may like the rest home. I know she will enjoy the good food and the care. She will make new friends. She will not have stress or the responsibilities she has had. The last time leads to a best first time. It all depends on how you look at it." My husband amazed me as I pondered what he said. I began to see last times and first times as part of life. When that loved one's body is put to rest in the ground it seems like the last time, but to God's child it is the "first time" to burst into the "Light."

It is the first time to experience the joy of eternal bliss, free from pain and all sorrow.

It all depends on how you look at it.

Dear precious Lord, thank You for Your wonderful grace. May each one of us have ever increasing faith, while knowing the "last time leads to the best time," because we will meet You face to face and live with You forever. It's all because of Jesus. We praise You today and every day for such a precious gift. In Him. Amen.

January 18 Read John 4:7-13

LIVING WATER

Bible Thought: "And he shall be like a tree planted by the rivers of water that bringeth forth his fruit in his season; his leaf also shall not wither; and whatsoever he doeth shall prosper" (Psalm 1:3).

A large main water pipe in our town broke in the freezing temperatures at midnight. Water came gushing out, covering streets with ice. The ice melted about mid-morning but the water had to be shut off for twenty-four hours before repairs could be made. Men worked all night in the cold. Stores sold out of precious water. Many drove to an adjacent town to wait it out.

How many times do we take God's gifts for granted," I pondered. In emergencies we realize how desperately the basics of life are needed. Some do not appreciate things until they are taken away.

I am so grateful for air to breathe, food to eat, and yes, good clean water to drink. More than that I want the "Living Water," the spring of the water of life. (Revelation 21:6)

I want to be a tree planted by the streams of water. I want to pray, study and receive "cleansing by the washing with water through the word." (Ephesians 5:26)

Are you thirsty? I am.

Let's drink from the "fountain of life" and never thirst again.

Dear God, thank You for water for our physical existence but more than that thank You for the "river of the water of life" You have prepared for us. In Jesus' beautiful name. A men.

January 19 Read 1 Thessalonians 4:14-18

I'M A BELIEVER

Bible Thought: "He that believeth on me, as the scripture hath said, out of his belly shall flow rivers of living water" (John 7:38).

In his day, my great-grandfather would have never believed a man could go to the moon. Certainly his ancestors didn't even dream of such a thing as an automobile. Some in Bible times didn't believe either, even when they witnessed miracles.

I'm a believer. Jesus lives in my heart. I have the blessed hope that when I leave this life, I will live with Him forever. No, I'm not perfect, but that is why Jesus came...to save us from the slavery of sin, and that includes me. That includes you. What ablessed hope. The grave is not the end. Jesus endured the cruelest form of torture for everyone who will accept His loving sacrifice. We cannot fathom the extent of His great love. He is a resurrected loving Savior.

I believe every person is born for a purpose. I want to fulfill my purpose in God.

I love to read about heaven in Revelation 22:5, "And there shall be no night there; and they need no candle, neither light of the sun; for the Lord God giveth them light and they shall reign for ever and ever.

Dear God, thank You for Your Word to teach us, Your Holy Spirit to guide us, and for Jesus, who died for us. What an awesome God You are. We praise You today with all our hearts. In that wonderful name of Jesus. Amen

January 20 Read Psalm 103:17-22

REJOICE...WE WIN

Bible Thought: "But let all those that put their trust in thee rejoice: let them ever shout for joy, because thou defendest them: let them also that love thy name be joyful in thee" (Psalm 5:11).

Jesus sees you as a person of great worth. He sees in you a person of great qualities, deep resources and capabilities. He sees the best in you with greatness and promise.

Should we not shout for joy and sing praises? Nothing can defeat you. You are a winner.

With Jesus you have peace, refuge, triumph, strength, restoration, encouragement, mercy, grace, forgiveness, life, victory, delight, hope, gladness, love, righteousness and wholeness. Should I say more?"

Let us rejoice. We have everything to be happy about. Living life with gusto brings many happy moments. Yes, we have trials in life but does a bad mood help?

Be happy today and thank God for His many blessings. Find something beautiful today and be grateful.

Dear precious Lord, thank You for watching over us and meeting our every need. We love and praise You today and give You gratitude with every fiber of our being. In Jesus' beautiful name. Amen.

January 21 Read Genesis 29:10-13

HUGS ARE SPECIAL

Bible Thought: "…Paul called unto him the disciples, and embraced them, and departed for to go unto Macedonia" (Acts 20:1).

My second grade students reached up as far as they could to hug me. I bent over to hug them back. I think hugs made them learn better.

I would be lost if I didn't have hugs from friends and loved ones. Hugs make me happy. Hugs tell me someone loves me. Hugs fill me with delight.

Hugging is one of the human ways to express affection. I'm so thankful we have arms that can hug and be hugged. That special touch restores well-being.

I learned to hug Jesus from my four-year-old granddaughter. Kallie was hugging herself one day. When I asked her what she was doing she replied, "I'm hugging Jesus. He's in my heart you know."

Kallie is right. Jesus lives in you and me and He deserves all of our praise and devotion for the sacrifice He made to give us eternal life.

When I have trouble relaxing and falling asleep, I think of the "everlasting arms" of Jesus surrounding me and holding me tight with hugs. The next thing I know it is morning…another exciting day to hug Jesus.

Dear God, we cannot express our deep love for You with mere words. May we embrace You with love and adoration with every breathing moment. Thank You for the unspeakable gift of Your love. In the name of Jesus. Amen.

January 22 Read Psalm 27:1-5

BLESSINGS IN YOUR HEART

Bible Thought: "Every good gift and every perfect gift is from above, and cometh down from the Father of lights, with whom is no variableness, neither shadow of turning" (James 1:17).

We have lived in the same house on the same corner for 46 years. The house is too small when our sons and families come home but it's home and I'm thankful.

Our yard is too big since our sons grew up but it is just right for grandchildren. Birds that stop for a while on their migratory journey remind me every season has its own and I love the way the snow adorns our pine trees in the beauty of winter. Spring comes with the fragrance of rain. Summer and autumn add to God's beauty and it makes me happy.

Our house is one of memories, triumphs, victories, hard places, laughter, tears and love. The Lord has been faithful and I bow my knees for my many blessings.

Let us be thankful for each day. Be thankful for the bountiful beauty of nature, for friends, for family and most of all for God's love. His guiding light guides His children through every conflict.

Pray and welcome Jesus in your home for where He is love abounds.

Make your house a house of blessings in your heart.

Dear precious Lord, our hearts spill over with thankfulness. We give thanks to You today and every day. Most of all we're thankful for our Savior. His name is Jesus. Amen.

January 23 Read Psalm 36:5-10

MAKE THE MOST OF YOUR DAY

Bible Thought: "...I am come that they might have life, and that they might have it more abundantly" (John 10:10).

Each day of life is a gift. Making the most of that gift is up to us. Creating happy memories leave no regrets. The time to love is all too short at best. Making the most of your day adds zest to your life and to those around you. Be thankful for today. Whatever is going on in your life, the good far outweighs the bad.

Find someone to bless. The blessing will return to you. I like to play the "smiling game." I have yet to find a person who will not smile back.

Sing a happy song. "Is anyone among you afflicted? Let him pray. Is he merry? Let him sing psalms." (James 5:13-14)

Embrace life. I call it "squeezing life." Life is delicious and each day brings a new adventure to live life with enthusiasm. Getting excited about life is contagious.

Living today is the day to make meaningful memories. Making the most of your day is within your grasp. After all, today has not been lived before. You can make everyday a good day because God has given you this gift.

Dear God, we thank You for life and for the many blessings You bestow. May we never take life for granted and may we always be ever so grateful for Jesus who died for us.

In His beautiful name. Amen.

January 24 Read Luke 13:24-30

A WASTED LIFE

Bible Thought: " For the nation and kingdom that will not serve thee shall perish; yea, those nations shall be utterly wasted" (Isaiah 60:12).

I watched a famous athletic celebrity talk to teenagers recently. With an emotionally packed trembling voice he told the crowd not to model after him. He had undergone a liver transplant caused from alcohol abuse. His voice trailed to a whisper as he talked about his wasted life.

My heart ached for the man. One of the realities of life is what one sows, one reaps. God forgives but consequences remain.

When we stand before God on judgment day and He asks us what we did with our lives we want to be able to say we made our lives count for His Kingdom.

All of us are memory makers. We have a sphere of influence, for good or evil.If you feel you have wasted your life it is not too late. God is merciful, gracious and forgiving. Turn from sin and turn to God. Your sins will be dropped in the sea of forgetfulness.

You can start a brand new life.

Dear gracious God, help us to realize time is fleeting and the real treasures are the ones we send to heaven. Thank You for Jesus and may we always follow His example in our time on earth. In Jesus' wonderful name. Amen.

January 25 Read Isaiah 62:1-5

MY BRIDEGROOM

Bible Thought: "Turn, O backsliding children, saith the LORD; for I am married unto you…" (Jeremiah 3:14).

I linger in Your presence.
Teach me how to love You.
Thank You for my secret place.
Who is like unto You, O Lord?
You make every day a masterpiece.
In the depths of my being, gratitude reigns.
May my every breath honor and glorify You.
You put a song in my heart and I'm filled with joy.
The joy I feel spills and runs over blessing me again.
I am not my own. In the deepest part of me I know I belong to You.
Without You I would be hopelessly lost, with no purpose for existence.

You watch over me with loving kindness. You will never leave nor forsake me.

You are the Strength of my life, my Refuge, my Rock. You hide me under Your wings.

I praise You with my whole being. I magnify You with every fiber of my mind, body and soul.

I love You, adore You and bow down before You. You are my beautiful bridegroom and I am married to You!

Dear precious Lord, You are our hidden treasure, more than silver or gold and more costly than diamonds we could hold. You are the Prince of Peace, our love, our hope and our destiny. Thank You for Jesus our beautiful bridegroom. In His name. Amen.

January 26 Read Psalm 26:8-12

GOD'S HOUSE

Bible Thought: "Blessed is the man whom thou choosest, and causest to approach unto thee, that he may dwell in thy courts: we shall be satisfied with the goodness of thy house, even of thy holy temple" (Psalm 65:4).

A godly house has love, joy and peace in it. This house is not moved because it is filled with God's Word.

God's house is washed in the blood of the Lamb and is sprinkled on the doorposts of the heart. This house shields and protects from outside wounds. The King of Glory reigns here for this house is a fortress from adversity.

This house has walls of forgiveness and rooms of love, clothed with garments of righteousness.

This house is filed with sunshine for the Light of the Son continually brightens lives. It is wired with the power of the Holy Spirit. It has doors and they open with arms of love. Other houses may crumble, but this house stands firm and secure for God is honored here. This house is cemented with God's faithfulness.

This house will live forever, for nothing shall ever tear this house down. It is engraved in the palm of God's hands.

Who lives in this house? Those who allow the Holy Spirit to live in these earthly temples.

Dear precious Lord, thank You for living in these temples of clay. May we strive to honor You in these temporary vessels. May we never grieve You, but praise and serve You all of our days. In Jesus' beautiful name. Amen.

January 27 Read James 1:1-8

PERSISTENCE IS THE KEY

BIBLE THOUGHT: "Because he hath set his love upon me, therefore will I deliver him: I will set him on high, because he hath known my name" (Psalm 91:14).

Nothing great is going to happen in this life without persistence. Persistence compels us to get up, dust ourselves off and keep going. Falling down doesn't make us failures…staying down does.

Be determined to stay in the winner's circle. Let's not get down in the dumps. Press on. Endure. Try again. Fight back. Keep going, no matter how hard the struggle. Run to win. Set your face like a flint and plow right through. Jesus did not quit. Praise God He didn't. He sacrificed for you and me.

I've been called "God's Cheerleader." My middle son calls me "The Preacher." To me those names are compliments. Please don't tell me I'm a dreamer…a distorter of reality. I call it faith. Please don't try to take persistence away from me…you can't. It is as precious as gold.

We are winners. We are on our way to that "Fair Land" with persistence. We will not put up, shut up or give up.

Get out of our way. We're coming through. The Greater One lives in us.

Look out world…here we come. We're persistent, and that's the key.

I've read the last page.

Yea! We win.

Dear God, You are our Champion and with Your armor and the sword of the Spirit we are over comers. In the power of Jesus' name. Hallelujah! Amen.

January 28 Read Malachi 3:1-6

THE ONE WHO NEVER CHANGES

Bible Thought: "Jesus Christ the same yesterday, and today, and for ever" (Hebrews 13:8).

The Bible reading today talks about changes, a time for different things to happen. I find I resist change. I like things the way they are. Changes challenge my comfort zone. Friends move away. Children grow up and leave. Changes in technology are hard for me to keep up with. My new computer is almost out of date. Technology has developed faster than I can learn it. Just when I feel I've mastered new concepts, they become obsolete. The advancement of technology in the last several decades is overwhelming. New devices demand the "know how" to go with it.

I find I must change in adapting to newer computer skills. However, this one thing I know. Jesus is my refuge and my fortress. In a changing world, He is my unchanging Lord. It gives me peace to know Jesus is the one factor in my life that never changes. He will never leave me. He is in control and will make good out of what seems to me a hardship. He is the One who never changes.

Dear precious Lord, thank You for Your steadfastness, faithfulness and love. We can trust You because You change not. You are the most wonderful "technology" of all. How we praise You today for Jesus. In His name. Amen."

January 29 Psalm 104:31-35

THE SEASONS OF LIFE

Bible Thought: "And he changeth the times and the seasons: he removeth kings, and setteth up kings: he giveth wisdom unto the wise, and knowledge to them that know understanding" (Daniel 2:21).

Our lives are like seasons. From babyhood to adulthood, middle age or older, each season brings unique rewards and blessings. A baby's birth brings such joy. Young adulthood is so exciting. Middle age brings another generation. Older age comes before we know it, yet for the believer, it is the best time of all.

So let's relish all the seasons in our lives. Be a happy memory maker as you go about your day. Take time to breathe deeply on that early morning walk. Enjoy God's landscape of many dazzling colors. We only have one chance at life. Let's make the most of it by making life a masterpiece.

The change of seasons gives me happiness and I savor each one. Let's live each season with love and thanksgiving. Count the daily blessings with joy and gratitude for another day of life.

Greet your day with joyfulness because it's another day to be happy in whatever stage of life you're in. With that attitude happiness comes with the changes in your life.Each day is a gift. Open it with wonder!

Dear precious Lord, we thank You for earthly life, but more than that we thank You for

Jesus. What a day it will be to be with Him in glory. In that name above all names…

Jesus. Amen.

January 30 Read Revelation 21:1-6

NEVER SAY GOODBYE

Bible Thought: "Precious in the sight of the LORD is the death of his saints" (Psalms 116:15).

Our beloved friend left this earth. His example and influence upon lives cannot be numbered. Although he had a business of his own, he managed to minister to others. His layman sermons and Sunday school lessons will long be remembered. His life demonstrated his love for his fellow man. In the "twinkling of an eye" our friend went from death to life...eternal life.

The child of God never says goodbye for the last time. For the believer death is a reward.

I shall know Jesus when I see Him. I shall look upon His face.
His eyes so filled with love, compassion and such grace.
I shall know Him when I see Him for there will be no tears.
All the trials and heartaches will be of yesteryear.
I shall know Him when I see Him this life long friend of mine
His love cannot be measured. It endures the test of time.

Dear heavenly Father, thank You for heaven, a place of pure delight. Thank You that we never say goodbye for the last time. We shall see our Savior face to face. In His glorious name. Amen.

January 31 Read Psalm 23

AFRAID TO DIE, AFRAID TO LIVE

Bible Thought: "For this God is our God for ever and ever: he will be our guide even unto death" (Psalm 48:14.

I knew a dear lady who had been told by her doctor that she didn't have long to live. The lady went to the funeral director and planned her funeral. When all the plans had been made she shook the man's hand and said, "Now that I've fixed my dying, I'm ready to live."

She revealed a lot of truth in that statement. The dear lady had no fear because she knew her risen Savior. She had secured her future many years before.

It has been said, "If you are afraid to die, you are afraid to live." This statement puzzled me. I finally realized that once I settle my eternity with Jesus. I am free from the sting of death. I live in Jesus and He lives in me. Knowing this makes my life joyful. Every day is an exciting adventure.

I see each day as an opportunity to share Jesus with others.

Have you told someone about Jesus lately?

Dear wonderful God, we pray for zestful living today. Empower us to witness to those who do not know You. Help us to tell the world of Your Son. His name is Jesus. In His beautiful name. Amen.

FEBRUARY

February 1 Read Psalm 146

A GIFT FROM THE HEART LASTS FOREVER

Bible Thought: "Children's children are the crown of old men; and the glory of children are their fathers" (Proverbs 17:6).

I unwrapped a gift to find a letter from Jody's heart. My voice broke and tears fell as my tall handsome grandson read it aloud to the family. "I am so thankful that my grandfather passed on a name to be proud of to my father, who in turn passed it on to me. How many grandfathers not only leave a legacy for their grandsons with a name they can be proud of, but also one they can read to their children's children? Not many. I am forever thankful that I am blessed with a Savior, Jesus Christ. Second to such a wonderful gift, I am thankful for grandparents who have helped guide me from my youth. Love, from Jody."

My gift from Jody's heart is embedded upon my heart forever. Yet there is another One I love who has given not only His heart, but also His life. His sacrificial gift has sealed my redemption. I am on my way to glory.

I have marked my descendants for the Lord Jesus. I will be with Jody and all my loved ones forever. We will praise our Lord for eternity.

You come too.

Dear wonderful Lord, Thank You for Your plan for the family. We love our loved ones but our love for You far surpasses this world. Thank You for so many blessings. Most of all thank You for Jesus, the gift to the world. In His beautiful name. Amen."

February 2 Read Psalm 112:1-6

WHAT IS IN YOUR TRUNK OF MEMORIES?

Bible Thought: "Then they that feared the LORD spake often one to another: and the LORD hearkened, and heard it, and a book of remembrance was written before him for them that feared the LORD and that thought upon his name" (Malachi 3:16).

Going through my trunk one day
I stopped to read and then
Memories of my life appeared,
Blessing me again.

I lingered on some photos
Of those no longer here.
I thanked God for the time
I had with those so dear.

I found my Granddad's Bible.
It's pages old and torn.
My name is written in that book
On the day that I was born.

I closed the trunk remembering
Our lives are short at best.
So fill your trunk with goodness
And God will do the rest!

Dear heavenly Father, we thank You for the life You have given us to live and for all the loved ones You put in our paths. May we look to You for guidance all along the way. Thank You for our precious Savior. His name is Jesus. Amen.

February 3 1 John 5:1-5

VICTORIOUS TESTIMONY

Bible Thought: "Cast thy burden upon the LORD, and he shall sustain thee: he shall never suffer the righteous to be moved" (Psalm 55:22).

If I worry, I am saying, "God, this is too big for you to handle," and it grieves Him. Please say with me: "From this moment on I put everything in God's hands. I relinquish my life to Him. I hide God's Word in my heart and I stand, immovable upon His promises."

God is on your side. You are sheltered in His arms of love. If God is for you and His name is higher than anything, what shall you fear? He will never leave you. You are His and He is yours. God spared His own Son and that makes you special and valuable.Because Jesus lives in you, you have His righteousness. Because Jesus has your heart, you can "jump through a troop and leap over a wall." Nothing is impossible for you. You "can do all things through Christ who strengthens you." Let Him walk with you and tell you of His love. You are the called according to His purpose and He will equip you for that purpose.

You "overcome by the blood of the Lamb and the word of your testimony."

Dear precious Lord, who is like unto You, O God? You are the sweetest Rose of Sharon, the Daystar in our lives, the Glory and the Lifter of our heads. Thank You for the overcoming victory. It's all because of Jesus. In His beautiful name. Amen.

February 4 Read Philippians 4:4-9

GOD IS STILL IN CONTROL

Bible Thought: "Nay, in all these things we are more than conquerors through him that loved us" (Romans 8:37).

I have never heard such bad news before in my lifetime. Bad news tries its ugly best to disturb our peace.

Disappointments and heartaches do come. Struggles and conflicts come unexpected in this journey of life and a daily diet of problems brings depression and despair. It makes me temporarily forget this planet is not our permanent home.

Good news is seldom told in the media and that blinds the beauty and blessings in life. I must say it again, "We always have more blessings than problems. We are rich in family, friends and most of all, Jesus."

Life is precious and it is beautiful. Despite the daily bombardment of calamities the sky is still blue and mockingbirds still sing. Have you ever noticed mockingbirds sing through life regardless of whatever happens? They never seem to lose their song, even when hungry cats sneak up. We can learn a valuable lesson from our feathered friends with their little birdbrains.

I am thankful to live in a wonderful place filled with loving, caring people. I am thankful for a God who will never leave or forsake His children.

The next time you hear disturbing news remember God is still in control.

Dear Lord, forgive us for not trusting You. Your promises are "Yes and Amen."

Empower us to keep Your Word in our hearts. In Jesus' beautiful name. Amen.

February 5 Read Proverbs 16:20-28

HAPPINESS IS KNOWING JESUS

Bible Thought: "Where there is no vision, the people perish: but he that keepeth the law, happy is he" (Proverbs 29:18).

I learned a valuable lesson in happiness from some special people. "Miss Bea" is a wonderful happy friend in the rest home. She is extremely active for her 93 years. She held me close the day I had to enter my two aunts in the nursing home where she resides. My tears were falling on her feet as she reassured me she would see after them.

Miss Bea never failed to give me a report in the weeks and months that followed. She noticed how my aunts were eating, how they were sleeping and how they were enjoying the activities.

My beautiful friend is everyone's favorite. She told me her source of happiness. "Honey, someone can have everything in the world and still be miserable. Take me; the Lord has blessed me so much. I have a wonderful place to stay, good food to eat and people to take care of me. That's why I'm so happy!"

Later in the day, my granddaughters were enjoying the fall beauty as they laughed and tossed golden leaves back to God. Suddenly they stopped and hugged themselves.

"What are you doing?" I casually asked.

"We're hugging Jesus. He's in our hearts you know. That's why we're happy."

Traci 6, Kallie 3, and Miss Bea 93, all have a lot in common.

Happiness is seeing Jesus everywhere.

Dear God, thank You for the joy You bring. May we be generous with our joy by sharing it with others. In Jesus' precious name. Amen.

February 6 Read Psalm 25:1-10

A PSALM TO MY GOD

Bible Thought: "Let every thing that hath breath praise the LORD. Praise ye the LORD"
(Psalm 150:6).

My God will never leave me He lives in me. He knows every hair upon my head. He knows my every heartbeat.

He knows me inside out with all my faults and loves me anyway. My God is always there in the darkest hour and in the brightest day.

He joys over me with singing. He fills me with joy and that joy bubbles up and runs over. He renews my strength and I soar like eagles.

No other god is like my God. He is healing to my flesh and health to all my bones.My God gives me peace, well being and sound mind. My God is the King of Kings and the Lord of lords.

When my physical body is laid to rest, my spirit will go to my God and I will be with Him forevermore. I shout hosannas and praise to the Lamb of God who died for me. I will sing throughout endless ages to my God.

The power of the cross,
Resides in you and me.
For on a dark and lonely hill
Jesus died at Calvary.

Dear heavenly Father, let Your mighty works flow through us and may You be exalted in every way. In that name above all names. Jesus. Amen.

February 7 Read Psalm 36:5-9

THIS IS THE DAY

Bible Thought: "O bless our God, ye people, and make the voice of his praise to be heard (Psalm 66:8).

Morning breaks with enthusiasm and all nature acknowledges God's gift of life. Dewdrops of God's love sprinkle the earth with the promise of a new day.

I am valuable today because Jesus died for me. I want to make my day count. I am not just a number. I am a person who has sold out to Jesus. I am a unique person in His sight.

I want every thought to be of Him, glorifying Him in all I say and do. When I stumble and fall He picks me up. I begin again with a stronger resolve.

He is on my side. He loves me. He guides my steps because I abide in Him and I dwell in the "secret place."

I awaken with heartfelt praise to my Savior. I sing to Him with joy. He restores my soul and lifts me to a higher place.

He is ever mindful of me. He joys over me with singing. I delight in Him and He gives me the desires of my heart.

This is the day to rejoice.

I am one day closer to heaven.

Dear Lord, may the joy that dwells within us bubble up and reach out to everyone we meet today. In Jesus' name…that wonderful name. Amen.

February 8 Read Psalm 37:1-7

A LESSON IN TRUST

Bible Thought: "Trust ye in the LORD for ever, for in the LORD **JEHOVAH** is everlasting strength"(Isaiah 26:4).

We found a little starved kitten whose fright kept him from food. After many days his hunger won out. He allowed the slightest touch while eating. Even though we were his refuge and his sustenance, he had decided no one was trustworthy.

Finally, little by little he allowed longer touches that let us pet him while hearing a faint purr. He became part of the family and brought us many blessings.

How much this little kitten has taught me about trusting. I must come to the Lord and trust Him. He nourishes and holds me up with His righteous right hand. He is the strength of my life. He is my Light in a world of darkness.

Like the kitten, the world comes crashing in around me at times. I run to the Lord to rest in Him, knowing He holds me up in His everlasting arms. He is always trustworthy.

My kitten ran with joy to greet me this morning. He trusts me.

I run with joy to my "Master" too.

Trust in the Lord and acknowledge Him,

No matter what you see.

Living by faith is the only way

To live in victory!

Dear God, may we trust you unconditionally each day. Thank you for Your everlasting love Thank You for Jesus who died for all of us. In His wonderful name. Amen.

February 9 Read Psalm 29

LISTEN TO THE STILL SMALL VOICE

Bible Thought: "And after the earthquake a fire; but the LORD was not in the fire; and after the fire a still small voice" (1 Kings 19:12).

We were leaving the restaurant when a lady stopped me. She told me her name and when she told me the name of the tall man beside her. I had a "glory" fit. He was one of my students in the second grade many years ago. I hugged him and said, "How did you recognize me?"

"When I heard your voice something in me clicked and I thought to myself, that is Mrs. Clayton." I had not seen my ex-student since the second grade but he remembered the sound of my voice.

I immediately thought of Elijah running from Jezebel's threats but the still small voice came to him with provisions.

I also thought about how we use our voice today. The tone of frustration, negativity, anger, anxiety and impatience brings hurt feelings and pain. I learned in a career of teaching that soft words solve many problems. I would have felt ashamed and sorry if my student had remembered me by loud critical tones.

The enemy of our souls comes with haste, impatience, and criticism. He compels us to hurry in making decisions. Let us take time to seek the Lord for prayer and wisdom. Listen today for that "still small voice."

Dear Lord, thank You for Your still soft voice that empowers us to listen in obedience and fellowship with You. In Jesus' name. Amen.

February 10 Read Isaiah 62:1-5

A NEW NAME

Bible Thought: "He that hath an ear, let him hear what the Spirit saith into the churches; To him that overcometh will I give to eat of the hidden manna, and will give him a white stone, and in the stone a new name written, which no man knoweth saving he that receiveth it" (Revelation 2:17).

We thought a long time about the name we would give each son. Each of our three boys are so special and the name had to be just right. Names have special meanings. My husband's name, "Emmit," means "diligent one." My name, Joan, "means "Gods gracious gift. I love that. I truly want to be a gift to Him.

In heaven we will have a new special name given to us by the Lord. Think of it. The Lord Himself will give us a name and only He and you will know the name.

Names seem to run in cycles and popularity in this life, but God will give us His own unique name with a special meaning.

Our God is so creative and original that no two of us will have the same name.

Truly, our God is an awesome God!

Give your heart to Jesus today. You will have a new name (born again) here and a new name in heaven.

Dear precious Lord, thank You that through Jesus we can have a new life and a new name. In His wonderful name. Amen.

February 11 Read Exodus 15:1-7

A NEW LIFE

Bible Thought: "But thanks be to God, which giveth us the victory through our Lord Jesus Christ" (1Corinthians 15:57).

You are forgiven. Gone are the sins that beset you. Your old life has died. Your life is hidden in Jesus. You no longer live but Jesus lives in you. That same power that raised Jesus from the dead lives in you. He is never defeated. Neither are you. He is the glory and lifter of your head. Through Him you can do all things. You are more than a conqueror.

Your enemies come at you one way, but they flee seven ways. A thousand fall at your side and ten thousand at your right hand, but they do not come near you. You are girded with truth and have on the breastplate of righteousness. Your feet are shod with the gospel of peace. You have the shield of faith, quenching all the fiery darts of the enemy. You wear the helmet of salvation and the sword of the Spirit.

You overcome by the blood of the Lamb and the Word of your testimony. Your God reigns. You abide under His shadow and dwell in the secret place.

Rejoice that your name is written in the Lamb's Book of Life.

Because of Jesus, you have a new life!

Dear wonderful Lord, praise rises up and spills to overflowing when we think of Jesus' sacrifice. Worthy and honor to the Lamb and blessed be the name...that name is Jesus. Amen.

February 12 Read Psalm 37:18-25

ANCHORED TO THE ROCK

Bible Thought: "Blessed is the nation whose God is the LORD; and the people whom he hath chosen for his own inheritance" (Psalm 33:12).

A legacy left to its citizens is a precious gift. My great grandparents, grandparents and parents did just that for me and I am thankful.

This chaotic world of today overflows with bad news. "Family values" are criticized. Disobedience, blasphemy and irreverence for God prevail. I wonder at times if there is a conspiracy to present sin as the norm. From the beginning of time mankind has had a sin problem. Sin is not an island. It always affects lives many of which are innocent.

I say to you there is only one safe place to be. Those anchored to the Rock are secured. That Rock is Jesus. More than ever we need to guard our faith. Guard it at all costs because we live in a world that continually seeks to erode it. Our faith is far too precious to have it demeaned.

We are in a fight to reserve and protect our faith. Faith filled people focus on Jesus. They have His Word in their hearts. They know where they are going and they will not bend an ear to the cries of doubt and unbelief. They do not give up, back up, let up or shut up about their faith.

When it comes to the end of life, faith filled people become spiritual millionaires. We have a priceless inheritance. So hold steady. You are anchored to the "Rock."

Dear wonderful Lord, thank You for Jesus, our "Anchor." Whatever the battle we are secure. We are calm in the storms of life with Jesus our Lord. In His beautiful name. Amen.

February 13 Read Psalm 92

SEE WITH YOUR HEART

Bible Thought: "The eyes of your understanding being enlightened; that ye may know what is the hope of his calling, and what the riches of the glory of his inheritance in the saints" (Ephesians 1:18).

For the last ten years we have helped Uncle Steve live alone in his own home. His ninety years-young on a walker and in a wheelchair has not damped his enthusiasm for life. His courage and faith adds to my memory book of love. A weak body and feeble knees have not blinded Uncle Steve's vision. He sees with his heart.

One day Uncle Steve will walk out of that body on strong, perfect knees. He will have no more pain. There will be no walkers, wheelchairs or crutches in heaven. For the Christian, death is a reward

So we press toward the mark. We meet conflicts head on with knowledge knowing this world is not all there is.

Have you ever wondered why you were put on planet earth? You are not an accident. God wanted someone special to love and you are that someone. The greatest thing we can do in this life is to love Him back. You make these great moments in your life. Please don't miss a single one.

Although we do not see our Lord physically, we see Him with our hearts through faith and that is the most beautiful sight of all!

Dear heavenly Father, You are holy. You are majesty. You are King of our hearts and we see You and feel You there. Thank You for living in us, loving us, redeeming us. Thank You for Jesus, the sacrificial Lamb. In His beautiful name. Amen.

February 14 Read Hosea 2:15-20

FALL IN LOVE WITH JESUS

Bible Thought: "Turn, O backsleding children, saith the LORD; for I am married unto you: and I will take you one of a city, and two of a family, and I will bring you to Zion" (Jeremiah 3:14).

Today is Valentine's Day. Do you remember your first love? I married my first love and I still see "skyrockets." The more I know my husband the more I love him. He has given me enough love to last a lifetime.

It is the same with Jesus. The more you know Him the more you love and want to obey Him. It is the greatest love ever known and that love lasts forever!

Love is the ultimate infinity. It is hard for humans to understand eternal love, yet a yielded heart receives eternal life.

"I'm in love with Jesus and He's in love with me.

He walks daily by my side and I have victory.

You can have that too. He's just a prayer away.

Give your heart to Jesus and love Him ever day."

Jesus is the "Sweetheart" of all time.

Dear precious Lord, we thank You for forgiving us, loving us, and dying for us. We are married to You forever. What an awesome God You are. In Jesus' beautiful name. Amen.

February 15 Read Psalm 138

WHISPERS OF LOVE

Bible Thought: "For the mountains shall depart, and the hills be removed; but my kindness shall not depart from thee, neither shall the covenant of my peace be removed, saith the LORD that hath mercy on thee" (Isaiah 54:10).

I cannot count how many whispers of "I love you" from my husband each day. I see my grown children whispering in their children's ears. I know what they are whispering.

I'm filled with joy when my children and grandchildren's whispers tell me "I love you" on the phone.

Do I take these blessings for granted? No. I have been blessed beyond belief and am forever grateful. Whatever problem seems so gigantic loses its significance in the security of unconditional love. Through illnesses, operations, teenage accidents and other difficulties, God never leaves His child alone. His love remains behind it all. Love always triumphs. Love wins. Why? God is love.

I love to give whispers of love to Him, thanking Him for the many blessings, the everyday things so often taken for granted, the beauty of the earth, the promise of spring, friends and neighbors and the joy of family…so many things to thank Him for.

Become a "whisperer" with me. Whisper throughout your day to the Lord. Tell Him of your love.

That still small voice answers, "I love you too."

Dear precious Lord we came to say, "I love You." In that mighty name of Jesus. Amen.

February 16 Read John 10:14-18

SHEEP NEED A SHEPHERD

Bible Thought: "He shall feed his flock like a shepherd: he shall gather the lambs with his arm and carry them in his bosom, and shall gently lead those that are with young" (Isaiah 40:11).

Our young son left a note that he had run away. We panicked until we saw the family dog's tail wagging behind a bush in the backyard. My husband ran and picked him up and smothered him with love and kisses. "You are important to us. We love you. you and your brothers have special places in our hearts. If you ran away we would have to go too because we want to be where you are."

That scene of my husband's love for his child is frozen in my memory. I saw a picture of God's love for His lost lambs that day. The Lord is our Shepherd and we are the sheep of His pasture. Without a shepherd we, like sheep, are helpless. Sheep wander into harm's way without a shepherd. So do we.

Lance is grown up now, but he still remembers his father's arms surrounding him with love for his seven year old child. When Lance calls we talk a bit and then he wants to hear his daddy's voice.

I feel the same way. I want to hear my "Father's" voice too.

I am a sheep and I need the "Good Shepherd."

Dear wonderful Lord, You are our Good Shepherd and we cannot praise You enough for reaching down to us, redeeming, loving and caring for Your lost lambs. What a mighty God You are. We give You the highest place in our lives. In Jesus' wonderful, beautiful name. Amen.

February 17 John 15:9-12

LOVE IS FOREVER

Bible Thought: "Set me as a seal, upon then heart, as a seal upon thine arm: for love is strong as death, jealousy is cruel as the grave: the coals thereof are coals of fire, which hath a most vehement flame. Many waters cannot quench love, neither can the floods drown it: if a man would give all the substance of his house for love, it would utterly be contemned" (Son of Solomon 8:6-7).

Love holds this world together. It's the reason to get up in the morning. It's the reason to go on living after a tragic loss. Love gives hope to life. As long as there are people there is a reason to live and to love.

Love heals the deepest hurts and brings peace in the midst of chaos. Love is the bridge over troubled waters. Love makes life precious. Take away love and you have taken away life.

Someone is deeply in love with you and His love surpasses all others and has stood the test of time.

I love the "sweetheart" story in today's Bible Thought. Our youngest son said those same words to his beautiful bride on their wedding day.

Love is spending time in a loved one's presence. I love it when my husband whispers, "When I'm away from you, you are all I think about." That's how God's love is. He even joys over you with singing" (Zephaniah 3:17). You are His beloved.

Love is the greatest gift. It is priceless. It cannot be bought, nor can it be earned.It is a precious gift from the One who loves you the most. The greatest love mankind has ever known went to Calvary for you and me.

Dear God, thank You for Jesus, our wonderful Savior. In His beautiful name. Amen.

February 18 Read Psalm 91:7-16

WATCHING OVER YOU

Bible Thought: "For the eyes of the LORD run to and fro throughout the whole earth, to shew himself strong in the behalf of them whose heart is perfect toward him…" (2 Chronicles 16:9).

Remember the day you enclosed your tiny baby's hand into yours?

Remember holding that toddler's hand when he or she took the first step?

Remember the first day of school when you had to let go?

Remember the teenager driving for the first time?

Remember the day they left home?

Through all the growing years we prayed and watched over our children.

God loves us even more than we love our children. We love so much it hurts, but who knows that love more than Jesus? It's a love we cannot fathom. His love has no end. He had you and me in mind when He endured he cruel cross. The love of God surpasses all understanding. It reaches to the highest high and the deepest low.

So let's remember a man who came from Galilee to set us free. He suffered pain. He took our shame. He paid a price…His sacrifice. He secured victory for our destiny. Life delights in light. Jesus is that "Light."

Let Jesus watch over you.

Dear Lord, thank You for watching over us. Thank You for sending Your only Son to save us. Thank You for coming back for us to live with You forever. What a day that will be! In Jesus' wonderful name. Amen.

February 19 Read Psalm 139:1-10

UNDER HIS WINGS

Bible Thought: "How excellent is thy loving kindness O God! Therefore the children of men put their trust under the shadow of thy wings" (Psalm 36:7).

Have you ever watched a mother hen and her baby chicks? In a storm or danger she spreads her wings and calls to her children. They know her voice and run to her.

The mother eagle bears up her baby eaglets when they are beginning to learn to fly. If they begin to fall she swoops them up on her wings.

I like the word "wings." That word reminds me of God's great wings. I cannot weather the storms of life on my own. The stress and pressures would blow me away. I want to be under God's wings. I want to be safe, warm and secure to be protected from the storm. I run to God and He lifts me up. My strength is renewed. Under His wings I run without weariness and I run without faint.

I'm thankful for those strong wings. There I find refuge, rest, strength, healing and peace.

God will cover you with His wings too.

Take refuge today and run to His wings.

Dear God, help us to overcome the storms of life because with You we are victorious. Guide us O thou great Jehovah! In Jesus' wonderful name. Amen.

February 20 Read 1 Peter 2:13-17

A GODLY LEADER

Bible Thought: "Righteousness exalteth a nation: but sin is a reproach to any people" (Proverbs 14:34).

George Washington and Abraham Lincoln are national heroes. I still see memories of their portraits in grade school. Principles for which they stood for still leave examples of diligence and integrity.

I am so thankful for godly leaders who stood for courage and conviction. We need those truths of the Bible to be our standard for living today.

Many civilizations have come and gone. Those who have forgotten God's laws have disintegrated because of ignoring the Bible.

The current phrase "politically correct" denotes a non-observance of God's laws. Behaviors that are strictly forbidden in the Bible are blatantly and openly practiced. Such lifestyles lead to the crumbling of a nation.

I'm so thankful to live in a country whose forefathers sacrificed for me to enjoy freedom. Freedom does not come cheaply. It is a precious thing.

Real freedom comes from knowing Jesus and living by His commandments.

Dear Father, we pray for our leaders in government. May their hearts turn to You for wisdom and guidance. Thank You for Jesus who became "flesh and dwelt among us."

In that wonderful name. Amen.

February 21 Read Job 12:7-9

SPIRITUAL FOOD

Bible Thought: "Behold the fowls of the air: for they sow not, neither do they reap, nor gather into barns; yet your heavenly Father feedeth them. Are ye not much better than they?" (Matthew 6:26).

We filled our new bird feeder and retreated to a safe distance from our swing. We settled down for a relaxing time of bird watching. We waited and watched. We did the same thing the next day and the next.

"What is wrong with those birds?" I impatiently exclaimed to my husband. "Here is this beautiful banquet of food and they are ignoring it. All they have to do is receive it."

Instantly in my heart I felt the Lord saying the same thing to me. God has provided a "banquet of food" for me in His Word. He satisfies the deepest longings of my soul. He has "spiritual food" for every need in my life and all I have to do is open His Word and receive it.

When I experience a "famine" in my life, I stumble around, until I remember my heavenly Father who feeds the birds of the air and the beasts of the field. He will surely feed me and meet my every need.

Let's be encouraged today. If God watches over my feathered friends, I know He watches over you and me.

"Look," I whispered to my husband one day. "The birds have found their food and they have told their friends." I will tell my friends too.

Dear Lord, thank You for being our "Jehovah Jireh," even for the birds and beasts. What an awesome God You are. We praise you today and every day. In Jesus' name. Amen.

February 22 Read 1 Samuel 30:1-6

ENCOURAGEMENT...A GIFT TO GIVE AWAY

Bible Thought: "No weapon that is formed against thee shall prosper, and every tongue that shall rise against thee in judgment thou shalt condemn. This is the heritage of the servants of the LORD, and their righteousness is of me, saith the LORD" (Isaiah 54:17).

Do you ever feel discouraged? Does life seem to surround you with problems on every side? Take heart dear reader. God's child has many, many promises that encourage the discouraged.

Every morning say the following statements to yourself:

"I will rise up and be successful...not failures because I am more than a conqueror. I am confident in my Lord. My inner being is renewed day by day. I have hope that something good is going to happen because I expect the best. I have a victorious attitude. I am not a "quitter." I am one of God's most prized possessions. God turns disappointments into His appointments. He loves me and I am highly favored because with God all things are possible."

Keep saying the above concepts until you believe them. Remember, "There is only one safe place to be in this world...in the arms of Jesus. If there is no cross, there is no crown. If there is no conflict, there is no conqueror."

I challenge you to encourage someone else today. Encouraging others return to you in many ways.

This life is exciting. I call it "delicious."

Be a gift to give away!

Dear precious Lord, thank You for blue skies and rainbows, roses and rain, sunshine and harvest. Most of all we thank You for Jesus, life's greatest gift. Blessed be His name.

February 23 Read 2 Samuel 22:47-51

PRAISE THE LORD ANYWAY

Bible Thought: "While I live will I praise the LORD: I will sing praises unto my God while I have any being" (Psalm 146:2).

Do you ever lose your song? I have. The "storms of life" can almost blow me away. I lose sight of the fact that I have a loving, heavenly Father who wants the highest good for me.

God has promised to never leave or forsake us. He is with that son or daughter who is far from home. He is in that hospital room. He is with you while waiting for the diagnostic tests. He is with you when the telephone rings with disturbing news in the middle of the night. And yes, He is there when that loved one is finally laid to rest.

Instead of looking at the "storm" and prevailing circumstances, cling to the Lord with all your might. Sing in your storm and praise Him. He will calm the storm and you will have peace again even in adversities.

What is left if we don't sing or praise Him? Then worry, anxiety, headaches and sleepless nights torment us.

Praise the Lord anyway. It brings peace and you will see sunny days again.

Dear Lord, thank You for Your incredible love. May we have ever increasing faith in this earthly journey, glorifying You each day. In that beautiful name of Jesus. Amen.

February 24 Read Ephesians 3:17-21

ROOTED AND GROUNDED

Bible Thought: "I can do all things through Christ which strengtheneth me" (Philippians 4:13).

My beautiful tree had been battered all night with fierce winds. It leaned over and we could see roots. This cedar tree had been growing many years, being at least twelve feet tall. Windstorms had gnarled its branches and despite its calamity it still looked alive.

My husband staked the tree back to its position with his pickup and chains. In a few days it began to show tiny buds and needles. It seemed to refuse the intimidation by the storms of life. It stands stately now and is reaching out its branches with beauty again.

What a lesson for me! My tree had sent down deeper roots that we were not aware of. Its roots had sustained it in the darkest hour.

This life has storms but if God's children send down deep roots while standing firm in their faith and His promises, victory is attained. God brings you and me through hard times with strength and power.

Are you going through a storm? Tell the storm, "Blow storm blow! You can't keep me down because I am rooted and grounded in the Lord Jesus Christ."

Dear God, thank You for Your steadfastness and everlasting love. May we keep pressing on, growing to spiritual maturity. In Jesus' name. Amen.

February 25 Read Psalm 36:5-9

CLOSER TO HEAVEN

Bible Thought: "O bless our God, ye people, and make the voice of his praise to be heard" (Psalm 66:8).

Morning breaks with enthusiasm and all nature acknowledges God's gift of life. Dewdrops of God's love sprinkle the earth with the promise of a new day.

I want to make this day count. Since Jesus died for me I am valuable. I am not just a number. I am sold out to Jesus. I am a unique person in His sight.

Every thing I say and do should glorify Him. When I stumble and fall He picks me up again.

God is on my side. He loves me. He guides my steps because I abide in Him and I dwell in the "secret place."

I awaken with heartfelt praise to my Savior. I sing to Him with joy He restores my soul and lifts me to a higher place.

He is ever mindful of me. He joys over me with singing. I delight in Him and He gives me the desires of my heart.

I rejoice today.

I am one day closer to heaven.

Dear God, may the joy that dwells within us bubble up and reach out to everyone we meet today. In Jesus' name. Amen

February 26 Read Psalm 138

DOES GOD KNOW WHERE I AM?

Bible Thought: "The LORD looked down from heaven upon the children of men, to see if there were any that did understand, and seek God" (Psalm 14:2).

My grandson had played all day to exhaustion. When twilight came he climbed up in my lap and asked,

"Does God know where I am?"

"Of course," I answered.

"But does he know I'm at your house and not at my house?"

"Yes, he knows where all of us are."

"Then will you sing me to sleep?"

I didn't sing very long because he quickly went to dreamland in my arms. He knew God was watching over him.

What a lesson for all of us. The innocence and faith of children bless me. I want that kind of faith. To go to bed knowing God sees and hears me thrills my soul. I like to think God is tucking me in bed like I did with my children and grandchildren. Sometimes I sing to God in my prayers. Many times God is singing over me because I awaken with a song in my heart. (Zephaniah 3:17)

Yes, God knows where we are, each one of us. May we be childlike in our faith especially when we close our eyes in life or in death.

Dear God, thank You for Your everlasting arms. May each day we live have everlasting faith. In that beautiful name of Jesus. Amen.

February 27 Read Numbers 27-30

WEED OUT NEGATIVITY IN YOUR LIFE

Bible Thought: "I said, I will take heed to my ways, that I sin not with my tongue: I will keep my mouth with a bridle, while the wicked is before me" (Psalm 39:1).

My husband bought a weed eater. It's one that I can start. Now I can "weed eat" any time I want to. I've learned something else from weed eating. When I cut them out, they are gone. I am resolved to do the same thing with negative thinking, speaking and all of those "weedy" thoughts and words.

I am so blessed that even a tiny complaint is most inappropriate. I resolve to stop it. It makes a heart ungrateful and we lose joy by failing to recognize the good. I think taking things for granted in this life is an offense to our gracious God.

We can stop negative thoughts by thinking on things that are honest, just, pure, lovely and good report. (Philippians 4:8).

I am clearing my mind of weedy, thorny, hateful, cutting remarks. I am after those weeds in my yard and those in my mind. You can do that too.

When a negative thought or word comes to mind, picture yourself with the weed eater...cutting it out.

It's great for your thought life and your garden too!

Dear precious Lord, we repent of wrong words that have slipped from our tongues. Thank You for the power to reject negativity, in words and in thoughts. Thank You for Jesus, our great Redeemer. In His beautiful name. Amen.

February 28 Read Isaiah 55:10-13

TODAY IS THE BEST DAY OF YOUR LIFE

Bible Thought: "Today is the day which the LORD has made; we will rejoice and be glad in it" (Psalm 118:24).

Today is a special day. You are alive! This day comes with blue skies, revealing fluffy clouds playing hide and seek. This gift comes wrapped in sunshine and is displayed in sparkling colors. You are presented multiple bouquets of flowers while the trees clap their hands, demanding an encore.

Music accompanies the production. Various notes from our feathered friends provide numerous sounds, thrilling and warming the soul. The heavenly concert begins. All that is required is your presence…be it in a swing, a front porch chair or a morning walk.

Alone with God in His morning theater is spectacular. The only ticket for the show is a listening heart. You will find beauty in ordinary things, peace in extraordinary circumstances, and the "peace that passes all understanding." (Philippians 4:7).

For those who seek Him will receive wisdom. The secret of a successful day is receiving your gift of today from God. This present is attached to ribbons of joy with sunbeams that burst with life.

Today is God's gift to you and it is wrapped in love. It's the best day of your life!

Dear wonderful God, we thank You for this day. May we be grateful for it and fill it with praise for You, knowing that You will never leave Your child. Blessed be the name of Jesus. Amen.

February 29 Read Matthew 6:5-8

A MORNING PRAYER

Bible Thought: "The LORD hath heard my supplication; the LORD will receive my prayer" (Psalm 6:9).

"Grant me the wisdom Lord, to know when to speak and when to be silent Forgive my pride and selfishness. Help me to see the good in others and to build upon their strengths.

Make me aware of every transgression and may I be quick to repent. May I be sensitive to the leading of Your Spirit.

I ask for wisdom in every thought, word and deed. May I encourage others in their journey of life. Fill me with compassion, forgiveness and mercy. May I impart those same qualities to everyone I meet.

Teach me to sing through the storms of life with my focus on You alone, my anchor holding fast and secure. Help me to know I am not walking blindly, but with You, I can do all things. I walk upon the high places of the earth because You guide my every step.

Help me to live in the "now" of my life, forgetting the past and pressing on to that wonderful day I will see You face to face.

When my earthly time is ended, may I be found faithful, meeting the dawn of Your glory with wondrous praise throughout eternity for Your wondrous love for me!

In that beautiful name of the King of kings and Lord of lords. His name is Jesus.

Amen.

MARCH

March 1 Read 1 Kings 19:11-12

ENJOY GOD'S MASTERPIECE

Bible Thought: "Be still and know that I am God: I will be exalted among the heathen, I will be exalted in the earth" (Psalm 46:10).

Our family had a picnic in the country recently. The sun touched the horizon and disappeared. I asked my granddaughters to close their eyes and listen. "Just listen to the quietness and you will be blessed."

"I hear it," Traci said. "I hear it too," Kallie exclaimed.

"What did you hear?" I asked. "It's something I hear in my heart," and Traci smiled. "It's Jesus in my heart," Kallie added.

I love to be in the country at twilight. There is something about the moment the sun goes down. The quiet speaks volumes. All the busy noises of the day are gone and only stillness remains. As dusk reposes nature is breathtaking.

It's time to rest while forgetting the problems of the day. It's time to relax in the presence of the "Holy Hush." I like to call it "God's good night" as He tucks nature into bed.

The next time you're in the country at sundown listen to your heart and admire God's magnificent sunsets.

Dear wonderful God, thank You for the beauty of our days and nights. Thank You for sweet sleep as we fall asleep in Your tender care. In Jesus' beautiful name. Amen.

March 2 Read 2 Corinthians 15:18

FEEL LIKE GIVING UP?

Bible Thought: "Many are the afflictions of the righteous: but the LORD delivereth him out of them all" (Psalm 34:19).

Trials come and trials go, but I've had a revelation. If I can't be happy today regardless of problems, then when am I going to be happy? When the trial is over? What about the next one? Life is full of obstacles but today's Bible Thought sums it up. God solves every thing if I allow Him to. So giving up is not an option!

Defeat comes with complaining, murmuring and criticizing. That makes a bad atmosphere causing bad feelings in the home, workplace or wherever.

Dare to make life the best it can be. Know you are a special creation. Of all the billions of people that have ever walked the face of this earth you are still a special person. What a boring existence it would be if we were all clones. You are "fearfully and wonderfully made." (Psalm 139:14) Each day you arise repeat Psalm 118:24: "This is the day which the LORD hath made; we will rejoice and be glad in it."

It is always too soon to quit in this race of life…"with God all things are possible" (Matthew 19:26).

Set your face like a flint and meet life head on.

Victory is just around the corner.

Dear precious Lord, You are our "problem solver." We repent today of trying to handle life on our own. Thank You for being our "burden bearer." It's all because of Jesus.

Blessed be His name. Amen.

March 3 Read Romans 5:1-5

A FRIEND OF GOD

Bible Thought: "And the scripture was fulfilled which saith, 'Abraham believed God, and it was imputed unto him for righteousness: and he was called the Friend of God'" (James 2:23).

Friends bring sunshine and sparkle into our lives. Whether young or old and all the way in between, friends are great blessings. Neighbors around me are such good friends they feel like family. I love to make new friends. Each time I make one they are "keepers."

My friend Marjorie knows all about me and loves me anyway. She comforts, encourages and brightens my day. Yet there is a friend that surpasses all friends for all time. His name is Jesus.

He is a friend that "sticketh closer than a brother" (Proverbs 18:24). He gives us peace in a troubled world. (John 14:27) If we keep His commandments he calls us "friends." (John 15:14-15) Nothing can separate us from His love. (Romans 8:38-30).

Jesus is a forever friend. He gave His life; a sacrifice for all that will receive Him. He is the joy of today and the hope for tomorrow. He will never leave nor forsake.

Will you not make Him your friend today? He loves you with an everlasting love.

Dear precious Lord, words are not enough to tell You of our love. The depths of such love is more than we can fathom, but we welcome You and praise You with all our hearts. Live Your life in us and may we walk in obedience, loving You more each day. In that name above all names, JESUS. Amen.

March 4 Read Exodus 15:6-12

HANDS

Bible Thought: "I have set the LORD always before me: because *he is* at my right hand, I shall not be moved" (Psalm 16:8).

It seems I have been holding hands with my husband forever. Those same hands carried my books at school. Those hands held mine on our wedding day and he pledged all his love to me. Those hands held mine at the birth of each son. Those same hands built our first home.

I think there is something spiritual about hands. In a battle with the Amalekites the Israelites prevailed as long as Moses held up his hands. When Moses became weary and dropped his hands to rest, the enemy became stronger. So Aaron and Hur held the hands of Moses up and won the battle.

The healing hands of Jesus have been with you and me throughout our lives. Yet the most precious hands of all are the nail-scarred hands of Jesus. Without those loving hands there is no hope for a sin-stained world.

Do you have a heavy burden today? Are you facing a problem? Put your life into the hands of Jesus.

Holding hands with Jesus is what life is all about.

Dear awesome Lord, thank You for those beautiful hands of Jesus, scarred for all of us. May we hold those hands in our hearts with every breath we take. Eternity is not long enough to thank You and love You. In that wonderful, precious name of Jesus. Amen.

March 5 Read Joshua 14:11-14

ENTHUSIASM

Bible Thought: "These things have I spoken unto you, that my joy might remain in you, and that your joy might be full" (John 5:11).

Don't you like to be around enthusiastic people? I call those with enthusiasm "world changers." We should be happy as kings because with Jesus "all things are possible."

Enthusiastic people see life as a gift from God and they share their gift of joy with others. They also see and appreciate things that are often taken for granted. They get excited about sunsets, flowers that bloom, clean air to breathe, fleecy clouds and rainbows, a horse running in the wind, or a dove's cooing.

Enthusiastic people make life "delicious." As for me, I like to see how many people with smile back at me. I love it when I have a former student recognize me. When my ninety years young uncle says "Thank you" for giving him a hug I am blessed.

This earthly journey of life has so many things to enjoy. I love the quote, "Money may not be a lot, but blessings cannot be bought."

Think big with faith and courage. You will enter a new life of hope. Your faith and belief in God are the greatest things you can ever have and that is something to be enthusiastic about.

Dear precious Lord, You are the greatest thing that ever happened to us and we cannot help but sing and live this life with enthusiasm. We get so excited about Jesus and we thank You with enthusiastic praise. In His wonderful name. Amen.

March 6 Read Psalm 119:97-104

PLEASANT WORDS BRING JOY

Bible Thought: "Pleasant words are as an honeycomb, sweet to the soul, and health to the bones" (Proverbs 16:24).

Wrong words are hard to retrieve. Angry words can hurt, harm and wound. They are not soon forgotten. Harsh words stir up strife, break down marriages and can even start wars.

Pleasant words restore the soul and soothe difficult circumstances. They also leave a sense of well being by calming down an angry person.

Words have power to hurt or power to heal. God has put within each one of us the ability to stop negative thoughts and words. With the Greater One in us, we can fight the battle and win with conquering thoughts and speech.

I want my words to bless, help and encourage. I have the choice of words that I use. So here are my words for you, dear reader:

"You are a wonderful amazing human being, created by God. May you be blessed today. May you know the height, depth and breadth of His overwhelming love."

Take your heart with you in everything you say. Your "mental sunshine" will bring many blessings to you and to others.

Dear gracious Lord, fill our minds and hearts with loving kind words to every one we meet. In that wonderful name of Jesus. Amen.

March 7 Read Psalm 46:7-11

A BLESSING BOOK

Bible Thought: "The memory of the just is blessed: but the name of the wicked shall rot" (Proverbs 10:7).

Some call it "journaling." I call it my "Blessing Book." I write down God's wonderful surprises with the date. My book is full to running over.

"Happy Mother's Day Mom. Will you marry me when I grow up?" "Teacher, you're the best teacher in the whole world."

A "Happy Birthday" long distance call from an eighty-four years young friend goes in my blessing book.

These are the things in my book It is filled with loving memories of those who have touched my life with loving kindness.

I have an even greater "Blessing Book." It is my Bible. It is more precious than gold. It has shown me the way of life. It is filled with unconditional love.

God tells me in His Word that I am special in His sight. He knew me before I was born. He knew that I would stumble and fall, yet He still came. He forgives, heals, restores and saves.

I will praise Him with every breath.

Open your Blessing Book today and read how valuable you are to God.

Dear God, Your Word is our blessing for all time. May we hide it in our hearts and honor You in every word, thought and deed. Thank You for Jesus, Your gift to all mankind. In His name. Amen.

March 8 Read Colossians 1:9-14

PRAY FOR OTHERS

Bible Thought: "And all things whatsoever ye shall ask in prayer, believing, ye shall receive" (Matthew 21:22).

Many years ago I sat in the doctor's office waiting my turn. The lovely receptionist answered the phone and began to cry uncontrollably. Her mother had just been taken to the hospital. In ER they could hardly find a pulse. I asked the doctor if I could take the hurting young lady to another room and pray for her and her mother. "Yes, please do," the doctor said. I prayed and the lady seemed to be comforted as she left the office.

For many years I thought of the lady and had vaguely remembered it when a beautiful woman and her elderly mother stopped me in a restaurant recently.

"Mrs. Clayton, do you remember praying for me in Dr. Smith's office many years ago? You prayed for my mother and me."

After the goodbye hugs and tears, the lady's mother said, "God answers prayer."In the midst of an illness or emergency many cannot pray for themselves and depend on others.

We may never know the results of our prayers like this incident but it demonstrated to me the importance of it all.

May we be bold to pray for others.

Dear Lord, may we always be available to help a hurting soul. Grant us the boldness to lift up others in prayer. Thank You for our Savior. His name is Jesus. Amen.

March 9 Read 1 Thessalonians 4:9-10

EXPRESSING GRATITUDE IS A VIRTUE

Bible Thought: "Let us come before his presence with thanksgiving, and make a joyful noise unto him with psalms" (Psalm 95:2).

Expressing gratitude is a great habit. Saying "Thank you" to the many people who do things for you brings joy.

The Israelites in Bible times forgot the fact God had delivered them from the brutal slavery of the Egyptians. God's people complained more about what they didn't have instead of appreciating what they had.

Each one of us can remember going though tough times. Did we express thankfulness for the solution of the problem? God gives us beautiful gifts of life, health, food, work and friends. Many blessings surround us!

Jesus healed ten lepers but only one returned to thank Him. There must have been nine ungrateful hearts. (Luke 17:17).

When you feel discouraged it's hard to be thankful, but looking at God's faithfulness in the past assures His provision for the future. He will see you through. He never leaves you where He cannot guide you. Embracing the good leaves little room for the bad.

Let's be thankful every day. So many blessings abound. Expressing gratitude makes life more positive, gracious, loving and blessed.

Dear God, we offer our lives as a living sacrifice. We want to make our lives a gift to You and we want to be thankful every day. In Jesus' beautiful name. Amen.

March 10 Read Mark 9:36-37

CHILDREN ARE GOD'S GIFTS

Bible Thought: "Lo, children are an heritage of the LORD: and the fruit of the womb is his reward" (Psalm 127:3).

I well remember when the nurse put each newborn baby in my arms. The love I felt I can't describe.

Of course my husband and I were the proudest parents ever. Emmitt gazed at his sleeping baby and asked everyone that passed by, "Isn't he a doll?"

I shudder to think of a world without children. They make the world go round. Our future depends on them.

Children have such wonderful traits. They don't hold grudges. They forgive and forget so easily. Children simply abandon themselves to life.

The students in my teaching career taught me many things but perhaps the greatest trait was their ability to trust. Their childlike trust, faith and humility are imprinted on my heart. "Whosoever therefore shall humble himself as this little child, the same is greatest in the kingdom of heaven" (Matthew 18:4).

Somewhere between childhood and adulthood, we lose that faith. Let's be determined to reclaim the faith of a child.

Aren't we all God's children?

Dear Lord, thank You for the children. Help us to train them in Your ways and may we have their childlike trust in You. In Jesus' beautiful name. Amen.

March 11 Read Jude 20-25

TIME IS GOD'S GIFT FOR YOU

Bible Thought: "Blessed is he that readeth, and they that hear the words of this prophecy; and keep those things which are written herein: for the time is at hand" (Revelation 1:3).

Each day is a gift made just for you. It is from the heart of God. If I empty my burdens and give them to God in my nightly prayers I awaken with a brand new day filled with wonders.

Time cannot be reclaimed and leaves no room for remorse or regrets. Harsh words, malice and strife are stolen by the thief of time. Brooding over past mistakes wastes the time I have been given today.

God's gift of time is a treasure box of jewels. They are precious stones that can make today memorable.

Keep praising and thanking God for today, even in the midst of a crisis. Victory is just a breath away. There will be joy in the morning. Pray for others. Everyone has problems. Give away God's diamonds of time by making the day sparkle for some weary soul. Give time to a bereaving family. Write an encouraging letter or note. God's jewels glow to the words, "I love you."

Open your gift of time from God today. Giving that gold away will make you a millionaire on earth and in heaven.

Dear Lord, thank You for the time we have. Teach us to number our days and make every day count for You. Thank You for sending Jesus to redeem us. In His glorious name. Amen.

March 12 Read Romans 16:24-27

AN AWESOME GOD

Bible Thought: "And there are also many other things which Jesus did, the which, if they should be written every one, I suppose that even the world itself could not contain the books that should be written. Amen" (John 21:25).

I'm thankful for my many blessings. My husband has taught me much about faithful, unconditional love. My children and grandchildren do the same. I have friends who love me. Can you imagine not having all those you love in your life?

I feel God's love when I look at nature's handiwork. I see a beautiful blue sky with white puffy clouds. Could the sky be any other color but blue or clouds white or grass green?

Have you ever noticed fields of waving grain just waiting to produce food for you and me? Smell the wonderful scent of a gentle falling rain, the laughter of children at play or the sound of singing coming from thankful hearts. Think of the great blessing to be married to your one and only.

What a great and awesome God we have. Blessings overtake us as we see His wondrous works everywhere.

He is awesome. I can't help but shout it!

Dear precious Lord, we thank You today with every fiber within us. You are mighty, glorious, beautiful and faithful. We love You. In that name of above all names. His name is Jesus. Amen.

March 13 Read Psalm 46:1-7

MAKE YOUR LIFE SECURE

Bible Thought: "Consider the ravens: for they neither sow nor reap; which neither have storehouse nor barn; and God feedeth them: how much more are ye better than the fowls?" (Luke 12:24).

I prayed earnestly for my husband as he climbed the weathered windmill. Crows had built a nest in the fan of the mill. Underneath the maze of twigs and sticks, unbelievably, the crows had woven old rusty wire in and through the blades of the fan, paralyzing the windmill even in the midst of fierce strong winds.

How can those crows with their birdbrains have that much sense? I thought. *They know how to build a strong home base in the midst of threatening storms.*

I can learn a valuable lesson from the crows. I need to build my "nest" securely too. I need to "wire" my faith with the Word of God and I need to "intertwine" my nest with obedience, trust and love for others. Then when the wind of adversity challenges my nest, I will be strong in the Lord.

With immovable faith your "nest" will stand the test of time in this span of life. At the end of your journey you will soar into the heavenlies to meet Jesus in the air.

Hallelujah!

Dear Lord, thank You for Jesus, our Redeemer and Savior. May our roots be anchored deeply in Him. thank You for the day we will "fly away" to live with Him forever. In His beautiful name. Amen.

March 14 Read Ephesians 3:14-21

THE GREATEST LOVE

Bible Thought: "The LORD hath appeared of old unto me, saying, Yea, I have loved thee with an everlasting love: therefore with loving-kindness have I drawn thee" (Jeremiah 31:3).

God is filled with love for you and that love goes beyond anything this world could ever offer. His love heals the deepest hurts and brings peace in the midst of chaos. His love is the bridge over troubled waters. Love makes life precious.

Many love stories in the Bible thrill me. Jacob loved Rachel so much he worked fourteen years for her hand.

Joseph was put into a pit and sold as a slave by his brothers because of jealousy yet his love and forgiveness won out.

What about Queen Esther? She was the only one who could save her people and with God's help she did.

Who of us can fathom the love of Ruth for Naomi, her mother-in-law?

I love the Scripture in Song of Solomon. It is a reminder of intense love.

The greatest love mankind has ever known went to Calvary for you and me. His love is priceless. It cannot be bought nor can it be earned. It's a precious gift from the One who loves you the most. He is love and His "Love Letter" to you is the Bible written in red.

Read your Love Letter today. It's the greatest love.

Dear wonderful Lord, we come to You today with joy in our hearts for Your incredible love. May our worship and love for You increase day by day. In that name of all names. His name is Jesus. Amen.

March 15 Read Romans 8:35-39

FOREVER FRIENDS

Bible Thought: "Behold, I have graven thee upon the palms of my hands; thy walls are continually before me" (Isaiah 49:16).

Aren't you Mrs. Clayton?" a polite Colonel asked me in a restaurant. "I was in your second grade class."

"Let me look at you," I exclaimed gazing at his brown eyes. Many of my ex-students keep the same facial features and are easily recognized. Others change yet whether I recognize them or not the thrill is still the same. It had been many years since this particular student had been in my class. The fact he recognized me was an extra blessing.

It is the same in God's classroom. However old I become I am still His child. He doesn't have to stop and try to remember who I am. I will always be in His class and I want to be that same trusting child trying to learn.

My students wrote me love notes. So has God. His love letters are in His Word, the Bible. Nothing can separate His love from me.

I learn in His classroom. Some of the lessons are hard, but my "Teacher" is gentle and kind...and He will never leave or forsake me. When I don't understand I ask Him for help and He patiently shows me the way.

Like my ex-students, God is my "Forever Friend."

Dear Lord, thank You for Your Word. It is the "School of life." May we be good students all of our days. In the wonderful name of Jesus. Amen.

March 16 Read Numbers 11:4-10

COMPLAINING IS A JOY STEALER

Bible Thought: "Do all things without murmurings and disputings" (Philippians 3:14).

Imagine our surprise when we saw a monkey in our tree. Our three boys ran to get a ladder. The monkey ran in the brush across the street and they couldn't find it.

The boys complained a long time. My husband and I sat them down to teach some profound lessons about that monkey. They wanted to catch it but we told them how dangerous that would be. A monkey bite can turn into a bad wound.

We also talked about how complaining is a joy stealer and a faith robber. Complaining causes one to never be satisfied with what they have, never remembering all of the many blessings God has bestowed. Complaining erodes faith in God. The boys changed their minds when they learned how serious monkey bites could be.

The Lord sent venomous snakes as punishment for the Israelites unbelief and complaints. Moses prayed for the people and God rescued them.

What a lesson for us. Instead of complaining, trust God and be willing to change behavior.

That's what the Israelites had to do. So did our sons.

Dear Lord, forgive our murmurings and complaints. We repent today and may we be transformed by the renewing of our minds. In Jesus' beautiful name. Amen.

March 17 Read Isaiah 51:7-11

A CHILD OF GOD

Bible Thought: "I will greatly rejoice in the LORD, my soul shall be joyful in my God; for he hath clothed me with the garments of salvation, he hath covered me with the robe of righteousness, as a bridegroom decketh *himself* with ornaments, and as a bride adorneth *herself* with her jewels" (Isaiah 61:10).

We are God's children and special in His sight. We were in His mind from the foundations of the earth. For you and me He went to the cross. For our peace He broke every partition, every wall. He watches over us while we sleep. He hears our heart's cry. He sees every tear and He knows our heart's desire.

He joys over us with singing and inhabits our praises. He takes delight in our prayers and it is His pleasure to give us the Kingdom and all things that pertain to life and godliness.

We are a unique creation, a special vessel, set apart. He causes us to ride upon the high places.

So let's go forth, conquering and possessing the land. We shall inherit His holy mountain and walk victoriously. We are His treasures in an earthen vessel.

"But unto you that fear my name shall the Sun of righteousness arise with healing in his wings; and ye shall go forth, and grow up as calves of the stall." (Malachi 4:2).

Dear wonderful Lord, You have blessed us more than we could ever say and with humble hearts we thank You. Our joy is overwhelming because of Jesus. Blessed be His name, now and forever. Amen.

March 18 Read Proverbs 16:19-24

BE A BLESSING

Bible Thought: "And even to *your* old age I am he; and *even* to hoar hairs will I carry *you*: I have made, and I will bear; even I will carry, and will deliver *you*" (Isaiah 46:4).

Senior citizens have brought us many blessings. Now it's our time to bless them. Daily contact with people is so important, especially the older population. Stimulation is vital. I watched my aunts improve mentally and physically when they had daily contact with people.

When that "housebound" person knows you will be visiting on a certain day, he or she looks forward to the visit with eager anticipation. Take a new baby in the family along with you and watch eyes light up. Allow your grandchildren to help make a cake or cookies. You will be teaching compassion.

Older Christians are filled with maturity and spiritual growth. They are of great value in telling children Bible stories and of course, they are never too old to pray. The Bible has many references about respecting and honoring the older saints.

Speak life to those older precious people. Hold one's hand and give a hug You will come away blessed.

Bless someone today.

Dear wonderful Lord, thank You for the good example and spiritual maturity our older seniors live before us. May we follow their deep love for You. In that name of all names.

His name is Jesus. Amen.

March 19 Read Proverbs 2:1-6

HIDE THE WORD IN YOUR HEART

Bible Thought: "Thy word have I hid in mine heart, that I might not sin against thee" (Psalm 119:11).

I have heard many adults say the scriptures they were required to memorize as children emerged at a crisis time in adulthood. The comforting and stabilizing in threatening situations gave them peace.

My ninety-two years young friend, a resident of the rest home told me, "I'm so thankful I memorized scriptures because they come to me in the night when I can't sleep."

The Word of God will keep you sane in a crazy world. God's Word will pick you up out of despair and enable you to soar like an eagle. His Word will keep you calm in a troubled sea.

This world and everything in it, including all the materials things we have worked so hard to accumulate, will pass away but God's Word will never pass away. His Word is truth and life. It sustains in the darkest hour. It ministers hope in the darkest night. It gives peace to troubled souls.

Love the Word of God. Cherish it. Memorize it. It is a priceless treasure.

Hide the Word in your heart.

Dear God, thank You for Your Word. It is light and life. Lead us to someone today to share "The Good News." In Jesus' beautiful name. Amen.

March 20 Read Hebrews 6:17-20

BE ANCHORED TO THE ROCK

Bible Thought: "Blessed is the name whose God is the LORD; and the people *whom* he hath chosen for his own inheritance" (Psalm 33:12).

My ancestors left me a legacy more precious than gold…a strong faith in God. To my great grandparents, grandparents and parents, I am forever grateful.

This chaotic world overflows with bad news. "Family values" are criticized. Disobedience, blasphemy and irreverence for God seem to prevail. I wonder if there is a conspiracy to present sin as the norm. From the beginning of time mankind has had a sin problem. Sin is not an island. It always affects lives, many of which are innocent.

Natural disasters come when least expected. It is a tumultuous world and there is only one safe place to be. Those anchored to the "Rock" are secured. That rock is Jesus. More than ever we need to guard our faith. Guard it at all cost because we live in a world that continually seeks to erode decency. Our faith is far too precious to have it demeaned.

We are in a fight to reserve and protect our faith. Faith filled people focus on Jesus. They have His Word in their hearts. They know where they are going and they will not bend an ear to the cries of doubt and unbelief. They do not give up, back up, let up or shut up about their faith.

When it comes to the end of life faith filled people are spiritual millionaires. We have a priceless inheritance. So hold steady! You are anchored to the Rock.

Dear Lord, Thank You for Jesus, our "Anchor." Whatever the battle is we are still anchored to Jesus our Savior. We are calm in the storms of life with Jesus. In His beautiful name. Amen.

March 21 Read Psalm 139:14-18

FEARFULLY AND WONDERFULLY MADE

Bible Thought: "Keep thy heart with all diligence; for out of it are the issues of life" (Proverbs 4:23).

Our bodies are amazing things. They are made of many cells, muscles, tissues, nerves and organs that all function together. God designed them to resist disease and illness while making a plan of recuperation from life-threatening forces.

I appreciate medical science and the great advances that have been made. However, I heard a relative's oncologist say, "I am only an instrument. There is a Greater Physician that brings health and healing to human bodies."

I watched a program on TV about a heart transplant. When the heart surgeon sutured the last stitch the heart moved and pulsated ever so slowly, beat by beat until the rhythm became normal.

How could anyone not believe? Did some cell from the primordial slime pit millions of years ago decide its descendants would turn into humans? Hardly!

Where there is a creation there is a Creator. Where there is a design there is a Designer.

Healing was a main aspect of Jesus' ministry and it's a comforting thought to know Jesus hears prayers.

Yes, we are fearfully and wonderfully made.

I am so glad God made you and me.

Dear Lord, thank You for "breathing into our nostrils the breath of life." In Jesus' name. That name is above all names. Amen.

March 22 Read Ecclesiastes 12:13-14

WHAT WOULD YOU DO ON YOUR LAST DAY?

Bible Thought: "And I heard a voice from heaven saying unto me, Write, Blessed are the dead which die in the Lord from henceforth: yea, saith the Spirit, that they may rest from their labours; and their works do follow them" (Revelation 14:13).

Life has a way of being daily. We sometimes slide into complacency taking it for granted. Yet life is not guaranteed for any number of years and we can readily agree with Job 7:6 that our "days are swifter than a weaver's shuttle."

It is so important to come to the end of our lives with no regrets. It would be sad indeed to not even be missed like the wicked kings in the Old Testament.

God has given the gift of time today. How we live our lives is the gift given back to God. So why should we wait until our very last day to spread kindness and love? Wouldn't it be better to be at peace with God and man, cheering others wherever you can? After all when life is over it is people you have influenced that makes a difference. Life is too short to waste. Make every day count.

Death is something that happens in a war. Christian believers may die in the battle, but live forever.

Dear Lord, we thank You for this day and every day You have given us. Thank You for our heavenly home waiting for us. May we be joyful while looking forward to Your coming. In the beautiful name of Jesus who sacrificed Himself for all of us. Amen.

March 23 Read Isaiah 62:2-5

MARRIED TO JESUS

Bible Thought: "Turn, O backsliding children, saith the LORD, for I am married unto you…" (Jeremiah 3:14).

I linger in Your presence.
Teach me how to love You.
Thank You for my secret place.
Who is like unto You, O Lord?
You make every day a masterpiece.
In the depths of my being, gratitude reigns.
May my every breath honor and glorify You.
You put a song in my heart and I'm filled with joy.
The joy I feel spills and runs over, overwhelming me.
I am not my own. In the deepest part of me I know I belong to You.
Without You I would be hopelessly lost, with no purpose for existence.
You watch over me with loving kindness. You will never leave nor forsake me.
You are the strength of my life, my Refuge, my Rock. You hide me under Your wings.
I praise You with my whole being. I magnify You with every fiber of my mind, body and soul.

I love You, adore You and bow down before You. You are my beautiful bridegroom and I am married to You!

Dear precious Lord, You are our hidden treasure, more precious than silver or gold. More costly than diamonds we could hold…the Prince of Peace, our love…our hope…our destiny. Thank You for Jesus, our beautiful bridegroom. In His name. Amen

March 24 Read Ephesians 1:16-19

LET GRATITUDE REIGN IN YOUR HEART

Bible Thought: "Every good gift and every perfect gift is from above, and cometh down from the Father of lights, with whom is no variableness, neither shadow of turning" (James 1:17).

We have lived in the same house on the same corner for 47 years. The house is too small when our sons come home with their families but it's home and I'm thankful.

Our yard is too big, but I find it a solace, a comfort to me. The birds stop for a while on their migratory journey and I am reminded that God does not even forget the sparrows. (Luke 12:6) I love the way the snow adorns the pine trees in the winter. The fragrance of spring rain makes me overflow with praise and gratitude.

Our house is blessed…a home of memories, triumphs, victories, hard places, laughter, tears and love. The Lord has been faithful and I bow my knees with thankfulness.

Let us be thankful for each day. Be thankful for the bountiful beauty of nature, for friends for family and most of all for God's love.

God is a song in the night, a guiding "Light" that guides us through every conflict.

I pray your house is filled with His presence, for where He is love abounds.

We are grateful people.

Dear wonderful Lord, our hearts spill over with thankfulness. We give thanks to You today and every day. Most of all we're thankful for our Savior. His name is Jesus. Amen.

March 25 Read 1 Samuel 12:19-23

PRAYER IS A LIFESAVER

Bible Thought: "Confess your faults one to another, and pray one for another, that ye may be healed. The effectual fervent prayer of a righteous man availeth much" (James 5:16).

I heard a story about a bald eagle soaring over a lake. He spotted his prey in the water below and swooped down into the water. The eagle sent his talons deep into the fish, but the fish, being far too heavy caused the eagle to sink lower into the lake. Just when it seemed hopeless, two other eagles appeared. Each one went under one of the wings of their comrade and carried him to safety.

What a beautiful picture of prayer. Prayer warriors intercede for others. They send prayers on wings of faith and love, "building a hedge and standing in the gap."

I like to think prayers build walls of love around those prayed for. The walls are built with sincere care and concern, promoting positive affirmations that enhance healing and well being.

Make a wall of love and prayers for someone today.

You may not know the results of your prayers, but know that God answers.

If eagles can help a friend so can we.

Dear God, thank You for answering even before we finish our prayer. We worship, adore and glorify You in every way. In the name above all names…Jesus. Amen.

March 26 Read Genesis 6:5-9

GRIEVING GOD'S HEART

Bible Thought: "And grieve not the holy Spirit of God, whereby ye are sealed unto the day of redemption" (Ephesians 4:30).

Have you ever thought about the flood in Noah's time? Mankind had become so wicked God had to send a flood to cleanse the earth. A sinful planet grieved the Lord with a heart filled with pain and sorrow. Because of Noah's righteousness, Noah and his family were the only ones saved. Of all the people on earth, only one family was left in existence.

Just the thought of God's grievance hurts me. I never want to grieve my Lord. I surely wouldn't want God to be sorry He made me.

What about today? Wickedness broke God's heart in Noah's day and it surely does in today's society. Though I know many people love God and obey His commandments, but what about the others?" Let's be quick to share the gospel.

God's rainbow is a signal that earth will not be destroyed by flood again. Yet we know today's culture has many sins. We don't know when Jesus will return, but we do know the only safe place to be is in His arms.

May we strive to live a righteous life and be quick to repent of transgressions. Let us never grieve His heart.

Dear Lord, we repent of our sins and thank You for Your forgiveness. Give us boldness to tell others about Jesus. In His wonderful name. Amen.

March 27 Read Amos 9:5

THE TOUCH OF THE MASTER'S HAND

Bible Thought: "For we know that the whole creation groaneth and travaileth in pain together until now" (Romans 5:22).

Our family cat had just about lived his nine lives. I took him to the vet for another antibiotic and as usual he had a fit. The smell and the cold table told him what was happening. Except this day something different occurred. In the midst of his adversity I reached out and touched his back, stroking his fur. Immediately he calmed down and was peaceful. He knew the touch of his master's hand.

I broke into tears. The vet thought I was crying over my cat and I did love my cat. Yet I had a revelation then and there. If my cat knew the touch of his master's hand how much more I should know the touch of mine.

I learned a lesson that day. Did I know the touch of my Master? I began to seek the Lord with all my heart. He was faithful then and He is faithful now.

The incident with my cat happened many years ago, but the lesson that I learned will be with me forever.

In any situation the child of God can find peace because of the touch of the "Master's Hand."

Dear Lord, thank You for the many lessons we learn through Your guidance throughout our lives. May we feel Your touch each day. In Jesus' name. Amen.

March 28 Read Malachi 4:2-3

BLESSINGS ALL AROUND US

Bible Thought: "Blessings *are* upon the head of the just: but silence covereth the mouth of the wicked" (Proverbs 10:6).

Jesus has provided the greatest gift in the history of the human race. He sacrificed His own life for our eternal salvation. Yet He sends beautiful gifts just waiting to be opened every day. Wonderful little surprises occur and unless we are tuned in they will go right on by and never be noticed. I think that offends our heavenly Father who lovingly wants to bless.

Let's have childlike faith. Children abandon themselves in life and their faith is so great. May we see with our heart. Seeing with the heart is the best sight of all. Seeing with your heart enables us to reach out in love without criticism or judgment.

Listening with the heart helps us to read between the lines. I must listen with my heart if I'm going to hear that gentle whisper. (1 Kings 19:12)

Realize love has no boundaries. Love is not based upon performance or "What's in it for me?" These special little blessings only come through unselfish love and acceptance without a thought of being reciprocated.

Praying without ceasing keeps us focused on what is the most important thing in life…the assurance of our destiny.

Receive God's blessings today and pass them on.

Dear God, thank You for the many blessings You provide. May we never cease to be thankful. In Jesus marvelous name. Amen.

March 29 Read Philippians 4:6-8

RUN TO GOD'S WINGS

Bible Thought: "Cast thy burden on the LORD, and he shall sustain thee: he shall never suffer the righteous to be moved" (Psalm 55:22).

What do we do when trials come? Run to His wings! God's Word is faithful and true. He has a solution for every problem. Whatever the circumstance there will never be lasting relief from the cares of this world through any other means. Only Jesus can set one free.

A wonderful pattern for life is given in Psalm 37. Fret not, trust, delight, commit and rest in the Lord. Following this guide would erase a lot of spiritual, mental and physical problems.

I'm not saying it is easy but a direct constant focus on these principles bring life and peace.

A mother hen doesn't run here and there trying to round up her baby chicks. She calls, spreads her wings and covers her children. They must run to her to be safe.

In the darkest moment of your life, please know God is there, waiting for you to run to His wings. Run there today.

Dear precious Lord, forgive us for worry and anxiety. May we face trials boldly knowing You are in total control. In Jesus' wonderful name. Amen.

March 30 Read Isaiah 43:1-5

YOU ARE FORGIVEN

Bible Thought: "But thanks *be* to God, which giveth us the victory through our Lord Jesus Christ" (1 Corinthians 15:57).

You are forgiven. Gone are the sins that beset you. Your old life has died. Your life Is hidden in Jesus. You no longer live but Jesus lives in you. That same power that raised Jesus from the dead lives in you. He is the glory and lifter of your head. Through Him you can do all things. You are more than a conqueror.

Your enemies come at you one way, but they flee seven ways. A thousand fall at your side and ten thousand at your right hand, but they do not come near you. You are girded with truth and have on the breastplate of righteousness. Your feet are shod with the gospel of peace. You have the shield of faith, quenching all the fiery darts of the enemy. You wear the helmet of salvation and the Sword of the Spirit.

You overcome by the blood of the Lamb and the Word of your testimony. Your God reigns. You abide under His shadow and dwell in His secret place.

Rejoice that your name is written in the Lamb's Book of Life.

How do I know? Because all you have to do is give your heart to Jesus and obey Him.

Do that today. Assure your destiny.

Dear Lord, praise rises up and spills to overflowing when we think of Jesus' sacrifice. We give you our hearts. May we strive to follow You all of our days. In Jesus' name.

Amen.

March 31 Read 2 Chronicles 32:6-7

ONLY BELIEVE

Bible Thought: "Jesus said unto him, 'If thou canst believe, all things are possible to him that believeth'" (Mark 9:23).

All through the Bible we read of the glorious feats God has performed. In today's reading we see Hezekiah's great belief and faith. Yet many today do not believe until they face a life or death experience. Only God can fill the vacuum in the human heart.

Ask someone who has been healed. Ask someone who has known the "peace that passes all understanding." Ask someone who sought God and all addictions left. Ask any of these if they believe.

God is bigger than any circumstance and bigger than any mountain. He is the core of being alive. Every thought, word and deed is subject to Him.

God's love is greater than any love known by man. If you doubt that love for you just remember the great sacrifice God gave for all of us…His only begotten Son.

Ask God how much He loves you and He will tell you.

All you have to do is "BELIEVE."

Dear wonderful God, You are faithful and true. You are "Joy in the morning, the Light of our lives and the Hope of eternity. We praise You today. In that wonderful name above all names. His name is Jesus. Amen.

APRIL

April 1 Read Philippians 2:1-5

MY PRAYER

Bible Thought: "Unto thee, O LORD do I lift up my soul"(Psalm 25:1).

"I cling to You O God. I cling with every fiber of my being, for without you I am hopelessly lost. Thank You for Your tender mercies and Your loving kindness. I thank You for deliverance.

Grant me the knowledge and wisdom to recognize the onset of the enemy's strategy. May I boldly resist temptations in the power of Your precious blood.

May I encourage others and in the midst of problems, may I bravely declare that through Your Son I am more than a conqueror.

Cause me to realize moment by moment I am living in Your divine will for my life.

Help me to run to You when I am tempted. May I die to self so You can rise up mightily in me. Empower me to forget those things in the past that I might make a new beginning this very day to "press on toward the mark of the high calling in You."

I want to be strong in faith and obedience while glorifying You in every deed and word. When I make my heavenly flight may I awake in Your wondrous presence.

You are everything to me and I love You! Amen."

April 2 Read Isaiah 42:10-12

WE ARE A JOYFUL PEOPLE

Bible Thought: "Cry out and shout, thou inhabitant of Zion: for great is the Holy One of Israel in the midst of thee" (Isaiah 6).

I call joyful people "joy givers." They persevere no matter what. They are too busy helping others. Blessings return to those who give themselves away and their joy makes happy hearts. Where does this joy come from?

His name is Jesus. He is peace for the fearful, refuge for the lonely, triumph for the trials, conqueror for the lowly, strength for the weak, restoration for the addicted, encouragement for the downtrodden, mercy for the suffering, grace for the sinner, forgiveness for the offender, comfort for the sorrowful, life for the lifeless, delight for the desperate, hope for the hopeless, love for the unloved, wholeness for the broken victory for the defeated and so much more.

I have noticed many characteristics in joyful people. One thing is above all other, "they let go and let God."

My granddaughter shouted loud when she sung her favorite song to others, "Glad to be a Christian, glad to be a Christian, glad to be a Christian...I'm trusting in the Lord." (And she sang it joyfully!)

Joyful people are excited about Jesus and that makes life delicious.

Let's shout aloud and sing for joy.

Dear Lord, may we sing of Your goodness and shout with joy for Your salvation. In Jesus' name. Amen.

April 3 Read Matthew 27:27-31

PAIN...THE PRICE OF LOVE

Bible Thought: "But God will redeem my soul from the power of the grave: for he shall receive me. Selah" (Psalm 49:15).

When Lane, our youngest son, portrayed Jesus in pageants, I had an emotional upheaval big time. When he came down that aisle shouldering that old wooden cross, I lost it. I sobbed out loud as I witnessed the beating, mockery, anguish and pain of just acting out the ordeal.

Lane stumbled beneath the load while soldiers beat him as he struggled to get up. The red stains on his clothing and body, the jeering of the soldiers, and the agony of it all pierced my heart. It seemed so real. I must have felt only a tiny part of the pain endured by Mary, the mother of Jesus.

Mary's Son became her Savior. I wonder, in the deepest recesses of her heart, if Mary realized it had to be. Her Son's sacrifice sealed mankind's only hope.

As Lane ascended out of sight, I felt once again the depths of God's love. If pain is the price for feeling love; Jesus thought you and I were worth it! He voluntarily gave His life, an atonement for our sins.

He went to the cross for you and me. He is the greatest love known to man.

Dear wonderful Lord, in the most humble way we know how, we thank You for Jesus.

We praise You today for Your love, guidance, care and favor. Grant us boldness in sharing the marvelous news of Jesus. In His beautiful name. Amen.

April 4 Read John 20:26-28

THE PERFECT LAMB

Bible Thought: "Saying with a loud voice, Worthy is the Lamb that was slain to receive power and riches, and wisdom and strength and honour, and glory, and blessing" (Revelation 5:12).

Can you hear the cries of the mob?

"Crucify Him! Crucify Him!"

Jesus stumbles. The rocks gouge the soles of His feet. The searing pain of the weight of the cross is excruciating. He cannot bear the weight. Simon is commanded to carry the cross. Jesus is brutally beaten until only shreds of skin are exposed on His back. The sound of nails being driven into His hands and feet echoes across the land.

Dark clouds appear to have won, but wait. The heavens roar. The veil is rent. Darkness is surrendering. Death has been conquered.

The world will never be the same.

From this moment on, darkness and death must bow their knees to THE PERFECT LAMB.

Dear precious Lord, thank You for Jesus The Perfect Lamb who gave His life for every one of us. May our lives reflect our thankfulness in everything we do and say. In Jesus' beautiful name. Amen.

April 5 Read Isaiah 53:3-7

RESURRECTION BRINGS NEW LIFE

Bible Thought: "Yet a little while, and the world seeth me no more; but ye see me: because I live, ye shall live also" (John 14:19).

Jesus resurrects hope, goodness and faith. The Resurrection symbolizes victory. It's victory over sin and victory over death. Jesus took our place on the cross to save you and me. We cannot save ourselves. The same power that resurrected Jesus will resurrect that body in the grave. The body isn't needed anymore. It has been transformed. Those who have gone on before us are alive in one form of life while we remain in another.

The path of Jesus from Gethsemane to Calvary was marked with His precious blood. It's been called the "Via Dolorosa," the way of sorrow. The agony Jesus endured cannot be fathomed. His love for you and me goes far beyond our understanding, a love that is stronger than death. No other event in human history has filled the believer with such hope and promise.

Jesus is risen! One day His faithful ones will receive a crown of righteousness prepared for those who have fought a good fight, finished the course and kept the faith. It is God's seal forever.

Let us rejoice and be exceedingly glad.

Dear precious Lord, thank You for Your incredible love. We praise You today with all our hearts. Teach us how to love You even more. In that name of Jesus. Amen.

April 6 Read Luke 23:44-47

PAID IN FULL

Bible Thought: "All we like sheep have gone astray; we have turned every one to his own way; and the LORD hath laid on him the iniquity of us all" (Isaiah 53:4-7).

Jesus bore it all. The sacrificial Lamb suffered in silence. In that horrendous time of suffering Jesus had to bear the painful agony of being alone.

Sin is a terminal disease, but Jesus is the cure. When a repentant soul receives Jesus, then "Forgiven" is written against the account of sin, reading "Paid in full."

"I had a dream, a frightful sight. It was so dark, as black as night.

Upon a cross there was a form. It was hard to see in such a storm.

Writhing in pain with jeers from the crowd...Roman soldiers looking proud.

I looked again and I gasped in tears. It was I on the cross for the sins of my years.

Then Jesus came and took my place. All was forgiven and my sins erased.

I awoke to proclaim the wondrous praise of that dear one, such boundless grace.

He chose the cross with agony. He paid the price for you and me!"

Dear wonderful Lord, thank You for Jesus. May every thought, word and deed glorify His beautiful name. In His name. Amen.

April 7 Matthew 13:37-42

PLANT GOOD SEEDS

Bible Thought: "But that which beareth thorns and briers is rejected, and is nigh unto cursing; whose end is to be burned" (Hebrews 6:8).

I think I'm the only one who can grow weeds year-round. If left alone they get larger, tougher and harder to get rid of. I find a similar parallel in my spiritual life. I must plant good seeds and weed out the bad.

Daily I must guard what I plant by my thoughts, speech and action. The enemy comes with all kinds of enticing scenes of beauty that results in ugliness. The enemy's undermining relentless tactics seem harmless at times, but behind every attack is a subtle, sabotaging sin. Sin is not an island, but a chain reaction. This puts a great responsibility on me.

I owe a debt not only to my husband, children, grandchildren and neighbors, but also to the world if I am trying to make it a better place. I have a long way to go and grow. I haven't made it by any means.

So I keep chopping "weeds."

As a child of the King, I pray my steadfast purpose includes the active determination to "weed out" things that do not honor my Lord.

Let's plant good deeds!

Dear precious Lord, may we be sensitive to bad seeds, we pray. May we be discerning in every thought, word and deed. Thank You for Jesus, our beautiful Savior. In His name. Amen.

April 8 Read Isaiah 41: 10-13

FINDING PEACE IN A TROUBLED WORLD

Bible Thought: "The LORD is my light and my salvation; whom shall I fear? the LORD is the strength of my life; of whom shall I be afraid? (Psalm 27:1).

Bad news seems to dominate the media and one might get a little depressed about all the wrongdoing across the planet. Those who trade their fears for faith can conquer fear of troubling times.

God has a plan for our lives. We are wanted and loved. He wants the highest good for all of us. God has made an investment. His incredible love for mankind is so great He sent Jesus to die for our sins.

When anxiety tries to attack, reading God's promises bring peace. I call it "feeding the faith." God's Word does not return to Him void. Nothing can happen to you or me that Jesus cannot handle. Underneath are His everlasting arms.

Trusting in Jesus enables one to meet fear head on because He has given us weapons to fight the enemy and win.

When fear comes knocking at your door, hang out a sign that says, "Wrong
Address. Faith Lives Here." That will enable you to win one more battle on your way to glory.

We can conquer fear in a troubled world. Why? We have an anchor that is faithful and true.

His name is Jesus.

Dear Lord, thank You for giving us "the spirit of power, love and a sound mind." May each day be filled with ever increasing faith with praise and thanksgiving. In Jesus' precious name. Amen.

April 9 Read Jeremiah 31:9-13

LET GOD LEAD YOU

Bible Thought: "Because strait is the gate and narrow is the way which leadeth unto life, and few there be that find it" (Matthew 7:14).

A mother cat dashed across the pavement. Behind her, all in a row, three tiny kittens tried to keep the pace. My husband stepped on the brake and came to a stop as we watched the touching scenario. Mother cat disappeared into weeds with two of her babies following. The last little kitten became confused and lost sight of his security. He turned around and ran in the opposite direction.

How much like we humans! Many of us lose our way and run from the One who loves us the most. Our security is in Him. By faith we run to Him for safekeeping.

Mother cat knew her baby needed her. She darted out of the weeds, ran to the kitten, surrounded him, and then sprinted to the weeds again with her baby following.

What a lesson for me. God knows where I am. I am not alone. I call out to Him and He leads me to safety.

Run to Him today. He will lead you too.

Dear precious Lord, we praise and thank You today for Your protection and safety. You are so beautiful, faithful and steadfast. May our love for You spill out and run over to everyone we meet today. In that name above all names. His name is Jesus. Amen.

April 10 Read Colossians 3:12-17

THE BIBLE...FOR ALL GENERATIONS

BIBLE THOUGHT: "For this God is our God for ever and ever: he will be our guide even unto death" (Psalm 48:14).

I love the Bibles relatives have passed down to me. Memories return when I think of the guiding force of life. God's Word is a blueprint for yesterday, today and the future.

This is the Book that proclaims the dignity of the individual and teaches we are created in the image of God.

This Book gives standards to live by to find peace and happiness.

This wonderful message of hope has changed all of history, bringing life and blessings wherever it is believed and obeyed. Once again it can bring hope to our nation and to you today.

Trust in the Lord and acknowledge Him. In His Word you will find golden nuggets that will help you on your way to heaven.

Read the Bible. Today could be a new beginning for you if you believe the message of God's Word.

The Bible...a precious gift for all generations.

Read it and be blessed.

Dear Lord, thank You for Your Word. Thank You for Your Son. Empower us to spread the Gospel and tell the world the "Good News!" In the wonderful name of Jesus. Amen.

April 11 Read Philippians 4:6-9

BATTLE OF THE MIND

Bible Thought: "For as he thinketh in his heart, so is he…" (Proverbs 23:7).

The enemy of our souls causes torment by worrisome thoughts. A perfectly good day can be ruined by the onslaught of allowing the enemy's "stinking thinking."

God has put within each one of us the power to stop negative thoughts.

To stop the negative thought process we deliberately saturate our minds with scriptures, studying and meditating. We are stubborn in our resistance. We refuse to accept or entertain the "what ifs" thoughts.

We count our many blessings and are grateful for what we have. The richest on the planet is the person who is rich in Jesus. He will never leave nor forsake you or me. The only way to safety is in Christ Jesus.

We pray without ceasing and think of the good things. We are optimistic because nothing is impossible with God. When things in the natural look the worst God comes upon the scene and changes the circumstances around.

We are fighting the enemy in the battle of the mind. Let's put on our boxing gloves and fight the good fight of faith.

God is on our side and that makes us winners!

Dear Lord, thank You for being our awesome King. With You all things are possible and we walk triumphantly. Blessed be You forever. In Jesus' beautiful name. Amen.

April 12 Read Joshua 14:10-12

FORGET YOUR AGE AND ENJOY LIFE

Bible Thought: "The hoary head is a crown of glory, if it be found in the way of righteousness" (Proverbs 16:31).

Getting older does not mean you are unacceptable. The golden years can be filled with things you never had time for previously. The world needs you because your prayers are high priority.

I love Caleb's attitude in today's Bible reading. His faith in God was awesome. He served God with vigor and optimism all of his life. Even in older years he said, "I am just as vigorous to go out to battle now as I was then." Yea Caleb!" What a guy. We may not be facing armies like he did but surely we can have a winning spirit like he had.

Remember, "...the joy of the LORD will make you strong" (Nehemiah 8:10).

"But unto you that fear my name shall the Sun of righteousness arise with healing in his wings; and ye shall go forth, and grow up as calves of the stall" (Malachi 4:2).

Be happy you're getting older.

Enjoy your life.

Make life "delicious!"

Dear precious Lord, thank You for giving strength for our days. A lifetime of serving You is a privilege. Thank You for our Redeemer, the King of kings. In Jesus' beautiful name. Amen

April 13 Read Proverbs 2:5-9

A FATHER'S LOVE

Bible Thought: "Trust in the LORD with all thine heart; and lean not unto thine own understanding" (Proverbs 3:5).

When I was a child severe nosebleeds left me anemic and I needed a blood transfusion. My earthly father, having the same blood type, quickly and willingly gave his blood to save me. My heavenly Father has done the same thing.

Godly fathers realize children are gifts from God and are a heritage of the Lord. Fathers are admonished to train their children in spiritual matters. Fathers show affection. They are not ashamed to tuck their child in bed with a goodnight kiss. Fathers like these bless their family and the memories last a lifetime.

A father who loves his child will move heaven and earth to help his child in need. To voluntarily give up a son is unthinkable and yet that is what God did. One might voluntarily give his or her life for their very own child but would they for another? Rarely, but that is what Jesus did.

Think of the pain that God endured having to turn His back on Jesus, who was dying on a cross for our sins. Can you fathom such love? Do you know that love? You can know today.

Come to Jesus. It's a Father's love.

Dear Lord, we thank You today for such great love. Teach us how to love You even more. In that beautiful name of Jesus. Amen.

April 14 Read Psalm 40: 8-11

LISTEN TO YOUR HEART

Bible Thought: "Be still, and know that I *am* God: I will be exalted among the heathen, I will be exalted in the earth" (Psalm 46:10).

My student had not completed his work. He offered many excuses, none of which were acceptable. Many compensatory strategies were utilized to no avail, including the withholding of recess.

As I silently prayed for wisdom, I surprised myself by saying, "Return to your seat and listen to your heart."

After a few my minutes my student came to my desk with the task completed. With a look of accomplishment he exclaimed, "I listened to my heart."

In this fast tumultuous world how many times have I stopped to listen to my heart? I learned a profound lesson that day from my student. When I make mistakes I must stop and listen to that still small voice.

My heart tells me God is on my side. Nothing is impossible with Him. His eyes run to and fro over all the earth finding those hearts that are tender toward Him. His children know His voice and another they will not follow.

Every one of us has a void, a vacuum that only God can fill. He sent Jesus to buy us back that we might spend eternity with Him. His love for us is the greatest love this world can ever know.

Let us stop and take time to listen to our hearts.

Dear Lord, please help us to realize You are the real "Teacher" who has the answers for the "School of Life."

April 15 Read Matthew 18:21-22

FORGIVENESS DISARMS THE ENEMY

Bible Thought: "As far as the east is from the west, so far hath he removed our transgressions from us" (Psalm 103:12).

During a misunderstanding with a fellow worker, I spoke in haste, my voice rising. Immediately my conscience convicted me and I felt remorse as I walked away. In shame and embarrassment, I hurried back to her.

"Please forgive me," I pleaded through tears. "I forgive you," came her answer.

Thankful for her forgiveness, I retreated to my office, but I couldn't shake what I had done. *How could I have done that?* I asked myself, *what kind of person am I?*

"Dear Lord, I am so sorry I talked to her like that."

I punished myself the rest of the week. Then on Sunday morning the preacher's words confirmed the truth: "Not only must we ask forgiveness, we must accept forgiveness for ourselves. We are all sinners saved by grace."

My friend had forgiven me, and God had forgiven me. I forgave myself and confessed my sin with a new determination to speak softly and turn away wrath the next time I have a misunderstanding.

Learning to forgive others as well as ourselves removes inner turmoil. True forgiveness does not keep bringing up the offense and relieving in the past about it.

God forgives us. Let's forgive ourselves.

Dear precious Lord, You are a forgiving, loving God. Thank You for forgiving our sins as we walk in the "Light" of Your love. May we be quick to repent, forgiving others and ourselves. In Jesus' beautiful name. Amen.

April 16 Read Hebrews 13:8-13

FIGHTING THE FIGHT

Bible Thought: "Nay, in all these things we are more than conquerors through him that loved us" (Roman 8:37).

Someone remarked to me one day, "Isn't it wonderful? We get to play until we win!" What a profound thought. I thought about her statement a lot and she is right. The score is not tallied up in this life.

We are in a daily war. It's a war of good versus evil. One by one, each one of us helps to push back the darkness. At times it may seem we are not getting anywhere but we press on, knowing this life is only temporary. Eternity lies in the unseen Kingdom. We are looking for a city whose Builder and Maker is God. We are in this world, but not of it. While we are in it, we do whatever we can while taking a stand for righteousness.

Adding action to faith yields great results. By not compromising, each day brings more strength and more progress.

Fighting the good fight of faith, obeying God's commandments, loving others and doing good brings a peaceful joyful life here and an eternal home with God.

Be encouraged. We are winning.

Keep fighting the fight.

Dear Lord, thank You for giving Your children the victory in this life. May we have boldness and an uncompromising stand in all that we do. Thank You for Jesus, our beautiful Savior. In His name. Amen.

April 17 Read Psalm 91:3-7

GOD'S SHELTER IN LIFE'S STORMS

Bible Thought: "The LORD shall preserve thee from all evil: he shall preserve thy soul" Psalm 121:7).

The winds roared like the proverbial lion, but that's how it is in eastern New Mexico.

Lady, our beautiful sorrel mare, seemed more like a person than a horse. She came galloping up eager to eat when I called, but she wouldn't get anywhere close to her trough. She stood several feet away, calling to me with her whinnies. "I'm too scared but I'm hungry too," she seemed to say.

The wind continued to clang against the barn and her eyes never left mine as she neighed pitifully.

"Come on Lady," I coaxed as I tried to tempt her by pouring her feed into her trough. "Don't be afraid I'm here and I will take care of you."

Then I thought, *how many times have I stood in the howling storms of life with fear when I have a "Master" that has always taken care of me?* Right then and there I repented and thanked God for His goodness. I resolved to trust, delight, commit my way, rest and be patient in His loving care.

Finally, Lady came cautiously to me and I put my arms around her beautiful neck.

If Lady can trust her master so can I trust mine.

Dear God, forgive us for getting anxious in life's adversities. We thank You for Your mercies. May we never take them for granted. In Jesus' beautiful name. Amen.

April 18 Read Matthew 18:2-6

BECOME LIKE A LITTLE CHILD

Bible Thought: "Children's children are the crown of old men; and the glory of children are their fathers" (Proverbs 17:6).

Children have within them the secret of life…unconditional love, forgiveness and complete trust.

The children's gift to me throughout my teaching career is forever embedded in my heart. The heart of a child is a precious treasure. It is no wonder Jesus held the little children in His arms.

To come to Jesus with an humble, forgiving, repentant heart with the faith of a child cannot be measured. We are to be child "like," not child "ish."

Children are gifts from God. They are something to be treasured, trained in God's way and led in His paths. We are to teach God's principles, "And ye shall teach them your children, speaking of them when thou sittest in thine house, and when thou walkest by the way, when thou liest down, and when thou risest up (Deuteronomy 11:19-20).

While we are training our children, let us become like them in simple childlike faith and trust in the One who gives us abundant life here and an eternal one in heaven.

Precious Lord, thank You for children. Help us to lead and train them in Your ways, giving glory and honor to You. In the name of our Savior Jesus. Amen.

April 19 Read Psalm 68:32-34

GRANNY SANG HER FAITH

Bible Thought: "O let the nations be glad and sing for joy: for thou shalt judge the people righteously, and govern the nations upon earth. Selah" (Psalm 67:4).

Granny's singing filled every facet of her life. I seldom have to look at a hymnal church. I know most of them by heart for I learned them on my Granny's knees. Many times I awaken in the night with some of those songs Granny sang.

Granny's daily advice still lingers in my file of memorable blessings, "The Lord is sure good to us. I love to sing about Him."

We were called to the hospital when Granny was released from a tired weary body. At ninety-two she had entered that "land" she used to sing about. She was as beautiful in death as she was in life. I felt sadness but joy knowing Granny sang her way to heaven.

As we walked to the car I stopped my husband, "Shhh. Shhh." Can you hear it?

"What? He asked.

I was sure I heard someone singing." I put my arms around him and looking at the breathtaking sunrise, I suddenly exclaimed,

"Isn't it a beautiful day to go to heaven?"

Dear wondrous Lord, thank You for the time we have on earth… time to love and time to pursue the plan You have for our lives. Thank You Lord, for grandmothers. Most of all thank You for our Savior. May we always sing praises for the many blessings You bring.

In that beautiful name. His name is Jesus. Amen.

April 20 Read Habakkuk 3:17-19

CONQUERING FAITH

Bible Thought: "For we walk by faith, not by sight" (2 Corinthians 5:7).

A pilot in a small plane remembered his instructor told him that if he ever found himself in a thick fog to remember this important statement: "The pilot's tendency in a fog is to fly downward, getting dangerously close to the ground. In that case, let the plane have full reign...let go and let the plane fly by what it was made to do."

One day the pilot found himself in just such a situation and he remembered his instructions. He let the plane fly what it was made to do. Immediately he felt the plane rise, gaining a safe altitude which initiated a safe landing.

We may not be pilots, but many times we find ourselves surrounded by problems with no visibility, dangerously close to crashing. It is important at these times to listen to our Instructor's voice: "Be careful for nothing; but in every thing by prayer and supplication with thanksgiving let your requests be made known unto God" (Philippians 4:6).

Conquering faith avoids many wrecks in life. Jesus, our pilot, knows our course and He will bring us to a safe landing.

Let's get in the plane of hope today and fly by conquering faith. That is what we were made to do.

Dear precious Lord, because of Your great sacrifice we fly and soar on wings of love.

May our faith be ever increasing. In that wonderful name of Jesus. Amen.

April 21 Read Hebrews 12:1-4

FAITH, OUR MOST PRECIOUS POSSESSION

Bible Thought: "For whatsoever is born of God overcometh the world: and this is the victory that overcometh the world, *even* our faith" (1 John 5:4).

Does life ever seem to be one battle after another? Do you manage to survive one hurdle only to be confronted by another? Welcome to the club.

We are in a fight to preserve and protect what we believe. Faith filled people focus on Jesus. They have His Word in their hearts and shut their ears to doubt and unbelief.

Faith-filled people do not give up, back up, let up or shut up about their faith. When it comes to the end of life, they have the hope of eternal glory.

The apostle Paul admonishes us to not only run this race of life with diligence, but to even "stretch" and "strain" forward to reach the goal and obtain the prize. (Philippians 3:14).

Remember with Jesus you have a love that can never be taken away and a joy that lasts forever. It's always too soon to quit. Quitters never win and winners never lose.

Keep the faith. It is your most precious possession.

Dear wonderful Lord, may we have incredible faith that will never be lost. Thank You for Your Word that empowers us to speak faith filled words to others. In Jesus precious name. Amen.

April 22 Read Mark 10:14-16

LOVE IN ANY LANGUAGE

Bible Thought: "For ye are all the children of God by faith in Christ Jesus" (Galatians 3:26).

"Hello Mrs. Clayton. I hope you remember me. I called to invite you to my graduation. Will you please be there?"

"Of course Bobby," I answered. "And I'm so glad you remembered me. Thank you."

I couldn't believe it was ten years ago that Bobby, this sweet little second grader, was in my class.

I found a seat and beamed with pride. I almost squealed when I saw Bobby's name on the program as valedictorian. All through the service I couldn't keep my eyes off Bobby.

He had written his own speech and he spoke it in English first and then Spanish. He told of his faith in God and how important it is to live by biblical principles.

"You will be leaving now," Bobby told his classmates. "Live your life with no regrets. Make every day count. Make your life count with purpose and love for others."

I couldn't catch all the words in Spanish but I surely did in English. I saw a lot of teary eyes. Those who didn't understand Spanish and those who didn't understand English all had something in common. Love happens in any language if you have Jesus in your heart.

Dear Lord, may we always walk in Your love and share it with others along the way.

Amen.

April 23 Read Psalm 46:1-5

REJOICE TODAY

Bible Thought: "Every day I will bless thee; and I will praise thy name for ever and ever" Psalm 145:2).

I love daybreak. So does my husband's horse. When Beauty sees her master coming to feed her, she has what I call a "happy fit." She rears up, frolics around and runs to meet the one who takes care of her every need. She stands in delight of her master's presence. Having eaten her fill, she quenches her thirst with cool water and heads for her green pasture.

What a picture for my Master and me. If I miss my daily feast upon God's Word, my thirst is not quenched and my day does not go as well. Being with my "Master" takes first place. Giving Him quality time keeps life in focus.

Many times I awaken with a song of praise in my heart. I like to think Jesus has been waiting for me. I tell Him of my love, thank Him for His faithfulness and delight in His presence. I linger in His "green pastures and still waters." Having feasted upon His Word, my thirst is quenched with "Living Water" and I am ready to start my day rejoicing!

You can do that too.

Dear wonderful God, we rejoice in this day You have given. May we share Your love and Your "Good News" to everyone we meet. May the joy we feel bubble up and overflow onto others. In Jesus' beautiful name. Amen.

April 24 Read Jeremiah 29:11-13

BE ENTHUSIASTIC FOR GOD

Bible Thought: "But I have trusted in thy mercy; my heart shall rejoice in thy salvation" Psalm 13:5).

I call enthusiastic people "world changers." Because of Jesus, they take courage in who they are and what they can become.

Since God has given us a gift, let's share love and friendship with others. Enthusiasm is contagious. It brings appreciation for things otherwise unnoticed. Get excited about sunsets, flowers blooming, clean air to breath, fleecy clouds with rainbows, horses running in the wind, or a dove's cooing. God made them all.

Enthusiasm for God makes me delight in how many people will smile back at me, ex-students recognizing me, or hugs from Uncle Steve at the rest home.

What opportunities will you have today to share the good things in life? Who will you meet to encourage? Share your enthusiasm.

With excitement I appreciate the many things I enjoy in this earthly journey. Money may not be a lot, but blessings cannot be bought. For a blessed life, think big with faith and courage. You will enter a new life of hope.

Your faith and belief in God are the greatest things you can ever have and that is something to be enthusiastic about.

Dear precious Lord, thank You for life. May we get so excited about life that we share it with everyone we meet. Thank You for the joy that overflows in Your love. In Jesus' beautiful name. Amen.

April 25 Read John 18:1-7

SACRIFICIAL LOVE

Bible Thought: "Hereby perceive we the love *of God*, because he laid down his life for us: and we ought to lay down *our* lives for the brethren" (1 John 3:16).

Jesus did no wrong, only good. He brought sight to the blind and healed the sick. He made cripples walk and restored the broken-hearted. He brought hope to a hopeless world. He radiated love. His teachings have stood the test of time. He demonstrated the importance of forgiveness, compassion for fellowman and gave instructions for the only way to true happiness.

For all of this He was mocked, scourged, beaten and crucified. He thought you and I were worth it. Yes He dreaded it. He agonized so much that His "sweat was as great drops of blood." His whole purpose for coming was to redeem mankind from the very jaws of the enemy, but He didn't count the cost. His sacrifice for every human being that has ever lived was worth it all in His eyes. We are His children and precious in His sight.

The sacrifice of the cross is the greatest love the world has ever known, because His love endured the cruelest form of pain, shame and rejection.

Jesus came to buy us back from destruction.

That is sacrificial love!

Dear God, we stand and weep, sorrow for our sins, but joy for forgiveness and salvation.

Thank You with every fiber of our being. In Jesus' wonderful name. Amen.

April 26 Read Psalm 100

LOVE MAKES HAPPY DAYS

Bible Thought: "These things have I spoken unto you, that my joy might remain in you, and that your joy might be full" (John 15:11).

When our youngest son graduated from high school, he walked across the stage, stopped and gave his Dad, the high school principal, a giant bear hug. The crowd cheered and I cried.

One unforgettable Christmas occurred when my husband took me in his arms and said, "Next to Jesus, you are my special gift."

On the second day of school one year, a cute little second grader came bounding in my classroom with a bouquet of flowers. The card read, "Teacher, I love being in your class. Love, from Don."

Yes, love makes happy days, but the happiest day of all is revealed in 1 Peter 1:8, "Whom having not seen, ye love; in whom, though now ye see *him* not, yet believing, ye rejoice with joy unspeakable and full of glory" (1 Peter:8).

If the world could only recognize the gift of Jesus, it would be a heaven on earth. Everyone has two choices. One leads to life everlasting. I pray we choose that one.

Until we see Jesus, let's make happy days on earth.

Dear precious Lord, thank You for happy days on earth, but they can't compare seeing You face to face. We will love and praise You forever and ever. In that beautiful name, the name above all names. His name is Jesus. Amen.

April 27 Read Philippians 4:4-8

ALL THINGS WORK TOGETHER FOR GOOD

Bible Thought: "And we know that all things work together for good to them that love God, to them who are the called according to his purpose" (Romans 8:28).

Do you ever worry? What's the worst thing that can happen to you? If you are in Christ Jesus, there cannot be a worst thing happening to you. Your trust is in the living God and He is mindful of you.

How can you lose? God loves you more than you can ever imagine. He is not going to ignore His children or their needs. You were in His mind before the foundation of the world. You were planned by God, loved by God and wanted by God. He will move heaven and earth on your behalf.

Do we love our earthly children? Would we not do every thing we could for that child in need? God loves us even more.

Believe the Lord Jesus today. Trust Him in every circumstance of your life. No matter what the problem or situation is He will take it and make it for your good.

Dear wonderful God, how we praise You today for Your faithfulness. Thank You for the victory in Jesus. Thank You for His sacrifice that we might live abundantly here and forever in eternity. We pray in that name above all names, that mighty name of Jesus. Amen.

April 28 Read Psalm 103:1-4

SHOUT THE GOOD NEWS

Bible Thought: "Make a joyful noise unto the LORD, all ye lands" (Psalm 100:1).

My God is bigger than any mountain. My God is bigger than any circumstance. He is the core of my inner being. Every thought, word and deed is subject to Him.

I stand strong in the Lord and in the power of His might. My heart is fixed. I am trusting in the Lord. I am not moved by what I see, touch or feel. I am moved by the promises of God, that He is faithful and true.

I will keep my eyes on Jesus. I will praise Him in every thought. I will praise His wondrous love with every breath. I will share that love and bless others.

The Lord is the strength of my life. That strength gives me joy and a merry heart. That joy is health to my bones.

I am happy in the Lord. I am whole. I am free.

I walk on golden streets and fly with joy on wings of love.

Blessed be my Lord, the Mighty One of Israel.

Dear God, You are the song in the night, an ever present Light. May our thoughts always be of Your kindness and steadfastness. A "thank you" is so small, but we give You our all. In Jesus' beautiful name. Amen.

April 29 Isaiah 40:9-11

SEEKING HIS CHILD

Bible Thought: "I am the good shepherd: the good shepherd giveth his life for the sheep" (John 10:11).

Our middle son accidentally caused his younger brother to fall and his head hit a rock. Blood gushed as we rushed Lane to the hospital. He was treated and sent back home. It was not as serious as it looked. In the excitement we forgot about Lance. When we returned home we found a note, "Dear Dad, I've run away because I am too much trouble."

We searched and searched for our lost "sheep." We were about to call the police when something caught my eye. Our dog's black tail wagged behind the butane tank.

I saw Jesus in my husband that day. Emmitt ran to Lance, picked him up and held him tight. "You are important to us. We love you. We could never be without you. You and your brothers have a special place in our hearts. If you ever ran away we would have to go too because we want to be where you are."

That scene of a father's love for His child is frozen in my memory. What a picture of God's love, seeking His lost child.

The Lord is our Shepherd.

Dear precious Lord, what a wonderful Shepherd You are. We praise You today for reaching down to us and picking us up with Your tender mercy. In Jesus' beautiful name.

April 30 Read Isaiah 43:19-21

WALKING THROUGH THE FIRE

Bible Thought: "Ye are of God, little children, and have overcome them: because greater is he that is in you, than he that is in the world"(1 John 4:4).

Life has a way of dealing some pretty hard blows. In the midst of a crisis, it is hard to make decisions. Many troubles pile upon troubles, blinding our thinking process. Yet, "There is nothing new under the sun" (Ecclesiastes 1:9)

Somewhere, sometime, someone has gone through the same situation. We either face the adversity with faith and courage or buckle under it.

Whenever you feel you have been put in a boxing arena, don't go down for the count, but come out swinging. Losers focus on the war. Winners focus on the victory. Dwelling on the negative is a real joy killer. I would rather have given life my best shot then to retreat in defeat.

With Jesus you have determination, courage and hope. So put on those boxing gloves and plow right through those obstacles in life. Show the world the stuff you're made of. Don't stop in the middle of the fire, but keep going and you will soon be the victor.

Let's be happy. We win. I've read the last page!

Dear precious Lord, with You we always come out victorious Help us to remind ourselves how blessed we are and that we are on our way to that "Fair Land." In that wondrous name of Jesus. Amen.

MAY

May 1 Read Matthew 10:29-31

A LESSON FROM MY FEATHERED FRIENDS

We watched the robins through our window. They looked so cute with their plump bright vests. They danced from tree to tree with exhilaration. However, the reflection of the sunlight on our window seemed to blind their path. Periodically through the morning we heard "thuds" as they flew right into the glare of the glass. Stunned, the robins fell to the ground but after a few minutes they regained their perspective and went on with life.

I find myself like the robins sometimes. If I neglect my quite time I, like the robins, hit invisible "pains." Starting my day with the Lord makes my day much better. It is there I seek direction, guidance and wisdom to make right choices and decisions.

I am thankful God is with me even when I am "stunned" by invisible pains of life. You may be facing something today that appears hopeless. You may feel there is no place to turn to…that you have reached the end of your rope. Not so dear reader! Take heart.

All things are possible with God. Be encouraged today because God's great love cannot be fathomed.

The robins have left but their joy, fortitude and resilience remains with me. If God watches over the sparrow and the robin, I know He watches over you and me.

Those who fly on wings of love soar on clouds of delight!

Dear God thank You for watching over us with Your everlasting love. In that beautiful name of Jesus. Amen.

May 2 Read 1 Chronicles 5:19-22

ACT LIKE THE BIBLE IS TRUE

Bible Thought: "Call unto me, and I will answer thee, and shew thee great and mighty things, which thou knowest not" (Jeremiah 33:3).

Do you believe your prayers are answered? Do you pray expectantly? Do you pray with enthusiasm?

God handed the Hagrites and all their allies over to the Israelites because His people cried out to Him. The Israelites trust in God brought the winning battle.

The Lord gives abundantly, exceedingly above all we could ask or think. He even answers while we are still speaking.

I wonder sometimes what would happen if we acted like the Bible is so? I think we live far beneath our privileges as God's children. Do we worry? We shouldn't. (Philippians 4:13) Are we fearful of new situations? (Romans 8:28). Are we just wandering aimlessly through life with no plan or purpose. No!

So if our steps are ordered aright and each step is guided by a loving Savior who holds everything together, what have we go to lose?

Let's act like the Bible is true.

Dear precious Lord, thank You for Your Word. Thank You for life. Thank You for Jesus.

In His wonderful name. Amen.

May 3 Read Proverbs 24:2-4

THIS HOUSE

Bible Thought: "Blessed is *the man whom* thou choosest, and causest to approach *unto thee, that* he may dwell in thy court; we shall be satisfied with the goodness of thy house, *even* of thy holy temple" (Psalm 65:4).

This house has people in it. This house has love, joy and peace. Yes, this house has had problems but God never left it because when storm clouds appear rainbows come into view.

This house is washed in the blood of the Lamb and is sprinkled on the doorposts of the heart. This house shields and protects from outside adversity. The King of Glory reigns here for this house is a fortress and a refuge.

This house has walls of forgiveness and rooms of love. It is clothed with garments of righteousness.

This house is filled with sunshine for the light of the Son continually brightens others. This house is wired with the power of the Holy Spirit. This house has doors that open with arms of love. Other houses may crumble, but this house stands firm and secure for God is honored here. This house is cemented with His faithfulness.

This house will live forever, for nothing shall ever tear down this house. It is engraved in the palm of God's hand.

Who lives in this house? The ones who allow the Holy Spirit to live in these earthly temples.

Dear wonderful Lord, thank You for living in these temples of clay. May we strive to honor You in these temporary vessels. May we never grieve You, but praise and serve You all of our days. In that beautiful name of Jesus. Amen.

May 4 Read Mark 2:25-28

THE SABBATH

Bible Thought: "And he said unto them, Is it lawful to do good on the sabbath days, or to do evil? to save life, or to kill? But they held their peace" (Mark 3:4).

A father's daughter was fifty miles from home when her car broke down and she realized she had forgotten her cell phone. As she sat praying, an elderly farmer stopped in his pickup. "Do you need some help, Maam?"

"Yes," the frightened young lady answered.

The man approached her car and pulled up the hood. After some prying here and there he said, "I think I know what's wrong but I don't have the tools. I have a friend in the next town and I'll call him on my cell phone."

After the call, the farmer walked to the driver's side and said to the lady, "My friend is coming to help. I'll stay in my pickup until he comes, and then I will follow you to the next town to be sure you are safe. It may be Sunday...a day of rest and worship, but God didn't mean it couldn't be a day of helping someone."

In the Old Testament, Pharisees were so attached to laws and rules they didn't dare help someone else, especially on the Sabbath.

I'm so thankful for Jesus and the examples of love He displayed for all of us.

I am thankful for the Sabbath too.

Dear precious Lord, may we open our eyes to someone who needs our help, even on the Sabbath. In the wonderful name of Jesus. Amen.

Read May 5 Read Psalm 63:1-4

A TIME FOR PRAISE

Bible Thought: "Let the people praise thee, O God; let all the people praise thee" (Psalm 67:3).

We live in the greatest country in the world. I believe many blessings have been bestowed to us because of our godly heritage. Yet how many of us take these blessings for granted? All of us have more blessings than problems. We can look back upon a life and see the hand of God guiding a path through difficult circumstances.

Let us count our blessings and be thankful. Regardless of hard times we can always find the good in our daily lives.

Being thankful for blessings evokes praise. Praising God keeps us joyful. It's a breath of fresh air to be around those who praise the Lord. I'm not referring spiritual name-dropping incessantly, but to hearts filled with praise and thanksgiving for a loving God.

Praise God for His willingness to guide us. Praise Him for eternal salvation. Praise Him for Jesus.

With so many wonderful truths, how can we lose? Praise is beautiful. It gives God joy because His greatest joy comes from our genuine worship and trust.

Make your life a life of praise.

It's time for praise!

Dear God, may every breath be a praise of thankfulness for You and the many blessings You send. We can never thank You enough here, but we will have an eternity to praise You forever because of Jesus. In His wondrous name. Amen.

May 6 Read Deuteronomy 7:9-13

COVENANT BLESSING

Bible Thought: "Turn, O backsliding children, saith the LORD; for I am married unto you; and I will take you one of a city, and two of a family, and I will bring you to Zion"

As my husband gave a "grandfather's blessing" for Ashley and Cody's wedding, I thought of our marriage to Jesus.

As a third partner in any marriage, we are to be loyal to Him. Being married to Him brings peace and harmony for couples in earthly marriages and heavenly bliss in the next life.

The following blessing given by Emmitt, will remain in the hearts of our family for a lifetime:

"As the patriarch of the Clayton family, Ashley and Cody, I declare unto you this day that as you live your lives together, your love for one another will be an inspiration for all to see. Because of your love for God, blessings will pursue and overtake you all of your days. Ashley, we are so proud to have you in our family and it is with love and open arms that we welcome you. Your love for each other will reach down to your children and your children's children, blessing them throughout eternity. As you live your lives together, no weapon formed against you will prosper and everything you say and do will glorify our blessed Lord. Let the record show that this marriage is sealed with love and honored by God. So be it, and let the people say, Amen!"

Dear God, how we thank You for marriage and families. Thank You for Jesus. In His beautiful name. Amen.

May 7 Read Nehemiah 2:18-20

PRAYER AND LOVE, A COMMON BOND

Bible Thought: "Evening, and morning, and at noon, will I pray, and cry aloud: and he shall hear my voice" (Psalm 55:17).

A recent medical study revealed that people who are prayed for recover faster than those who are not prayed for. Those not prayed for required more medication and treatment.

Prayer connects us with God who is always ready to hear and to answer. Prayer demonstrates love for God and others. Prayer and love form a common bond. Prayer is a reminder that we are never alone. In this huge, vast gigantic universe, we are never alone.

Prayer is vital to our lives. Prayer is a way of life. The journey of living on earth is too complicated without it. Prayer guides us through problems and hard places, giving peace in the midst of the storms of everyday circumstances.

Those heroes of Bible times depended on God's faithfulness. Through prayer Nehemiah carried out his plan to rebuild the walls of Jerusalem. Through prayer the early church stood strong in persecution. Through prayer Stephen was able to face death triumphantly.

Pray today and everyday. Give God your every care. It's such a wondrous blessing to start your day with prayer.

Dear wonderful Lord, thank You for the privilege of prayer. May we listen to Your "still small voice" in reverence and love. Thank You for loving us, forgiving us and most of all for Jesus who has redeemed us. In His beautiful name. Amen.

May 8 Read 1 Peter 1:3-5

GOING TO HEAVEN

Bible Thought: "Henceforth there is laid up for me a crown of righteousness, which the Lord, the righteous judge, shall give me at that day: and not to me only, but unto all them also that love his appearing" (2 Timothy 4:8).

Her funeral was a beautiful celebration of life. My beloved sister-in-love yearned to go home to heaven. A granddaughter had asked her previously who was the first person she wanted to see. "Jesus" she exclaimed joyfully.

Family members told of favorite incidents in her life. One son said, "I'm jealous. She got to go to heaven before I did." Yes, we all miss her but we rejoice she is home at last.

My husband and I have been caregivers for a number of relatives. We have been blessed. Each one went home in peace. I shall never forget what my mother said, "I see the heavenly lights."

These experiences have taken away the fear of death. "Precious in the sight of the LORD is the death of his saints" (Psalm 116:15).

Dear Lord, thank You for coming back for us to live with You forever. What a wonderful awesome God you are. In Jesus' name. Amen.

May 9 Read John 19:25-27

THE TENDER LOVE OF JESUS

Bible Thought: "When Jesus therefore saw his mother, and the disciple standing by, whom he loved, he saith unto his mother, Woman, behold thy son!" (John 19:26)

As the mother of three sons, my heart is filled with tears when I read today's Bible reading. Jesus is on the cross, suffering in the worst kind of pain, yet He looks down at His earthly mother and makes sure she is taken care of. I just love the tender heart of Jesus!

The Bible has a lot to say about mothers. Imagine the heart-wrenching moment for Moses' mother when she put him in that little basket on the banks of the Nile River. Or think about the pain of Mary as she witnessed the death of her Son.

Who can know a mother's love? Only a mother knows.

My mother knew my every fault, mistake, and wrong doing, yet she loved me anyway. I'm sure I hurt her feelings many times. I rejected her wisdom but she still loved me.

Godly mothers see infinite possibilities in their children. Children can accomplish amazing feats because of mothers encouragement. I wonder how many people owe their lives to the prayers of mothers and grandmothers.

I'm a mother and my love for my children cannot be expressed.

It's almost the tender love of Jesus.

Dear precious Lord, thank You for making us emotional. Love is deep and wide covering us with Your precious blood. Thank You for bottling our tears and You know every tear.

We love and praise You today and everyday. In Jesus' lovely name. Amen.

May 10 Read Matthew 7:1-5

WRONG WORDS CAN HURT FEELINGS

Bible Thought: "A soft answer turneth away a wrath: but grievous words stir up anger" (Proverbs 15:1).

"I really wanted this shoe leather on my boots," he grumbled. That ruffled my feathers. My husband could have said, "You really cooked this piece of ham well." When I saw him sharpen a cutting knife and then attack that piece of ham like a chain saw, I couldn't help but laugh.

It's hard for me to deal with criticism. Keeping my cool when criticized is emotionally draining. I said, "Okay, so I left the ham in the oven too long. Let's not waste it. Go ahead and tack it on your boot!" Now he laughed.

I've discovered flaws I find in others are flaws I see in myself. Since that time I have tried to learn from criticism, but if I become defensive, things get out of control and I become upset. Looking at my own faults motivates me to forgive others and overlook their offenses. If I send out criticism it returns to me. "If I give it, I receive it." Criticism comes in many ways. Reacting to it in the wrong way brings defeat.

Love enables us to see the good in others, thereby blocking critical remarks and cynicism.

Dear Lord, help us to see the beam in our own eye and realize soft words bring peace. In Jesus' beautiful name. Amen.

May 11 Read Genesis 32:22-30

BE PERSISTENT

Bible Thought: "And he said, Let me go, for the day breaketh. And he said, I will not let thee go, except thou bless me" (Genesis 32:26).

Like Jacob, all of us should be persistent not only in areas of our physical lives but in our spiritual lives too. Nothing in life is gained without persistence. Jacob persisted and received a blessing.

Have you ever been down for the count? How do you respond? Falling down doesn't make a failure...staying down does. I've heard that bulldogs' mouths are short and flat so they can breathe while they bite and hang on. Stay in the fight. Dust yourself off and keep on keeping going on. It's always too soon to quit.

Have you known anyone who has never had a problem? Troubles come and troubles go. A poor attitude is, "Well, that trial is over... wonder what the next one will be?" What a way to live.

God has given us weapons to fight evil. We use every piece of God's armor to resist attacks and when it's all over you will still be standing.

So we don't whine and resign. We press on. We endure. We try again. Jesus didn't quit. (Thank God He didn't).

Be encouraged today.

Never give up!

Dear God, forgive us for not trusting You. No matter the trial, You will never leave nor forsake us. Empower us to be persistent and strain forward for the "prize of the high calling in Christ Jesus." In His name. Amen.

May 12 Read Isaiah 45:2-3

MY SECRET PLACE

Bible Thought: "He that dwelleth in the secret place of the most High shall abide under the shadow of the Almighty" (Psalm 91:1).

In the stillness of the night I find the Lord waiting in my secret place. He receives me with gladness and joy. His presence satisfies the deepest longing of my soul. I am sheltered in His arms. I am precious in His sight.

He tells me of His everlasting love. My innermost being knows this is true as I hear His gentle whisper, "I will always be there…in the sunshine and in the rain, in the storms and in the pain. Hold my hand. Did I not make you? Did I not send my Son to save you? My love for you is endless."

The heavens and the stars reflect His glory, but He has time for me. I want to stay in His presence.

It's such a wonderful place, the "secret place of my heart."

You can have a secret place too.

Dear precious Lord, we run to our secret place and meet you with excitement. We love to be in Your presences. All through the day and night You are still with us. What a beautiful and awesome God You are. In that name above all names. It's the beautiful name of Jesus. Amen.

May 13 Read Revelation 22:1-5

TREE OF LIFE

Bible Thought: "And he shall be like a tree planted by the rivers of water, that bringeth forth his fruit in his season; his leaf also shall not wither; and whatsoever he doeth shall prosper" (Psalm 1:3).

If you know where I live, you can tell I love trees. Our sons were small when we first planted trees and like our sons, our trees have grown tall and stately too.

Trees remind me of God's Kingdom. In Psalm 52:8, David compares himself to an olive tree.

In Genesis 3:24 after Adam and Eve were banished from the Garden of Eden for disobedience, God placed an angel with a flashing sword to guard the way to the "Tree of Life."

In life, storms come to people and trees alike. Both trees and people are buffeted by adversity, but like the trees, we send down stronger roots. Those roots enable us to "press on toward the goal to win the prize." (Philippians 3:14)

When I awaken each morning I see the tops of our trees swaying in the breeze. I think of Isaiah 55:12..."all the trees in the fields will clap their hands."

I clap my hands in praise for God's many blessings and for the "Tree of Life." It's the best tree of all.

Dear God, thank You for so many blessings. We can't name them all but we send our hearts of love back to You. Thank You for Jesus. In His wonderful name. Amen.

May 14 Read Luke 12:22-29

WORRY...A REHEARSAL OF MISERY

Bible Thought: "Be careful for nothing; but in every thing by prayers and supplication with thanksgiving let your requests be made known unto God. And the peace of God, which passeth all understanding, shall keep your hearts and minds through Christ Jesus." (Philippians 4:6-7)

Worry has been defined as interest gained on torment. That being true, where does worry comes from? It is certainly not from God.

Whatever the situation, does worrying help? Does it give comfort? Does worry give peace? Does worrying give control of the situation? If you answered, "Yes" to any of the above, you must not be a member of the human race.

Worry is a joy stealer, a health robber and a dark cloud that hides the sunshine from our lives. Worry is like riding a ferocious tiger!

The same God who created the heavens and the earth knows all about our needs. We don't walk by what we see in this natural world. We live by faith and faith moves God. Conflicts do come in this life and if we dwell on them we slip into despair and do not see the real blessings.

My battle cry is "We always have more blessings than problems." We are rich in family, friends and most of all, Jesus!

Dear wonderful God, forgive us for worrying. We resolve to trust in You and live each day with ever increasing faith. Thank You for Jesus who makes us free. In His beautiful name. Amen.

May 15 Read Matthew 4:1-6

ANGELS AMONG US

Bible Thought: "For he shall give his angels charge over thee, to keep thee in all thy ways" (Psalm 91:11).

We had a terrific tire blow out. A man and his teenage son stopped immediately. The man worked in the heat and humidity for quite a while taking off the flat tire and replacing the spare.

We tried to pay him, but he said, "No. My mother had a flat and someone helped her so I'm paying back a good thing."

The Bible has many references about angels. Angels watch over children. (Matt. 18:10) Angels announced that Sarah would have a child. (Gen. 18:10) Angels shut the lions' mouths in Dan. 6:22) Angels announced Zacharias would have a son. (Luke 1:11-19) Angels warned Joseph to flee to Egypt. (Matt. 2:13-15) Angels announced Mary would have a son. (Luke 1:26-35) Angels announced the second coming of Jesus (Acts 1:10-11) An angel rolled away the stone of Jesus' tomb. (Matt.28: 2-4) Angels rejoice over one sinner who repents. (Luke 15:10) Angels are not to be worshiped by man. (Revelation 22:8-9)

I thanked the man and told him he was an angel to help us.

We can read many things about angels in the Bible and I love them all. However, the one that really stands out for me is in Luke 16:22. Angels carry us home when we fall asleep in Jesus.

Dear God, thank You for angels who are ministering spirits and who will escort us to heaven where we will live forevermore. Thank You for Jesus who made it all possible. In His name. Amen.

May 16 Read Hebrews 12:1-2

BE A CHEERLEADER FOR GOD

Bible Thought: "But Jesus beheld them, and said unto them, With men this is impossible; but with God all things are possible" (Matthew 19:26).

Let's face each trial with hope and faith in our hearts. Let's be a carrier of the "Good News." Today's reading causes me to get excited. I can almost hear the heavenly cheerleaders shouting as I run toward the finish line. To me they seem to say, "Go! Go! Go! Give it all you've got. Heaven is worth it all."

We win. I've read the last page of the Book. Jesus is our all in all. So let's run the race.

Jesus is rest for the restless, victory for defeat, peace for unrest, faith for the fearful, refuge for the lowly, triumph for the trials, gladness for sadness, conqueror for the loser, strength for the weak, restoration for the lost, encouragement for the fainthearted, forgiveness for the offender, life for the lifeless, victory over death and grace for the sinner.

Be a cheerleader for God. Shout it from the rooftops.

Say, "Jesus loves you!"

Dear Lord, grant us boldness to spread the "Good News." Thank You for Jesus and our eternal home. In His marvelous name. Amen.

May 17 Read 1 Samuel 30:1-6

BLESSINGS COME FROM ENCOURAGEMENT

Bible Thought: "Now therefore fear ye not: I will nourish you, and your little ones. And he comforted them, and spake kindly unto them" (Genesis 50:21).

My day had not gone well. At the end of the school day, I thought, *did I get anywhere? Am I a good teacher?*

I felt like a failure. At three o'clock my students lined up for a goodbye hug. The last little boy held out his hand, "Teacher, thank you for all your hard work," and he shook my hand vigorously.

That was all I needed. If my little second grader thought I had done my best, then I would accept that and look for a better day tomorrow. His encouragement changed my entire perspective.

We may never know the effects of supporting encouraging words, but they make a great difference. In the midst of trials our encouraging words bring out the best in people.

David encouraged himself in God and kept his faith. I will do that too.

Turn to the Psalms the next time problems seem overwhelming. They are filled with encouragement.

God is on our side.

Dear precious Lord, thank You for Jesus who encourages us. We are forever grateful. In Jesus' beautiful name. Amen.

May 18 Read John 14:13-16

PRAYER CHANGES THINGS

Bible Thought: "Hitherto have ye asked nothing in my name: ask, and ye shall receive, that your joy may be full" (Psalm John 16:24).

I like to greet others with a smile on my face and a prayer in my heart. I may not see or hear a reaction, but that's okay. That's not what I'm after. I strongly believe every prayer we pray for others will be answered in unusual ways and I may never know it.

Prayer has been so important in my life. Prayer sustained me through my husband's five major surgeries. Prayer sustained me when our oldest son was in a mowing accident. Prayer sustained me when our middle son was in a butane explosion. Prayer sustained me when an evaporative air conditioner fell on our youngest son's head. Prayer sustained me when my dying mother said, "I see the heavenly lights."

Jesus is in the "people" business. He soothes, comforts, redeems and saves. One of the most important things we can do in life is to pray for others.

You can send prayers anywhere. I silently send prayers to others while waiting in the doctor's office, at football games, on a city sidewalk or any other number of places.

Begin to send prayers to people. Sometimes they will suddenly look at you and smile. You will be surprised by joy. Lose yourself and think of others. Those prayers will come back to you when you need them the most.

Dear Lord, thank You for Jesus and the privilege of prayer. Empower us to live our lives in such a way that others see Jesus in us. In His wonderful name. Amen.

May 19 Read Mark 9:34-37

THE PATHWAY TO LASTING HAPPINESS

Bible Thought: "Happy *is that* people, that is in such a case: *yea, happy is that people, whose God is the LORD"* (Psalm 144:15).

Any bookstore will have books on being happy. TV commercials are filled with "things" guaranteed to satisfy. You only need their products to make your life perfect.

For some, happiness is attained only when "this or that happens." Yet the bottom line is that after the possession of fortune or fame is achieved, reality comes into play. "Is this all there is?"

Only the Bible contains the path to lasting happiness. Without God there wouldn't be kindness unselfishness and most of all, love for others.

Material things satisfy for a season, but real joy comes from a loving God. Pursing happiness is vain without knowing the secret of life.

Whether it is time, talent or other resources, everyone can give something to help a hurting soul. Giving what you have brings happiness to you and someone else when you give with the spirit of generosity as the poor widow did in Mark 12:44.

Know God and obey His commandments. That's "the secret" to the pathway of lasting happiness.

Dear God, thank You for the road to happiness that Jesus has paved for us. In His wonderful name. Amen.

May 20 Read Psalm 128:3-6

CHILDREN ARE PRECIOUS TREASURES

Bible Thought: "Lo, children *are* an heritage of the LORD: *and* the fruit of the womb *is his* reward" (Psalm127:3).

The world of children is such a wondrous thing. Their days are filled with sweet abandonment and trust. I need the same thing. The world has a way of badgering us with wounds and hurts leaving us cynical and caustic with no trust in others.

One of my students pinched another's arm. I had the offender to sit down and think about what she had done. It took only a few minutes for her to make amends with her friend. "I'm so sorry."

"That's okay," the offended said as she put her arms around her classmate. (Lesson number one for me: ("Forgive quickly those who offend you.")

One student described love to me. "It's something that makes you feel good when you listen to your heart." How I need to listen to my heart. Somewhere in the midst of difficulties I temporarily lose my patience. Lesson number two for me: (Listen and be patient.")

Another student didn't complete his work. I assured him that he could do it. In a few minutes he brought his work to me and said, "Here, I rememborized this time." Lesson number three for me: (Everyone needs reassurance and patience.)

Let's recognize that children are gifts from God and may our faith be rekindled as a little child's.

Dear precious Lord, we thank You today for children. May we recapture their faith and zest for living. In Jesus wonderful name. Amen.

May 21 Read 1 Thessalonians 5:16-23

GOD'S SURPRISES

Bible Thought: "A merry heart maketh a cheerful countenance: but by sorrow of the heart the spirit is broken: (Proverbs 15:13).

Every day God sends beautiful gifts just waiting for us to open. Living in the "now" of life brings many wonderful surprises. Unless we are tuned in these blessings we will go right on by and not be noticed.

My Aunt Mary lived to be 92. Although legally blind, she still found joy in simple things. She always said, "Others see with their eyes but with God many see with their hearts, and that brings many secret surprises."

Let's be a blessing gift to everyone we meet today. We can give ourselves away. Realize love has no boundaries. Special blessings come through unselfish love and acceptance without a thought of reciprocation.

Starting and ending our day with prayer makes a happy existence. Living one day at a time and trusting in God brings happiness. I like to talk to God all through the day. By the way, God's telephone number is Jeremiah 33.3

"Now throw away your troubles and have a happy face.

For God is always with you with His amazing grace!"

Dear Lord, You sent Your Son for our salvation and that makes our hearts sing because the "best is yet to be." We can't thank You enough. His name is Jesus. Amen.

May 22 Read Matthew 6:30-34

GIVE GOD YOUR TROUBLES

Bible Thought: "Trust in the LORD with all thine heart; and lean not unto thine own understanding" (Proverbs 3:5).

Of all the things you have ever worried about, tell me something good that came about as a result. What is worry? I define it as "rehearsing calamity" or meditating on the worse thing that can happen. I also think it's a sin because there is no trust.

How long could one feel this way and still have good health? Worrying is fear trying to conquer faith. Consider worrying a tormenting plague from the enemy.

Let's stop the enemy. We want to believe and act on God's Word knowing He is on our side. Nothing takes Him by surprise. Take the energy you use in worrying and replace it with overwhelming positive thoughts.

The greatest antidote to worry is Jesus in you, the hope of glory. In Jesus you have a love that can never be taken away, an eternal life that will never die, a righteousness that dwells in you, a peace that passes all understanding, a rest that can never be disrupted, a joy that lasts forever, a hope that can never be disappointed, a glory that shines, a light that can never be extinguished and a wisdom that will always lead your path.

We win!

Dear God, we repent today of worrying. Help and guide us to give all problems to You. Thank you for Your grace and mercy. In the precious name of Jesus. Amen.

May 23 Read Genesis 6:1-4

WE ARE GREAT GIANTS

Bible Thought: "And it repented the LORD that he had made man on the earth, and it grieved him at his heart" (Proverbs 6:6).

It grieves my heart to. From ages of giants to people of today sinful ways have gone rampart. The populace doesn't seem to get it. Immorality destroys humanity.

It seems an explosion of evil. From high levels to low we are tempted to go with the flow. In biblical times the Nephilim, (giants) had a physical advantage and they used it to oppress people. The giants today are dishonesty, theft, fraud, adultery, fornication and idolatry to say a few.

So here we are again but we can win. We resist the enemy. Jesus did not die for us in vain. We are bought with a precious price. We walk with joy for His joy is our strength. Our weakness becomes His strength. We soar like an eagle above the "storms of life," for He has caused us to walk upon the high places of the earth. We are more than a conqueror for the "Greater One" lives in us.

We overcome by the blood of the Lamb and the word of our testimony.

If our head is in heaven while our feet are on the ground we conquer every foe.

Dear Lord, may we become giants of faith and righteousness. Grant us boldness to witness to others. In Jesus' name. Amen.

May 24 Read Jeremiah 29:11-13

SCHOOL IS NEVER OUT

Bible Thought: "Take my yoke upon you, and learn of me; for I am meek and lowly in heart: and ye shall find rest unto your souls" (Matthew 11:29).

Remember those wonderful days of childhood when the last day of school arrived?

"I've got to hurry home and get to playing, "our youngest son would say. He couldn't wait to make every summer day count.

In my memory bank I thought high school would never end. Then the long-awaited day of college graduation happened. I thought surely school was out then, but I discovered something. In "life's school" there is always more to learn.

Some of the man-made rules in life's classroom are unfair. I may suffer injustices but my "Teacher" knows my pain and He comforts me and tells me how much I mean to Him.

Whatever stage of life you are in He will still be your Teacher. He is on your side.

What a wonderful way to live. I love this "School of Life." Every day is a day of adventure and excitement in Jesus. To that I say again, "Life is delicious."

Finally when we celebrate our final Graduation Day we will hear, "enter thou into the joy of thy lord."

Dear precious Lord, we thank You for our time to live, but most of all we thank You for eternal life because of Jesus. We praise You today with grateful hearts. In Jesus' marvelous name. Amen.

May 25 Read John 1:1-5

JESUS IS THE LIGHT

Bible Thought: "Ye are the light of the world. A city that is set on an hill cannot be hid" (Matthew 5:14).

I like to look out my window when I awaken early on a winter morning. I see lights of distant farmhouses. They seem so warm and inviting. One morning I asked the Lord, "Why am I drawn toward the light?" A thought answered, "Because I am the Light."

When my husband and I travel at night I see little lights in houses as we pass by. I say to myself, "That light looks so cozy and so secure." Then it occurs to me again. "He is the Light!"

Jesus is the Light in a world of darkness. No matter how dark the darkness it can never overcome the Light. When the Light of the Lord is in a life, the darkness cannot stay.

The glorious gospel of the Lord Jesus Christ is a "Lighthouse" for drifting sinners.

Look for the "Light" today.

Jesus is the Light!

Dear God, thank You for Jesus, the "Light of the World." Help us to be lights in a world of darkness. In Jesus' mighty name. Amen.

May 26 Read Psalm 46:1-5

MY PROFESSION OF FAITH

Bible Thought: "O clap your hands, all ye people; shout unto God with the voice of triumph" (Psalm 47:1).

My God is bigger than any mountain or circumstance. Since I have made Him Lord of my life happiness has come to me. He takes all my burdens and I leave them there. He is the core of my inner being.

I bring into captivity every thought that exalts itself against God. I have settled in my heart that God is God. I stand strong in the Lord and in the power of His might. My heart is fixed. I am trusting in the Lord. I am not moved by what I see touch or feel. I am moved by the promises of God. He is faithful.

The Lord is the strength of my life. That strength gives me joy and a merry heart. Joy is health to my bones. I am happy in the Lord. I am whole. I am free.

Therefore I will keep my eyes on Jesus.

I will praise Him with every thought.

Blessed be my Lord, the Mighty One of Israel!

Dear precious Lord, You are my love, my life, my redeemer, my healer, my comforter, my all in all. You are my God and I will praise You forevermore. In that beautiful name of Jesus. Amen.

May 27 Read Psalm 93

GOD LOVES YOU

Bible Thought: "The LORD reigneth; let the earth rejoice; let the multitude of isles be glad *thereof*"(Psalm 97:1).

You are important today because Jesus died for you. Make your day count. You are not a nobody. You are somebody who has sold out to Jesus. Make every waking thought be of Him, glorifying Him in all you say and do When you stumble and fall He picks you up. He is on your side. He guides your steps because you abide in Him and you dwell in that "secret place." He is ever mindful of you. He joys over you with singing. (Zephaniah 3:17) Delight in Him and He will give you the desires of your heart.

If you awaken in the night watches, praise the Lord with all your being. Sing to your Maker. He restores your soul and lifts you to a higher place. Fall asleep in His arms of love.

You will find morning breaking with enthusiasm and all nature acknowledging Gods' creation. Dewdrops of God's love sprinkles the earth with the promise of a new day.

This is the day to rejoice. Why?"

You are one day closer to heaven!

Dear precious Lord, thank You for the gift of joy and singing. May our voices bring You joy and pleasure. We meet You today in that secret place of our hearts and it is with love and adoration that we approach Your throne. In that name above all names. His name is Jesus. Amen.

May 28 Read Deuteronomy 30:14-19

RIGHT CHOICES BRING BLESSINGS

Bible Thought: "But as many as received him, to them gave he power to become the sons of God, *even* to them that believe on his name" (John 1:12).

Giving God control of one's life enables the believer to make good choices. God's promises give the power to change a life. We can place confidence in Him, knowing His way is the only way to be happy.

God's gifts depend on how we use them. We decide. It is not what we have or don't have. Things never supply lasting happiness, but love, family and friends are precious gifts that money cannot buy.

Time is fleeting. Today is the time to live, love, laugh and be happy for "He has made everything beautiful in his time: also he hath set the world in their heart, so that no man can find out the work that God maketh from the beginning to the end" (Ecclesiastes 3:11).

So choose to be happy today, tomorrow and everyday. Choosing God's way will make a lot of happy days and a lot of happy memories.

Right choices bring blessings.

Dear precious Lord, we thank You for each day that comes as a gift and it is wrapped in Your love. May we make right choices so we can return that gift back to You. We love You with all our hearts, body and soul. In that beautiful name above all names. His name is Jesus. Amen.

May 29 Read Psalm 46:1-5

A WINNING SPIRIT

Bible Thought: "Humble yourselves therefore under the mighty hand of God, that he may exalt you in due time" (1 Peter 5:6).

I well remember the day my husband went off to war. The big Greyhound Bus waited while we held each other one more time. Emmitt's winning spirit assured me we would come through as over comers and winners.

A winning spirit enabled my parents and grandparents to be married sixty-five plus years. I witnessed first hand the meaning of faithfulness, unselfishness, sacrifice and love. Hardships only brought them closer together and made them winners.

We honor those many heroes of 9-11. What the enemy meant for evil has resulted in a united determined supportive oath of affirmation of what Americans are really made of. Courageous God-fearing people are bouncing back with strength, enabling victory as we go forth as "One Nation Under God."

Jesus loved you and I enough to die in our place and that makes us pretty special. He nailed our sins to the cross. You and I are forgiven. That makes us winners.

I feel like a cheerleader with a cheer coming on.

"With a winning spirit, we conquer every foe.

The Greater One is Captain.

Go Team Go!"

Dear God, You are Lord. You are King. You are the Champion. You are the most wonderful thing that ever happened to us. It is Christ in us, the hope of glory. We praise You today, lest the rocks cry out. In Jesus' beautiful name. Amen.

May 30 Read 1 Corinthians 23-27

MEMORIALS

Bible Thought: "Greater love hath no man than this, that a man lay down his life for his friends" (John 15:13).

I am thankful for those in my heritage who left a spiritual legacy for me. Their examples for overcoming problems taught me many lessons of deep faith.

This legacy they left me has made me realize the depth of Jesus' love. He died that I might live. He paid a debt I could not pay. He gave His life for my freedom and my eternal salvation.

Recounting the faithfulness of my Lord makes me want to love Him every moment. He is always there to encourage, sustain, comfort and give me peace. It is hard to see the way clear when I go through the valley but even in the darkest night I am not alone. God has said, "...I will never leave thee, nor forsake thee" (Hebrews 13:5).

Whenever I think about what the Lord has brought me through, how can I help but sing about His goodness and mercy? I will remember every day the price Jesus paid on the cross and I will thank Him for that great sacrifice again and again.

Dear Lord, thank You for Jesus. With every fiber of our being we thank You. Words cannot express our deepest love and gratitude. In His beautiful name. Jesus. Amen.

May 31 Read Isaiah 55:11-13

JOYFUL, JOYFUL

Bible Thought: "Make a joyful noise unto the LORD, all ye lands" (Psalm 100:1).

I like to be joyful. It makes me happy. Just to know I'm redeemed. I want to shout it from the rooftops!

Someone once said, "Life is like a bicycle…stop peddling and you fall off." Well, I want to keep peddling with those who do. Regardless of hardships they keep on keeping on. You will not catch them in the "self-pity" trap. Somewhere in their hour of trial they still find the strength to help others. These people are my heroes.

I think being joyful is contagious and I'm going to share it. Jesus went to the cross to give us life and give it more abundantly. I want abundant joy! Those who worry have to walk in defeat, depression and discouragement. Who could have joy in the midst of that?

Joy is good medicine. It lowers blood pressure, cholesterol and friction. It reduces stress. Joy anticipates hope and optimism.

Each day is a joyful day and you will find wondrous beauty in it.

Have a heart full of joy.

Spread sunshine.

Put on your best smile.

Make people wonder why you're so happy. Then tell them about it.

Dear precious Lord, thank You for the joy of salvation. You make our hearts sing and we love and adore You. In that name above all names…Jesus. Amen.

JUNE

June 1 Read Psalm 65:9-11

GOD WEATHERS LIFE'S STORMS

Bible Thought: "Blessed *are* they that they do his commandments, that they may have right to the tree of life, and may enter in through the gates into the city" (Revelation 22:14).

My plants took a beating from the hot windy days we had at the beginning of summer. They curled up their leaves and wilted. It appeared all of my efforts had been wasted. Yet I refused to become discouraged. My garden reminded me to keep the faith with patience. Sure enough fall brought a beautiful harvest. The beauty of God's handiwork gave an awesome scene.

In the heat of life's battles winds of adversity can look harmful. Times of dryness prevail. Hope seems to fade and shadows block the sunshine. Yet remembering God's promises promote peace. Hiding God's Word in the garden of our hearts bring great dividends. God sustains any situation. He is "Living Water."

This world will pass away but at that "Great Harvest" we will see beautiful gardens of the soul.

Plant your garden with seeds of love, kindness and faith. God may weather life's storms but you will have a wonderful harvest.

Dear God, may the seeds we plant in this life lead to a wonderful harvest in heaven. In Jesus' name. Amen.

June 2 Read 1 Chronicles 16:33-36

A BELIEVER NEVER SAYS GOODBYE

Bible Thought: "And I saw a new heaven and a new earth: for the first heaven and the first earth were passed away; and there was no more sea" (Revelation 21:1).

People arrived and departed. We watched as my husband and I waited for our flight. The tears, hugs, handclasps and endearing words…all revealed love from someone's heart. All too soon it came time to say "goodbye."

Wouldn't it be great," I thought, *"if all of us could be this loving every day. Would it not be wonderful to hold each moment as precious?* This present moment is all we have to live. God's gift of time is a wondrous thing, yet time waits for no one. Today is the day to spread God's love.

Successful living comes when we make our days count. When it comes our time to make our heavenly flight we may say goodbye to those we leave, but as our middle son said to me when he left home, "Don't cry Mom, a Christian never says 'goodbye' for the last time.'"

When the child of God goes home, it's never a "goodbye" but another "hello" in heaven.

"Precious in the sight of the Lord is the death of his saints" (Psalm 116:15).

Dear Lord, may we use our time on earth living in service to you. Help us to spread Your amazing love, In that name, the sweetest name of all. His name is Jesus. Amen.

June 3 Read Isaiah 50:7-10

GOD IS BIGGER THAN ANY CIRCUMSTANCE

Bible Thought: "My help *cometh* from the LORD, which made heaven and earth" (Psalm 121:2).

Imagine you are in a spaceship and you can see our planet suspended in space. Looking down you see a small little blue ball called earth with millions of people on it. God knows everyone by name, even the number of the hairs on their heads. Now that is a big God!

The next time you find yourself getting anxious, remember that God is big enough to handle any situation in your life. He cares about you. Letting go and letting God brings peace to the soul. Compared to this planet, we are just tiny little dots, yet God is mindful of you and me.

Technological advances are awesome. Scientists are discovering knowledge every day. As wonderful as that is, knowledge eventually comes to an end. God is the essence of all knowledge.

Forget the trials that come your way. You will find peace and comfort if you will only say, "God is big!"

Dear God, forgive us for not trusting You. May we lay down every care at Your feet, knowing You know best. In the wonderful name of Jesus. Amen.

June 4 Read 1 John 3:1-3

OUR IDENTITY IN JESUS

Bible Thought: "Put on therefore, as the elect of God, holy and beloved, bowels of mercies, kindness, humbleness of mind, meekness, longsuffering" (Colossians 3:12).

Everyone wanted to see the newborn twins. "How do you tell them apart since they are identical?" someone asked.

"I have trouble sometimes, "the father replied. Just then the mother looked at her precious babies. "That one is Bobby and this one is Billy." She knew immediately which was which. Who can fathom a mother's love for her child or children?

Only Jesus. He knows our names, our hearts, and our thoughts. His love never ceases.

We have our real identity in Jesus. Knowing who we are in Him makes all the difference.

We are children of the King. The sacrifice of His great love makes everyone a winner.

With Jesus we can soar to immeasurable heights. With Him nothing is impossible.

We are born again spiritually when we come to Jesus. We arise from a sinful life to a spotless child of God.

Keep your identity in Jesus!

Dear Lord, thank You for our freedom in You. May we live each day with joy because of Your great love. In Jesus' wonderful name. Amen.

June 5 Read Psalm 89:13-16

DISCOVER GOD'S WONDERFUL SURPRISES

Bible Thought: "Whereby are given unto us exceeding great and precious promises: that by these ye might be partakers of the divine nature, having escaped the corruption that is in the world through lust" (2 Peter 1:4).

Every day God sends beautiful gifts just waiting for us to open. They are wonderful surprises and unless we are tuned in, these blessings will go right on by and not be noticed. I've discovered many but here are a few:

Have childlike faith. When our youngest son had a tonsillectomy he didn't know pain was awaiting him. Yet he had no fear because he knew he would not be left alone. He also knew how much he was loved. Is it not the same with us grownups?

See with your heart. Aunt Mary, although legally blind, found joy in simple things. One day she said, "Look at those beautiful fall colors." I gasped and said, "Aunt Mary can you see that?" She answered, "Not with my eyes, but there are things God shows you with the heart."

Forgive. Unforgiveness is a bitter poison.

Start and end your day with prayer. It starts your day right and ends your night right because it keeps your focus on Jesus.

Look for God's wonderful surprises today. They are all around you.

Dear precious Lord, thank You for the many blessings You send us each day and may we never take them for granted. In Jesus' beautiful name. Amen.

June 6 Read 1 Kings 19:11-12

BE STILL AND KNOW

Bible Thought: "Be still, and know that I *am* God: I will be exalted among the heathen, I will be exalted in the earth" (Psalm 46:10).

I complained to a preacher that I had never heard the voice of God. He replied, "No wonder. You talk too much." I laughed and agreed with him, but it made me realize that I talk more than I listen when I pray.

Many voices compete for our attention, leaving little time for quiet time in our busy schedules.

I often see signs in doctors' offices that read "Relax." This is humorous to me because it's hard to relax while waiting for test results or a certain diagnosis. Yet finding quiet time in our prayer and thought life is of utmost importance for our bodies and souls.

Keeping silence restores inner peace. After all life can only be lived one day at a time. We can only accomplish one task at a time, and that takes some silence.

Now I am specifically designating a quiet time for God. I pray and then listen.

Maybe you can find a quiet place where you can focus your mind on God. Let His peace minister to you. You will find a blessing. It's a beautiful gift.

Be still and know that He is God.

Dear God, may we remember to be still and know that You are God. In that beautiful name of Jesus. Amen.

June 7 Read Psalm 92:13-15

BEAR GOOD FRUIT

Bible Thought: "Either make the tree good, and his fruit good; or else make the tree corrupt, and his fruit corrupt: for the tree is known by *his* fruit" (Matthew 12:33).

Our growing sons spent many hours among our trees. Tree houses and swings made happy days. They loved the peach and apricot cobblers the fruit provided. I am reminded that if I am to leave something good in the world I need to produce good fruit too.

Our lives are books other people read. How do we react in conflicts? Do we use a soft answer to turn away wrath? Are we patient and longsuffering?

God knows our weakness. It is a comfort to know Jesus is at the Father's right hand, interceding for you and me.

Let us forget those things that are past and "press on to the mark of the high calling in Christ Jesus." (Philippians 3:14)

I have heard it said, "If we think we're ripe, we're rotten. But if we stay fresh and green, we are still growing in God's guidance.

After all, no one likes a rotten apple!

Dear precious Lord, may we be cleansed by the washing of the Water of the Word, striving to be like You each day of our lives. Thank You for Jesus, who died in our place. In His beautiful name. Amen.

June 8 Read John 17:23-26

YOU DON'T COUNT THE COST

Bible Thought: "For God so loved the world, that he gave his only begotten Son, that whosoever believeth in him should not perish, but have everlasting life" John 3:16).

Childbirth is a painful thing, but when you hold that precious bundle, you don't count the cost.

There was a man of Nazareth who walked this earth only thirty-three short years Yet He turned the world upside down. He did no wrong...only good. He brought sight to the blind and heal to the sick. He made the lame walk and restored the broken hearted. He brought hope to a hopeless world.

For all of this He was mocked, scourged, beaten and crucified but He didn't count the cost. He agonized so much he had sweats of blood.

Jesus came to redeem mankind from the jaws of destruction. His sacrifice for every human being was worth it in His eyes.

Like a mother's love for her child, the cost was not considered because you and I are precious in His sight and we are His children.

The sacrifice of the cross is the greatest love the world has ever known, because when it comes to love, you don't count the cost.

Dear wonderful Lord, thank You for Jesus, the perfect Lamb. We will praise You throughout endless ages for so great a gift. In His precious name. Amen.

June 9 Read Habakkuk 3:17-19

AS THE DEER

Bible Thought: "He maketh my feet like hinds' *feet,* and setteth me upon my high places" (Psalm 18:33).

While driving through the pasture one day we came to the top of a hill. My husband quickly stopped the pickup and turned off the motor. About 200 yards below, we saw four deer foraging the grass beneath the snow. What a beautiful sight! One buck had antlers and a mother deer had twin fawns surrounding her. They seemed oblivious to us as they simply grazed peacefully. We watched in amazement and I felt a little sadness as they began to walk away. Their big brown eyes and graceful bodies brought praises to our awesome God and we thanked Him for these beautiful creatures.

I thought of Psalm 42:1, "As the hart, panteth after the water brooks, so panteth my soul after thee, O God."

God made animals, providing everything they need. He also made you and I, providing everything we need. Our lives are totally dependent upon Him too. I am always thirsty for Him and I want to know Him more and more.

In today's thought, He makes "my feet like hinds' feet" and I "walk on the high places of the earth." My feet are steady and I will not fear.

The next time I am faced with a problem I will remember the deer. I will stop to praise my Lord and I will have His peace.

Dear God, fill us with Your presence and lead us to everlasting life. In the name above all names. His name is Jesus. Amen.

June 10 Read Colossians 4:3-6

SALT YOUR WORLD

Bible Thought: "Ye are the salt of the earth: but if the salt have lost his savour, wherewith shall it be salted? It is thenceforth good for nothing, but to be cast out, and to be trodden under foot of men" (Matthew 5:13).

My grandfather used to say, "A man is worth his salt if he works hard." I thought about the meaning of that statement every time I picked up the saltshaker. In Bible times soldiers carried a pouch of salt on their belts to replace salt loss from intense perspiration. My great grandparents preserved meat with salt.

Salt is necessary for our lives, physically and spirituality. Salt preserves against corruption, but it can lose its flavor. I want to preserve the good in this world, to be salty and bring flavor to life and keep it from spoiling. I cannot do that if I break my part of the covenant with God.

I found an old piece of salt in my husband's pasture. It was still together despite the elements, erosion and time. As salt clings together, I am reminded of God's covenant with me.

I want to salt this planet with the message of God's love, to be "tasty" and gracious when I tell others about Jesus. Will you help me?

By the way, bring along your saltshaker and be a witness.

It's the "Good News!"

Dear Lord, enable us to salt the world with Your love, being examples of godliness. May we bring light where there's darkness and hope where there is hopelessness. It's all because of Jesus. In His name. Amen.

June 11 Read Ecclesiastes 9:7-9

HOW WILL WE BE REMEMBERED?

Bible Thought: "The memory of the just *is* blessed: but the name of the wicked shall rot" (Proverbs 10:7).

It was a perfect Sunday afternoon for a drive in the country. As we passed familiar farms, I couldn't help but notice the changes in peoples' lives. Some occupants were gone. Others had simply moved away leaving an abandoned house. I wonder what stories could be told if houses could talk.

How did they live their lives? Did they leave with regrets? Were words left unsaid? Were words should not have been said? Were opportunities to witness gone?

We are given; just so many years with the gift of life. Will we leave this world better when we take that final flight? Will we have discovered the real secret of life? "It is more blessed to give than to receive" (Acts 20:35).

Today is the day to leave good memories with those you love and with those you meet. Take your heart and witness the love of Jesus.

Make a difference to a hurting soul. You may the one who changes a life for eternity.

Embrace those special moments. Help someone who needs an unforgettable memory.

Dear wonderful Lord, thank You for our time to live. Empower us not to waste the gift of life but to make every day count. Thank You for Jesus, the greatest gift of all. In His beautiful name. Amen.

June 12 Read Proverbs 9:1-6

WISDOM BUILDS YOUR HOUSE

Bible Thought: "Except the LORD build the house, they labour in vain that build it: except the LORD keep the city, the watchman waketh *but* in vain" (Psalm 127:1).

Build your house with love and joy that leads to peace. If God is honored He will never leave your house. A home committed to God has happy hearts. When storms come let singing break forth with faith.

Acknowledging and depending on God preserves our earthly bodies of clay. The storm crashing against this house will not move, for those in this house are temples of God.

Your house will be calm in the eye of the storm, a refuge from the weary trials for your house abides in "the Secret Place" and under the "Shadow of the Almighty." This house is a fortress from the storms of life because God is the Landlord.

Sunshine will be filled within for the "Light" of the "Son" continually brightens those who live here. Your house is wired with the power of the Holy Spirit. This house has doors that open into arms of love. Your house will not crumble.

If you do not live in this house, you are welcome. Just knock on the door of your heart and invite the special guest in.

His name is JESUS!

Dear Lord, may our prayers never cease but be filled with compassion and forgiveness while being changed from glory to glory. In the name of Jesus. Amen.

June 13 Read 2 Chronicles 1:7-12

ABUNDANT LIFE

Bible Thought: "For whosoever hath, to him shall be given, and he shall have more abundance: but whosoever hath not, from him shall be taken away even that he hath" (Matthew 13:12).

It has been said, "The happiest heart is one that beats for others." I agree. Preoccupied with oneself brings misery. I learned this truth from 31 years of teaching little children. Their transparent childlike trust and forgiveness gave me a child's heart and more.

Solomon's unselfish prayer in today's reading surely must have been one of thinking of others.

We only have "x" amount of time on earth and we can make it count by giving ourselves away. Giving a helping hand to someone in need brings a warm happy feeling back to you.

Jesus came to give the abundant life. (John 10:10) I want to shout it to the world "Wake up world. We're alive in a beautiful world." God's nature wonder is spectacular. Live life to the fullest. Embrace it with open arms. Fill your heart with God's love. Praise and thank Jesus for His great sacrifice. That makes today a happy day.

It just doesn't get any better than that.

I wouldn't have missed it for the world.

Dear precious Lord, You have made today special and we will live it with gusto because our joy in You makes us strong What an awesome God You are. We love You to infinity. In that name…blessed be that name…Jesus. Amen.

June 14 Read Exodus 14:13-21

YOU HAVE ONLY TO STAND STILL

Bible Thought: "The LORD shall fight for you, and ye shall hold your peace" (Exodus 14:14).

One of my favorite stories in the Bible tells about the Israelites crossing the Red Sea. The people looked over their shoulder and shook with terror when they saw Pharaoh and his chariots coming. Yet Moses reassured the people God was still in control.

How does this apply to us today? Do you ever look over your shoulder and see enemies pursuing you? Being occupied with worrisome problems causes physical ailments and sleepless nights. These times can be just as fearful to you as they were to the Israelites.

Your faith is in the Lord. You do what you can, leave the rest to Him and after you have done all…stand. Stand when the doctor's report is not good. Stand when the nightly news has nothing but bad reports. Stand when everything in the natural looks the worst. We have a God who makes the best out of impossible situations.

Stand unshakeable and unmovable with mountain moving faith.

You have only to stand still!

Dear God, thank You for being our "Refuge and Fortress." We stand on the "Rock" of faith, unmoving in our stance, because You are greater than any enemy. In His beautiful name. Amen.

June 15 Read Matthew 7:7-11

SHARE YOUR SPECIAL GIFT

Bible Thought: "For the LORD God is a sun and shield: the LORD will give grace and glory: no good *thing* will he withhold from them that walk uprightly" (Psalm 84:11).

You are valuable and important to God. You have a gift within you, given especially by Him. Your gift becomes apparent through conversation, compassion, attitudes and personality.

One of my friends has the gift of encouragement. She seems to know when I need it the most. Another has the gift of laughter. He teases me about my peanut brittle. He likes to ask about my new "highway formula for black topping."

My teacher friend is sensitive to my need of prayer. My sister-in-law has the gift of caring. Her children know the depths of her love.

Other friends have gifts in special professions. They love what they do and are so good at it. Deep down in every person is a God-given gift. I believe that gift is given for a specific reason…to bless others. Our happiness comes from sharing that gift.

I could not be happy if I didn't write about God's love. It is burning within me and I can't lock it up inside. I feel if I didn't share it, I would lose it.

Stir up your gift today. It takes perseverance to share your God-given gift, but the world needs you and I need you too!

Dear Lord, thank You for the many gifts You have placed within our hearts. Most of all, we thank You for Jesus, the "Gift" of all gifts. In His mighty name. Amen.

June 16 Read Isaiah 12:1-6

SINGING PRAISES BRING RELIEF

Bible Thought: "Sing unto the LORD, praise ye the LORD for he hath delivered the soul of the poor from the hand of evildoers" (Psalm 20:13).

It's easy to sing when I'm happy. When everything is going just right, singing comes easily, but what about singing when things aren't going so well?

God doesn't leave us in trials. Singing praise to Him at all times displays happiness.

Many references about singing can be found in the Bible. God even sings over us. "The LORD thy God in the midst of thee is mighty; he will save, he will rejoice over thee with joy; he will rest in his love, he will joy over thee with singing"(Zephaniah 3:17)

Singing to God shows your faith in Him. You are demonstrating your confidence that He is indeed faithful and He is an awesome God.

Be joyful in God. Sing in the good times. Sing in the hard places. Sing when you're happy. Sing when you're sad.

Psalm 149:5 even talks about singing loud upon their beds. I love that.

I will sing anywhere with confidence because God delivers me.

He will deliver you too!

Dear God, thank You for the joy of singing and as we sing we praise the many wonderful blessings You have given. Thank You for the peace that passes all understanding. It's all because of Jesus. Blessed be His name. Amen.

June 17 Read Jeremiah 29: 4-10

LIFE IS A PRECIOUS GIFT

Bible Thought: "But none of these things move me, neither count I my life dear unto myself, so that I might finish my course with joy, and the ministry, which I have received of the Lord Jesus to testify the gospel of the grace of God" (Acts 20:24).

Life is a precious gift with a God-given purpose. The saddest thing to me is a life wasted, unappreciated or just thrown away. Effective living requires a study and knowledge of God's Word, while applying its principles in daily living. How I need to realize and pursue God's purpose for my life. My future is determined by how I have lived in the past. My faith must change the way I live. When I stumble and fall, I must repent, ask forgiveness and "strain toward the mark." An ungodly lifestyle to me is more dangerous than anything because my eternal destiny is at stake.

David taught Solomon to seek God's wisdom as the most important choice he could ever make. It is ours too. The apostle Paul considered life worthless if it is not used for God's purpose.

Trusting God in faithful obedience brings the "Light" of His glory in every situation. Walking in His Light annihilates fear and brings peace and rest to the soul. Living for God's purpose has no regrets on the deathbed.

What better way to live, being valuable to God and following His purpose!

Dear precious Lord, may we praise You, thank You for loving us, forgiving us and saving us. You are our God and we love You! In Jesus beautiful name. Amen.

June 18 Read Psalm 63:1-7

I LOVE YOU LORD

Bible Thought: "Set me as a seal upon thine heart, as a seal upon thine arm: for love is strong as death; jealousy is cruel as the grave: the coals thereof are coals of fire, which hath a most vehement flame" (Song of Solomon 8:6).

You are my song in the night…a guiding light that sees me through every conflict. You tenderly watch over me. You love me with an everlasting love and I am special in Your sight.

You gave Your life for me and I am valuable. You tell me of Your love in the night watches. You are my Shepherd and another I will not follow. My weakness is Your strength. I stand strong in You and in Your might.

You are my High Tower. I run to You and I am safe.

You fill me with beautiful things and I am pursued and overtaken with blessings from Your bountiful hand.

You knitted me together in my mother's womb. I'm so glad You planned for me to be born. I would have never known the joy of being Your child.

Thank You for dying for me…on Calvary…in victory.

Thank You for guiding me…setting me free…for my destiny.

Thank You for coming back for me…to be with you…eternally.

You are King of my life, my joy, my delight…and I love You!

Dear God, You are the reason to live and to love. You make life "delicious." With You we walk on golden streets and fly with joy on wings of love. Thank You for Jesus, our Redeemer, Counselor and Savior. In His glorious name. Amen.

June 19 Read Psalm 136:1-5

MY FATHER IS BESIDE ME

Bible Thought: "For the mountains shall depart, and the hills be removed; but my kindness shall not depart from thee, neither shall the covenant of my peace be removed, saith the LORD that hath mercy on thee" (Isaiah 54:10).

Kallie was supposed to stay all week. For three days my vivacious granddaughter and I played every game imaginable. On the fourth day Kallie began to get homesick. She longed to be swept up in her daddy's strong arms and she longed for the security of his presence. Just being with her daddy brought extreme happiness and made everything all right in her world. Lane sensed her loneliness and came to get her. She ran to her daddy's arms.

Kallie taught me a lot about a father's relationship with his child. An absence of time spent with my Father could create a loneliness in my life and I would find myself like Kallie, longing for the security of His presence. I cannot be too busy for meditation and prayer time for I need wisdom and guidance. I love to be in the Lord's presence and hear His still small voice.

I can be as joyful as Kallie, knowing my Father is right beside me and that makes everything all right in my world too.

Dear Lord, You are our Father and we praise and adore You. "As a deer pants for water," so our souls long for You. You fill our hearts with overwhelming joy. Thank You for Your love and we give You all our love. In Jesus' beautiful name. His name is "Jesus." Amen.

June 20 Read Deuteronomy 11:18-21

GOD'S CHILDREN

Bible Thought: "Lo, children are an heritage of the LORD: and the fruit of the womb is *his* reward" (Psalm 127:3).

I love the honesty and innocence of children. A career of teaching little ones brought many blessings. Children have within them the secret of life…unconditional love, forgiveness and complete trust. They renew hope and promise for our lives. To be trained in God's way with His love is the greatest gift a child can have. The support and love of a strong family builds successful children in life.

Spend quality time with your child and praise him or her for efforts, improvement and the smallest accomplishments. Let your child know you are on his/her team and that you are there whatever the need.

Us grownups are God's children. We need to spend quality time and praise Him too. After all we are in the school of life and we have the greatest "Teacher" of all. We are on His team and He is there whatever our need.

Let's pray together. No other single activity will have as profound an effect on your child's life or yours.

Dear Lord, we thank You for the gift of children. May we guide our children in Your way and seek You for wisdom in all our ways. We are grateful to be Your children and we thank You for Jesus. In His beautiful name. Amen.

June 21 Read Hebrews 11:1-3

YOUR FAITH IS A TREASURE

Bible Thought: "But that no man is justified by the law in the sight of God, *it is* evident: for, The just shall live by faith: (Galatians 3:11).

Every day you and I read or hear about crime, wars, double standards and every kind of dishonesty. More than ever we need to guard our faith. It is more precious than gold.

We are in a fight to preserve and protect our faith. We keep our eyes on Jesus. We have His Word in our hearts. We know where we are going and we will not bend an ear to the cries of doubt and unbelief. We do no give up, back up, let up or shut up about our faith. When it comes to the end of life, people of faith are spiritual millionaires. Their counterparts are spiritually bankrupt. Growing and maturing in Christ is the goal of the Christian.

In Jesus we have a love that never ends, a soul that never dies, a peace that passes all understanding, a joy that is never ending, a hope that is never disappointed, a light that shines forever, a wisdom that can never be erased, a beauty that can never be changed, resources that are never ending, righteousness in Him and an assured destiny.

Your faith is a treasure of immeasurable wealth.

Keep and guard your faith.

Dear God, may we have ever increasing faith and may every thought, word and deed glorify You. In Jesus' beautiful name. Amen.

June 22 Read Psalm 13

ANTIDOTE TO WORRY

Bible Thought: "Which of you by taking thought can one cubit unto his stature? (Matthew 6:27).

I define worry as "rehearsing calamity" or meditating on the worse thing that can happen. How long could one feel this way and still have good health? Instead of "cardiac thrombosis" written on a death certificate many doctors could write "worry" as the cause of death.

Worry is contagious. I have heard that a worry person's pet develops the personality of its owner. What a terrible thing to put on a pet!

What is the antidote of worry? Count your blessings. Live one day at a time. Break the habit of negative self-talk. See worry as fear trying to conquer faith. Believe and act on God's Word. To do otherwise is destructive. Believe God is big enough to take care of every part of your life. He is on your side.

Take the energy you use in worrying and replace it with overwhelming positive thoughts. Be worry free with God's help and then be successful, prosperous and be at peace.

The greatest antidote to worry is Jesus, your hope of glory. It's a love that can never be taken away.

Dear Lord, we repent of worrying and we replace it with Your promises. Thank You for Your grace and mercy. In Jesus' wonderful name. Amen.

June 23 Read 1 Chronicles 29:18-20

TO KEEP I MUST LET GO

Bible Thought: "I have shewed you all things, how that so labouring ye ought to support the weak, and to remember the words of the Lord Jesus, how he said, It is more blessed to give than to receive" (Acts 20:35)

When our last child left home I found myself with the "empty nest" syndrome big time. "Let's get in the pickup and go for a drive," my husband said, brushing away my tears.

After a few miles I saw it. A piece of gnarled white driftwood lay by a country road. It had deep scars from life's adversities. The deep white wood reflected in the glistening sunlight. Thoughts ran through my head. *The storms of life have surely scarred this structure but it has stood its ground.*

The next day we put our prize in the front yard. Why do I treasure that piece of wood? Its scars and wounds bring out the brightness of the sun. The scars and wounds of my life bring out the brightness of the "Son" who died for me.

My driftwood is still standing, reminding me the best things in life are free, simple things that mean so much. I learned a lot about life that day. Even though changes occur God is faithful and you get to keep what you give away.

Letting go of my children was hard, but as a friend remarked, "To keep them you must let them go."

Dear precious Lord, thank You that we get to keep forever the love we have given to others. Even more, we thank You for Jesus who gave the most love of all. In His wonderful name. Amen.

June 24 Read Habakkuk 3:17-18

WITH GOD WE WIN

Bible Thought: "I press toward the mark for the prize of the high calling of God in Christ Jesus" (Philippians 3:14).

My understanding of football is not the greatest but this much I do know. The object of the game is to lay hold on the ball and run toward the finish line. I find that similar to the game of life. Sometimes we have setbacks and lose the ball. We can even be tackled and run over. Though we may be down we're not defeated. We get up and try again. We keep on playing the game of life because the prize at the end of the race is worth everything.

I think about characters like Moses, Abraham, Job, Naomi and Elijah. Adversity came upon them but despite their troubles they stood steadfast until the end. What an example for us.

Every day you and I have a choice. We play the game of life according to God's "rulebook," the Bible. God is our Coach and He instructs His team with love and patience. He has given angels to watch over us and He will never leave nor forsaken us. At the end of life's game, He has prepared a place for us to live with Him forever.

With God we win. Let's keep running toward the finish line. Let us run the race with faith, hope and calm assurance.

Dear Lord, we thank You today for Your Word. We also thank You for those who have gone on before us leaving encouragement and examples. Most of all, we thank You for our Savior. His name is Jesus. Amen.

June 25 Read Proverbs 17:24-28

TIME IS PRECIOUS

Bible Thought: "Take therefore no thought for the morrow: for the morrow shall take thought for the things of itself. Sufficient unto the day *is* the evil thereof" (Matthew 6:34).

Today is all we have. We cannot go back and relive yesterday. Neither can we live tomorrow today. Psychologists agree that one of the main hindrances to victorious living is looking back.

Past hurts, guilt and remorse lead to despair. Dwelling on the past impedes moving forward, stifles success and promotes illness.

Each day is an opportunity to be happy. All of us have the same amount of time. God is in the "now" of life. We can only live one day at a time. We cannot save, loan or borrow time. Time is a precious commodity to be spent well. Every day is the day to love Jesus. Thank Him and appreciate salvation.

Today is a new day. Now is the time to live…right now…this very moment. Savor it. Relish the time. Make today count. God has given you life on earth and an eternal home.

We should be happy as kings!

Open God's gift today. There's a happy day inside.

Dear precious Lord, thank You for Jesus. Thank You for life and its abundance. Thank You for joy. Thank You for our heavenly home. Blessed be Your name. Amen.

June 26 Read Psalm 78:53-55

GOD'S BOUNDARIES MAKE SAFETY

Bible Thought: "If the Son therefore shall make you free, ye shall be free indeed" (John 8:36).

Imagine my surprise. A fluffy fat white rabbit sat in my flower garden. His long pink ears and twitchy nose made him look like a mechanical toy. He hopped along happily as if to say, "Look at me. I'm free!"

Visiting with a dear neighbor later that day I jokingly asked, "Could I give you a white rabbit?"

"Our rabbit is here? We've been looking everywhere for him."

Her children finally caught him and I began to see a spiritual lesson from the experience.

The rabbit had enjoyed freedom but sooner or later that freedom would have led to his destruction. Traffic is heavy on our street. We live at the edge of town and hungry stray dogs appear from time to time.

Yes the rabbit was free, but far from the safety his owner provided.

The same thing can happen to me. If I go beyond God's boundaries and do my own thing by disobeying his commandments I can be lead to all kinds of danger. Out of God's boundaries are many traps and snares that could be avoided by obedience.

I am not my own. My Owner paid an inestimable price for me. Within His boundaries I am provided safety and that is a great place to be.

Dear Lord, thank You for Your commandments. May we strive to obey them in thought, word and deed. In Jesus' name. Amen.

June 27 Read 1 Peter 3:12-15

GOD HEARS PRAYERS

Bible Thought: "But know that the LORD hath set apart him that is godly for himself: the LORD will hear when I call unto him" (Psalm 4:3).

My husband and our oldest son had gone to check the windmill. Mark suddenly stopped with one foot in mid-air. "A rattlesnake." He moved back quickly.

To me, this incident was not an accident. Every morning I pray for my family. I call each name and thank God for His protection and safety.

I recall many other incidents when a family member was in danger yet prayer kept them safe.

God answers prayers. There is no distance in the spirit and our prayers "avail much." Please don't leave home without them.

God's love for you and me is amazing. Think about how much you love your family. God's love is greater.

God changes things. Sometimes it's slow in coming or maybe the answer isn't like I thought it would be, but He always answers and His answers are the best.

Does God hear prayers?

A resounding "YES!"

Dear wonderful Lord, we cannot find words to express our love. We praise You today for You are the only One. You are the Morning Star, the Rose of Sharon and the King of kings and Lord of lords. In Jesus' name. Amen.

June 28 Read 1 Chronicles 16:8-12

A DANCING HEART

Bible Thought: "…for the joy of the LORD is your strength." (Nehemiah 8:10).

I like the refreshing smell after a rain or viewing the morning's dew from my windowpane. I love to watch powder-puff clouds in a soft blue sky or the spectacular sunsets with strokes of pink and golden hues. My heart dances because of God's many blessings. I find joy in simple pleasures.

I believe a dancing heart for Jesus is a happy heart. It reduces blood pressure, cholesterol and stress. Each morning I say "This is the day *which* the LORD hath made; we will rejoice and be glad in it" (Psalm 118:24).

You will never be a wallflower if you dance with Jesus in your heart. In my heart I want to dance every dance wit Jesus because He tells me,…"I am the light of the world: he that followeth me shall not walk in darkness, but shall have the light of life" (John 8:12).

His truths keep my heart dancing!

Dear God, the joy of knowing You fills us to overflowing. Our hearts dance in thankfulness. We praise You today with love and adoration." In Jesus' precious name. Amen.

June 29 Read Song of Solomon 2:14-17

ON THE WINGS OF MY DOVE

Bible Thought: "Though ye have lien among the pots, *yet shall ye be as* the wings of a dove covered with silver, and her feathers with yellow gold" (Psalm 68:13).

"Mrs. Clayton, we have your husband in the emergency room," an ER said on the phone. I grabbed the car keys and rushed to the hospital. "Lord, You are my anchor and I put all my trust in You." I reached the hospital to find Emmitt in a head and body brace. Another car had hit him in the middle of the pickup.

Each night I prayed for his recovery. The sight of his wounds and the agony of his pain brought tears I tried to hide. We were high school sweethearts and the book of Song of Solomon described our love.

After several days I brought him home. One night my tears began to flow uncontrollably. I went to bed half crying and half asleep, praying "Lord, I feel like a little dove with a broken wing."

Somewhere in that twilight I had a dream. I had a beautifully wrapped gift in gold paper and shining ribbons. I tore into it and there lay a dove's wing, shining in gold and silver. The next morning I found my dream in Psalm 68:13.

Emmitt recovered.

We were on the "wings of my dove."

His name is Jesus.

Dear Lord, thank You for walking with us through the trials of life. Thank You for never abandoning Your children.

June 30 Read Psalm 56:10-13

JESUS IS WAITING FOR YOU

Bible Thought: "Cast thy burden upon the LORD, and he shall sustain thee: he shall never suffer the righteous to be moved" (Psalm 55:22).

Life's journey has many experiences and some are hard to endure. Where do we run when our heartache is so great and the pain is unbearable? The blessed hope is Jesus.

He loves us so much we cannot fathom it and He knows what is best for all of us. Whatever the circumstance or situation, there will never be lasting relief from outside sources.

The promises of God are true. I must believe and cling to them if I am to have peace. I have faith in so many earthly things, faith the sun will come up and the sky won't fall.

In the darkest hour of your life Jesus is waiting for you to run to His wings. The Greatest One who ever lived in human form has paid the supreme sacrifice.

I believe the Lord sends roses with thorns to remind us of the painful yet wondrous beauty of Jesus' sacrifice of love.

Though you are impatient
And anxious in life's cares
Just renew God's promises
For He is always there.

So if you are discouraged
When troubles come your way,
Thank God for His promise
And you will be okay!

Dear God, thank You for Your steadfastness and grace. Thank You too, for Your patience. In Jesus' wonderful name. Amen.

JULY

July 1 Read Exodus 20:1-6

TO THE FOURTH GENERATION

Bible Thought: "Keeping mercy for thousands, forgiving iniquity and transgression and sin, and that will by not means clear the *guilty;* visiting the iniquity of the fathers upon the children, and upon the children's children, unto the third and to the fourth *generation"* (Exodus 34:7).

Have you ever thought about the way you live today will affect your descendants to the fourth generation? It is a sobering thought.

Hamar, Ahab and many others left terrible legacies for posterity. What an awful gift to leave for anyone. Sins of selfishness bring on pain and misery. Unless repentance is sincerely given an eternal destruction is waiting.

It breaks my heart to hear of neglect and child abuse. I saw this many times in my teaching career. An innocent child born in unwanted situations suffer immensely. I used to think "hate" was the opposite of "love." I now realize the opposite of "hate" is "selfishness."

Millions of dollars are spent and many programs are provided for children in dysfunctional families. It seems society doesn't want the answer. I read an unknown quote that is an awakening call, "Why is it our children can't read a Bible in school, but they can in prison?"

Obedience in God and love for children is the only answer.

Dear Lord, may we be a nation who has love and training for our children to all generations. In Jesus' beautiful name. Amen.

July 2 Read Isaiah 43:1-7

TODAY IS THE DAY THAT COUNTS

Bible Thought: "I press toward the mark for the prize of the high calling of God in Christ Jesus" (Philippians 3:14).

Many years ago we planted a small tree in our drive around driveway. It has survived treacherous storms because we anchored it to a strong support. Each storm has made it more beautiful. The gnarled tree trunk and wind blown branches have molded it into a thing of beauty and a shape one could not have grown.

Storms come to our lives too but we have the greatest support of all. Jesus takes our "windblown lives" and makes something beautiful. Anchoring to Him brings strong roots and they grow deep, anchored to His solid Rock.

Cling to Him when storm clouds come and the wind of adversity sways you to and fro. With Jesus you will emerge victorious.

Each day is a gift made just for you from the heart of God. Live it to the fullest. Again I say, "Life is delicious!"

Praise and thank God for today and every day.

Today is the day that counts. Make tomorrow count. Make all your days count.

How happy you will be!

Dear precious Lord, thank You for today. We fill this day with gladness and gratitude. We are so thankful for Jesus, our beautiful Savior. He is the bright and morning star, the lily of the valley, the fairest of the fair and we praise and bless His name. It's the name of all names. His name is Jesus. Amen.

July 3 Read 1 Samuel 17:32-37

CRITICISM

Bible Thought: "He that keepeth his mouth keepeth his life: *but* he that openeth wide his lips shall have destruction" (Proverbs 13:3).

How do you react to criticism? I do not react well, especially from my husband. Instead of saying, "I really wanted this shoe leather on my boots," he could have said, "You really cooked this piece of ham well."

It is hard to deal with criticism. Keeping our cool when criticized is emotionally draining but the wrong reaction brings defeat. David didn't let the jeers and mockeries of the crowd stop him. He took Goliath with one pebble.

I've discovered flaws I've been tempted to find in other people are flaws I've found in myself. So I've tried to learn from criticism. If I become defensive, things get out of control and I get upset. It's better to keep quiet than to fight back. I try to consider criticism as a lesson to be learned. My husband's comment about "shoe leather" caused me to learn to cook.

When a snappy reply occurs learn to really listen. Listening to others can be a path of wisdom.

God's love enables us to see the good in others, thereby blocking criticism.

Dear Lord, may we seek to be like You, every day in every way. Help us to keep the right statement by overlooking offenses and seeing the good. In Jesus' wonderful name. Amen.

July 4 Read Isaiah 61:1-5

REAL FREEDOM

Bible Thought: "Stand fast therefore in the liberty wherewith Christ hath made us free, and be not entangled again with the yoke of bondage (Galatians 5:1).

Today we celebrate our country's birthday and the freedom of this great land. As wonderful as that is, I know a greater birthday and a greater freedom. I celebrate Jesus every day. He came to earth to save sinners like me. Freedom in the Lord is freedom indeed. Living within His boundaries and commandments truly makes us free.

It's just too wonderful. I want to ask everybody, "Do you know Jesus? Do you know He loves you? Do you know He is coming back for His own? Do you know He will take His children home to live with Him forever?"

By reaching out to others and bringing them to Jesus, they too can receive freedom and pass on the good news, fulfilling the Great Commission.

What a wonderful way to welcome His coming.

Jesus came to set the captive free.

That is real freedom!

Dear wonderful Lord, how we praise You today for the real freedom…freedom from the bondage of sin, bringing the hope of everlasting life with You. Thank You for Jesus who made it all possible. In His mighty name. Amen.

July 5 Read Philippians 4:4-9

HOW IS YOUR THOUGHT LIFE?

Bible Thought: "And be not conformed to this world: but be ye transformed by the renewing of your mind, that ye may prove what is that good, and acceptable, and perfect will of God" (Romans 12:2).

It has been said, "We are what we eat." Someone has also said, "We are what we think." The writer in Proverbs 23:7 said it first, "For as he thinketh in his heart, so is he." Our thoughts affect our life. Negative thoughts have adverse positive reactions. Thoughts can bring smiles or tears, gladness or sadness, peace or anxiety.

It takes determination to stop negativity. Many ailments such as depression, blood pressure and insomnia to name a few, had a beginning with plain old "stinking thinking." That kind of thinking ruins a perfectly good day or night.

To change our lives, we must change our thoughts. It is easy to praise the Lord in good times, but it takes real faith and courage to raise Him when things are not going well.

We block the enemy's intent when we meditate on the Lord in spite of the circumstances. Keep your thoughts on the Lord when you are tempted to worry, especially in the still small hours of the morning. Praise the Lord in the midst of adversity. Exercise your faith and trust. In a trial think of Psalm 56:3 and let it be your battle cry. "What time I am afraid, I will trust in thee."

That makes a happy thought life.

Dear Lord, we pray to be transformed today by the renewing of our minds. You are a positive God and we walk, talk, and have our being in You. Thank You for Jesus, our beautiful Redeemer. In His name. Amen.

July 6 Read Psalm 63:2-8

REACHING UP

Bible Thought: "Salute one another with an holy kiss…(Romans 16:16).

When our sons were small a hug and kiss made every thing better. It still does now that they are grown.

I have been reaching up to hug my husband for many years. I had to reach even higher when our sons became teenagers Now I have to stand on tiptoes to hug our grandsons. Hugs and kisses make well being.

A hug or pat on the back went a long way with my second grade students. "A hug a day makes a happy day," they said as they came to school each morning. At the end of the day they hugged as far as they could reach.

There is something about a touch. Jesus held the little children. His touch healed the sick. He is a God of love and His love extended to His crucifixion on a cruel cross for you and me. The first thing I'm going to do when I see Jesus will be to kiss those nail-scarred hands and feet.

Meanwhile, I will praise Him, love Him and yes, I will give kisses toward God!

Dear precious Lord, Your love brings so much joy. We return that joy to You today and everyday of our lives. We will even have more joy when we see You in heaven. In that beautiful name. His name is Jesus. Amen.

July 7 Read 2 Samuel 7:22-26

UNDER NEW MANAGEMENT

Bible Thought: "Jesus Christ the same yesterday, and to-day, and for ever" (Hebrews 13:8).

I see the sign "Under New Management" many times and wonder what happened to the previous manager. Yet I know a "Manager" who is the "Manager" of all times.

To me new management implies something different. In a world of darkness God's new management is a welcome sign. The sacrifice of Jesus, nailed to a cross for the sins of mankind, gives assurance to troubled souls. Jesus endured sorrow for our joy. He trades peace for our anxiety. He exchanges a cross for a crown of righteousness. He gives hope for the hopeless, a home for the aching heart. He turns disappointments into God's appointments. The child of God is "under new management." The old life is gone.

We are living in tumultuous times. Economy looms, terrorists threaten, homes are lost if not by bankruptcy by physical disasters, plagues appear and problems seem to be a heartbeat away. God is ready to hear the heart's cry for a hurting soul and He is the best "Manager" for your problems.

Resolve to be "Under The New Management" today.

Dear Lord, thank You for making us brand new. Thank You for being our "Manager" in this life and throughout eternity. Amen.

July 8 Read Psalm 150

SING TO THE LORD

Bible Thought: "O sing unto the Lord a new song: sing unto the LORD, all the earth" (Psalm 96:1).

We have our devotional early in the morning. I lead the songs because my husband thinks he can only make a joyful noise but before you know it he joins in. Singing to the Lord brings joy.

Have you ever awakened in the morning with a song in your heart? I have many times. Each song seems to stay with me all day. It reminds me of a gracious loving God who is right there with me and will never leave me.

When I was a young Christian waiting for anesthesia in the surgical room I began to sing in my heart. I awakened in the recovery room singing.

I sung many hymns while rocking my babies. I sung over my husband after many operations and I sung to my dying mother as she flew to heaven on wings of love.

Sing to the Lord today.

It blesses and soothes your soul.

Dear God, we worship You with singing and thankfulness for Your incredible love. In Jesus' beautiful name. Amen.

July 9 Read 1 John 4:7-12

GOD IS LOVE

Bible Thought: "Set me as a seal upon thine heart, as a seal upon thine arm: for love *is* strong as death; jealousy *is* cruel as the grave: the coals thereof *are* coals of fire, *which hath a* most vehement flame" (Song of Solomon 8:6).

"Is this Mrs. Clayton?" a young man's voice asked. "This is Jimmy. It's been five years since I was in your second grade, but I still think of you a lot. We're moving to Missouri and I just wanted to call and say, "I love you!"

"I love you too Jimmy, and you will never be out of my heart or prayers."

The need to be loved is one of mankind's basic needs. It has been noted that newborn babies cannot thrive without love. Husbands and wives will surely fail without love for each other. Their children will suffer even more.

God so loved that He gave us Jesus. That is the greatest love. Let us tell the others about Jesus. May we love each other by reaching out to a hurting world.

We were created and wanted by God. He loves you and me. Knowing this enables us to return that love.

It only takes three words.

Is there someone you need to call today and say, "I love you."

Dear heavenly Father, thank You for loving us. Thank You for Jesus. May we reflect that love to everyone we meet. In Jesus' mighty name. Amen.

July 10 Read Revelation 21:1-4

HOW BIG IS GOD?

Bible Thought: "Unto him *be* glory in the church by Christ Jesus throughout all ages, world without end. Amen (Ephesians 3:20).

The vastness of God's creation is overwhelming. From outer space, planet earth is but a little blue marble, yet God provides every need for the earth's inhabitants.

God knows each one of us. He knows every hair upon our heads. Realizing the sovereignty of God difficulties can turn into opportunities. All things are possible for you and me because He lives mightily in us.

God is bigger than the illness of a loved one, a misunderstanding, a financial crisis or any other problem that plagues the human soul.

God is able. He never grows weary and His supply never runs out. He is big enough to renew strength and to hear and answer prayers. He restores well being. Nothing can compare to our God. He is unequaled.

The next time you have a problem, step outside and look at the sky. Only God can make such magnificence, yet He has time for all of us.

How big is God? GOD IS BIG!

Dear wonderful God, we thank You for the wondrous beauty You have made. May we share the beauty of Your love with everyone we meet. Amen.

July 11 Read Psalm 122

BE A HAPPY ECHO

Bible Thought: "Now unto him that is able to do exceeding abundantly above all that we ask or think, according to the power that worketh in us" (Ephesians (3:20).

On a mountain hike one morning, Lance shouted to his brothers, "I'm the king of the mountains." He beat on his chest like Tarzan. Imagine the surprised look on his face when he heard, "I'm the king of the mountains" coming back to him.

"Who are you?" Lance yelled.

"Who are you?" came back the answer. All three of our boys took turns. When it became my time I shouted, "I love you," and the same words came back to me.

Immediately I realized the impact of what I had just witnessed. I began thinking about the words I say and things I do. Life gives back what I give, just like an echo does.

If I want more love in my life, I must create more love in my heart. If I want to be blessed, I must be a blessing. If I want to be truly happy I will try to make others happy. What I give to life returns to me.

A life that gives love, kindness, unselfishness, forgiveness and happiness is a blessed life indeed.

Make a "happy echo" today.

Dear precious Lord, may we say kind words to those we meet and may they see You in everything we do. Thank You for our beautiful Savior. His name is Jesus. Amen.

July 12 Read 2 Corinthians 4:16-18

PERSISTENCE

Bible Thought: "And Jesus looking upon them saith, With men it is impossible, but not with God: for with God all things are possible" (Mark 10:27).

Do you ever experience failures? Welcome to the crowd. When I make a mess of things I feel defeated. I have to remind myself I'm not perfect. Human beings do make mistakes but learning from those mistakes enables one to pursue success.

Just because you have failed in the past doesn't means you will keep failing. See yourself succeeding because with God all things are possible.

Pursue that dream God has put into your heart. Be patient. Expect the best. Say, "I can do all things through Christ which strengtheneth me" (Philippians 4:13).

You are a unique person with a special gift, just waiting to be shared. Share that gift God has given. It will return blessings to you.

Try it today. What seems unsuccessful to you may be the very thing that brings fulfillment in your life.

Be persistent. Turn your failures into success because God is on your side.

Dear Lord, thank You for leading us in the way we should go. It is the guidance of Your Spirit and the overwhelming victory we have in You. Thank You for the most precious gift of all. His name is Jesus. Amen

July 13 Read Proverbs 3:21-26

WISDOM FROM A CHILD

Bible Thought: "Keep thy heart with all diligence; for out of it *are* the issues of life" (Proverbs 4:23).

My second graders seemed to enjoy "neighborhoods" in my social studies class. The need for rules and fairness to all, regardless of race, creed or color, was explored and explained.

Children have quick insight. One student, after repeating exuberantly with his hand proclaimed most enthusiastically, "It doesn't matter what's on the outside. It's what's on the inside that counts!" What wisdom from a seven year old.

The attitudes of our minds and hearts make all the difference. God is no respecter of persons. If we allow Him to mold our lives we will have an "inside" that is tender and yearning for righteousness.

Blessings always follow obedience. Pain always follows disobedience. Pursuing wisdom brings common sense that enhances a life of peace and safety.

Seek the Lord today. Let's pray and give thanks for another day to praise and follow Jesus. Read the Bible. Commit special passages to memory. "Hide the Word in Your heart." Fill your thoughts with good things.

Reach out and touch someone today with love and kindness.

Remember, "It's what's on the inside that counts!"

Dear Lord, may we have the faith of children. Grant us wisdom in this journey of life. In Jesus' beautiful name. Amen.

July 14 Read Genesis 2:24-26

ANIMALS ARE GIFTS FROM A LOVING GOD

Bible Thought: "And God made the beast of the earth after his kind, and cattle after their kind, and every thing that creepeth upon the earth after his kind: and God saw that it *was* good" (Genesis 1:25).

I am always amazed at the many blessings and gifts God has bestowed upon mankind. I am also fascinated with Adam's intelligence in being able to name every animal.

With three lively sons we had our share of pets. Although I took care of the feeding and vet visits I became attached to all the pets we had. I learned a lot.

"Lady," my husband's horse didn't know she was a horse. Instead of a "horse whisperer" she was a "horse loud talker." We had a strong sandstorm one day and it made the tin over her stall rattle. She talked to me in her loudest "whinny" that she couldn't eat in her stall. Her fear was evident. I moved her trough out of the stall and she began to eat peacefully. She trusted me.

Old Tom became a tiger on the vet's cold steel table but when he felt the touch of my hand he relaxed and began to purr. He knew the touch of his master's hand.

My husband found seven little lost sheep on our porch one night. He led them to the backyard and enclosed them safely until he could find the owner. They followed him everywhere as he became their shepherd for a while.

When I lose my way I run to "The Good Shepherd" and He brings me safe to the fold. Yes, God's animals are gifts!

Dear God, thank You for all the provisions You have made. In Jesus' name. Amen.

July 15 Read Isaiah 56:5-7

PRAYER IS OUR AVENUE TO GOD

Bible Thought: "And it shall come to pass, that before they call, I will answer; and while they are yet speaking, I will hear" (Isaiah 65).

Planet earth is experiencing unprecedented challenges. We have made great strides in technology, but so has our enemies. Now, more then ever, we need wisdom guidance and direction.

You can read about how God confused the Philistines in 1 Samuel 14, directed Joshua in Joshua 6. Deborah led God's people in Judges 4. Gideon had 32,000 soldiers but God chose 300 and sent the rest home. Gideon had victory because he depended on God.

Dependence upon God produces a cutting edge in battles. Prayer is the mighty weapon. It is a privilege to pray, not just in hard times, but all the time. God is the strength of life, the fortress and refuge in life's battles. With Him on our side nothing is impossible.

Our lives are a testimony of God's saving grace. We awaken with eyes that can see, ears that can hear and strength to get out of bed. We have food to eat and clean water to drink. We have family and friends that love us. We're thankful we can pray every day for those loved ones, committing and trusting them in His care, and praising Him for our many blessings.

Prayer is our avenue to God, an eternal refuge.

Precious Lord, may we seek You every moment, loving and thanking You for Jesus, our Savior. In His beautiful name. Amen.

July 16 Read John 11:21-27

IF JESUS HAD NOT COME

Bible Thought: "The thief cometh not, but for to steal and to kill, and to destroy: I am come that they might have life, and that they might have *it* more abundantly" (John 10:10).

Have you ever thought about how this world would be if Jesus had not come to earth? I shudder to think about it. This world would be a terrible place to be with no absolutes of right and wrong. We have the choice to choose life and goodness. Otherwise it would bring untold heartache, not only to one's self, but to everyone else. Wrong choices imprison the soul. There will be no "do overs" or second chances in heaven.

There are those today who would try to rewrite the Bible to suit their own lifestyle. The truth remains. God's Word is still God's Word and it will never pass away.

The good news is that Jesus did come. We are saved from the ravages of sin.

Two thousand years have come and gone but He still reigns. He lifts the hearts of the downtrodden. He heals the brokenhearted. He removes the pain of yesterday and brings joy for tomorrow.

Jesus came and forever changed the world.

Allow Him to change your life today.

Dear precious Lord, thank You for sending Your only Son to save us. Such sacrificial love is beyond our understanding, but we give our hearts to You for all our days. May we live in obedience to the everlasting way of Your love. In Jesus' wonderful name. Amen.

July 17 Read Psalm 149:1-5

JOY IN THE LORD

Bible Thought: "...the joy of the LORD is your strength" (Nehemiah 8:10).

Today is all you have. Make the most of it. Say, "I love you" to someone dear. Please don't wait until "this or that happens." Be happy because we know who holds our future. Our trust in Him gives peace. That is something to be joyful about.

I like to call life "delicious." If I had never been born, I would have missed everything. I love the cooing of doves, the sunrise and the sunsets. The sound of rain against my window pane soothes me. The depths of love with my husband, three wonderful sons and six grandchildren are blessings!

I'm so glad to be alive. Aren't you? Every day I think the Lord for my time to live and the time I've had to love others.

When our youngest son graduated from high school he walked across the stage then stopped and gave his Dad, the high school principal, a giant bear hug. The crowd cheered and I cried.

One forgettable Christmas occurred when my husband took me in his arms and said, "Next to Jesus, you are my special gift."

These are just a few happy memories that make my happy days.

Joy comes from Jesus.

Let Him make you joyful today and every day.

Dear Lord, living for You is like living in heaven already. We will be there someday for ever and ever. Oh happy day! In Jesus beautiful name. Amen.

July 18 Read Isaiah 43:1-5

TRUST GOD

Bible Thought: "Be careful for nothing; but in every thing by prayer and supplication with thanksgiving let your requests be made known unto God" (Philippians 4:6).

Do you dread a trip? Do you imagine the worst, creating a scenario with all kinds of mishaps? We rob ourselves of peace by rehearsing calamity. Today is the only day we can live. Packing around all the woes of the past and dreading the future is an offense to a loving God. Trusting in God is essential. To do otherwise is living a miserable life.

Yes, all of us have stress. The trick is dealing with it. As one of my grandsons said, "You're only as stressed as you allow yourself to be." What wisdom for Jody's young adult years.

Why should we allow the enemy to rob the peace and joy of today by rehearsing some disaster? Why subject ourselves to heart-wrenching experiences? Why suffer all emotional pain and misery?

Whatever problem you are experiencing today let go and let God. He is bigger than any circumstance. After all, there is just so much you can do. Worrying doesn't accomplish anything and destroys a lot of peace and unrest.

God is able. Trust Him today!

Dear wonderful Lord, we lay our anxieties at Your feet today. Forgive us for not keeping our minds on You, trusting You, praising You and loving You. In Jesus' mighty name. Amen.

July 19 Read Isaiah 9:6-7

YES, I'M A BELIEVER

Bible Thought: "And the LORD their God shall save them in that day as the flock of his people: for they *shall be as* the stones of a crown, lifted up as an ensign upon his land" (Zechariah 9:16).

The scripture reading was written centuries before Jesus came, yet scoffers still existed then and now.

I'm a believer! I believe there is a void in the human heart, a vacuum that only God can fill. Jesus lives in my heart. I have the blessed hope that when I leave this life, I will live with Him forever. No, I'm not perfect, but that is why Jesus came to save mankind from the slavery of sin and that includes me. That includes you.

I believe every person born is not here by accident, but for a purpose. I want to fulfill that purpose in my life. Had you or I not been born, we would have missed the greatest love ever given to the human race and I would not have missed that for the world.

I love to read about heaven in Revelation 22:5, "And there shall be no night there; and they need no candle, neither light of the sun; for the Lord God giveth them light: and they shall reign for ever and ever."

Yes, I'm a believer!

Dear precious Lord, thank You for that great day! Seeing You face to face will be our greatest joy. What a great reunion it will be. Thank You for Jesus who is coming back for us. In His wonderful name. Amen.

July 20 Read Revelation 5:11-14

OUR GOD REIGNS

Bible Thought: "And there shall be no night there; and they need no candle neither light of the sun; for the Lord God giveth them: and they shall reign for ever and ever" (Revelation 22:5).

I am confident for the Greater One lives in me. Through Him I can run through a troop and leap over a wall. I am the redeemed, the healed, the child of God. I do not see through natural eyes. I see in the faith realm. In every situation I see possibilities.

Everywhere I put my foot I take dominion for Jesus rises strong in me. My enemies flee from me seven ways.

I break generational sins. I stop them in my generation. I build the bridge for my family and descendants. "As for me and my house, we will serve the Lord."

I do all things through Jesus because His strength is my strength. His health is my health. His riches are my riches. My God supplies all my needs and I am thankful.

Let all the earth proclaim. Let the mountains shout it. Let the seas roar it. Let all earth rejoice.

"I'm in love with Jesus
And He's in love with me.
In every facet of my life
He keeps me constantly.

My life is filled with purpose
Each day of life I sing.
I'm on my way to glory
Forever with my King!"

Dear precious Lord, thank You for Your steadfastness, Your love, You're everything we need. Blessed be Your name. In Jesus. Amen.

July 21 Read Psalm 56:10-13

JESUS IS WAITING FOR YOU

Bible Thought: "Cast thy burden upon the LORD and he shall sustain thee: he shall never suffer the righteous to be moved" (Psalm 55:22).

Life's journey has many experiences and some are hard to endure. Where do we run when our heartache is so great and the pain is unbearable? The blessed hope is Jesus. He loves us so much we cannot fathom it yet He knows what is best.

Whatever the circumstance or situation, there will never be lasting relief from outside sources. The promises of God are true. I must believe and cling to them if I am to have peace. I have faith in so many earthly things. It's easy to have faith the sun will come up and the sky won't fall. In the darkest hour of your life and mine Jesus is waiting for us to run to His wings.

The Greatest One who ever lived in human form has paid the supreme sacrifice. I believe the Lord sends roses with thorns to remind us of the painful yet wondrous beauty of Jesus' love.

"When the battle's over
So happy you will be.
His strength enables you
To walk in victory!"

Dear Lord, thank You for waiting with grace and patience. Thank You for Jesus who sacrificed for the way to heaven. In His beautiful name. Amen.

July 22 Read Psalm 118:14-17

JESUS DID NOT DIE IN VAIN FOR ME

Bible Thought: "Precious in the sight of the LORD *is* the death of his saints" (116:15).

Jesus did not die in vain for me. His death on the cross covers every area of my life. His crown of thorns cover my thought life and I am transformed by the renewing of my mind.

When the enemy tries to penetrate my mind, Jesus' crown of thorns become my crown of victory, for those thorns become a fortress.

The thirty-nine stripes on Jesus' back cover my physical body and every disease, every germ, every harmful thing that comes against my body must surrender. All malevolent forces stand powerless in the light of the cross.

Since I belong to Jesus, He gives me every good and perfect gift that pertains to life and godliness. He makes all things work together for my good. He sends the precious Holy Spirit to counsel, lead and guide me.

Oh happy day! I am more than a conqueror…and I do it by the blood of the Lamb and the word of my testimony.

I receive and walk in His great love for Jesus did not die in vain for me.

Dear Lord, thank You for loving us, dying for us and coming back for us. In the blessed name of Jesus. Amen.

July 23 Read Jeremiah 29:4-10

OBEDIENCE AND PURPOSE

Bible Thought: "But none of these things move me, neither count I my life dear unto myself, so that I might finish my course with joy, and the ministry, which I have received of the Lord Jesus, to testify the gospel of the grace of God" (Acts 20:24).

Life is a precious gift with a God-given purpose. The saddest thing to me is a life wasted, unappreciated or just thrown away. Effective living requires a study and knowledge of God's Word, while applying its principles in daily living.

How we need to realize and pursue God's purpose for our lives. Our future is determined by obedience. I must keep my faith. If I stumble and fall, I must repent and ask forgiveness to "strain toward the mark." An ungodly lifestyle to me is more dangerous than anything because an eternal destiny is at stake.

God's wisdom is the most important choice we could ever make. The apostle Paul considered life worthless if it is not used for God's purpose.

Trusting God in faithful obedience brings the "Light" of His glory in every situation. Walking in His Light annihilates fear and brings peace and rest to the soul.

Living for God's purpose has no regrets on the deathbed.

What better way to live, being valuable to God and following His purpose.

Dear God, may we always trust and obey You. Thank You for our purpose in life.

Jesus' wonderful name. Amen.

July 24 Read Joshua 1:6-9

NEVER ALONE

Bible Thought: "For the LORD will not forsake his people for his great name's sake: because it hath pleased the LORD to make you his people" (1 Samuel 12:22).

We are never alone in this world. There is an all caring, loving God who sacrificed His own Son. He will never abandon His children. This fills our hearts with hope and calms our fears. Even though we often fall short, God loves us anyway. Many trials are experienced from the cradle to the grave, but God sees, provides and lovingly watches over His own.

I can see the hand of God in every event of my life. He is faithful. He has a plan for every life. Those led by His Spirit and walk in His plan are blessed indeed. In the darkest hour, He is there. He even sends His angels to watch over His beloved.

Who would not want the security and peace that God brings? The world may crumble around you, but "the name of the Lord is still a strong tower" (Proverbs 18:10).

Get to know God today. Trust Him. Love Him. Serve Him.

With Him, you are never alone.

Dear precious Lord, thank You for the life You have given. May we spend our days on earth loving and praising You for Your great love. In that wonderful name of Jesus. Amen.

July 25 Read Revelation 21:1-5

FOCUS ON THE VICTORY

Bible Thought: "And let us not be weary in well doing: for in due season we shall reap, if we faint not" (Galatians 6:9).

Do you ever feel like life has put you into a boxing arena? Do you ever feel like you're out for the count? In the heat of battle, it takes real courage to persevere, to keep the faith, to focus on the victory. It is so easy to think our case is isolated and we are the only one in the world our situation is happening to. Yet somewhere, sometime, someone else has met a similar circumstance.

We do have the choice of our attitude. We can find the good things and think positively, or we can cower in defeat and misery along with negativity. It all depends on how you look at it. I would rather give life my best shot than to retreat in defeat. I would rather have tried than not to have tried at all.

Losers see only an ongoing battle. Winners see the end result, because they have read the last page.

One reason the enemy fights so hard is because just around the corner victory is waiting for you. You aren't down for the count. Champions get back up.

Losers focus on the war.

Winners focus on the victory.

Dear Lord, thank You for making us more than conquerors. "We can do all things through Jesus." In His mighty name. Amen.

July 26 Read Genesis 2:21-25

LOVE FOR A LIFETIME

Bible Thought: "O magnify the LORD with me, and let us exalt his name together" (Psalm 34:3).

I watched the elderly couple through misty eyes. He led her on his arm into the cafeteria. After he seated her he went through the serving line. He lovingly brought her food and sat down beside her. Then he gently cut her meat. His every move was to see that her needs were taken care of before he started eating.

I could tell they had spent a lifetime together. His devotion, commitment and love dominated the whole scene. Although he was not too strong himself, he used what strength he had to care for his mate whom he adored.

My parents and grandparents were married sixty-five years. I witnessed first-hand the meaning of faithfulness, unselfishness, sacrifice and love of each other. The hardships they endured only brought them closer as they looked to God for guidance. Their love became "stronger than death."

In this world of selfish humanism it is refreshing to see a husband and wife still committed after so many years.

God's plan for marriage and the family still rings true in spite of liberal philosophy.

Love for a lifetime. There is no greater concept!

Dear precious Lord, thank You for Your plan for marriage and the family. May each family recognize You as the foundation for successful living. In that name above all names, the name is Jesus. Amen.

July 27 Read 1 Timothy 4:8-15

EXERCISE THE SOUL

Bible Thought: "And herein do I exercise myself, to have always a conscience void of offence toward God and *toward* men" (Acts 24:16).

Physical exercise is mandatory for good health. Medical authorities highly endorse it. There is another aspect of my life that is even more important.

Another aspect of my life is even more important. If I admonish me to exercise my spirit in a right and godly way my Spirit will live forever. The Christian life is one of growth and maturity. It requires training conscience, senses and mind to discern good from evil. Prayer, study and meditation builds "spiritual muscles. They must be exercised daily. When a major problem occurs, there is no time to exercise on the spur of the moment. Having exercised spiritually on a daily basis enables you to not only cope but to know God is in your midst.

So while you're taking that walk or working out with weights, do your spiritual exercises too. Praise and thank God for both…a body and a Spirit!

You can start today.

Dear God, thank You for sound minds and bodies. May we exercise our spiritual muscles as well as our physical ones. In that beautiful name of Jesus, our Savior. Amen.

July 28 Read Revelation 5:4-8

IMPATIENCE

Bible Thought: "In your patience possess ye your souls" (Luke 21:19).

Impatient people want short cuts. "The steps of a good man are ordered by Lord: and he delighteth in his way" (Psalm 37:23). Our steps cannot be ordered if we are impatient.

There are no short cuts to victory. Patience keeps us from running ahead of God. Patience enables us to speak with wisdom instead of regret.

Impatient proceeds full speed ahead with no thought or planning. Impatience is harsh and unkind in conversation. Impatience offends, hurts and strains relationships. Impatience is not the greatest thing for blood pressure. We pay a high price for impatience.

Let's do ourselves a favor. Be patient. Patience is good for our bodies and good for our souls.

I'm so glad the Lord is patient and merciful with me. I must strive to be more patient with others.

The next time you feel impatient, take a deep breath and thank God for being patient with you.

Dear Lord, thank You for Your patience with us. Empower us to be patient with others.

In Jesus marvelous name. Amen.

July 29 Read Psalm 89:15-19

THANK YOU GOD

Bible Thought: "Giving thanks always for all things unto God and the Father in the name of our Lord Jesus Christ" (Ephesians 5:20).

She was 102 years young. Other nursing home residents voiced many complaints about living in a nursing home but this lady had overwhelming gratitude. She began to tell me how she and her husband had worked so hard during their lives together. She had been a widow many years and what was left of family lived far away.

"I'm so thankful I have such a nice place to live, and people to take care of me." She hugged me and thanked me for coming.

I wondered if her "attitude of gratitude" had something to do with her alert mind and longevity.

How often do I take things for granted? Have I ever thanked God for blue skies, green grass, rich brown earth and eyes to see? Have I ever thanked God for ears to hear "I love you?"

The apostle Paul was thankful in whatever stage he found himself, whether lack or abundance, he continually thanked God.

Whatever situation you may be facing today, there are still many things to be thankful for.

May all of us have an "attitude of gratitude."

Dear precious Lord, thank You for the time we have had to live. Thank You for providing everything we will ever need. Most of all, thank You for Jesus. In His wonderful name. Amen.

July 30 Read Isaiah 62:3-5

HEAVENLY MARRIAGE

Bible Thought: "And I will betroth thee unto me for ever; yea, I will betroth thee unto me in righteousness, and in judgment, and in loving kindness, and in mercies" (Hosea 2:20).

Today is our wedding anniversary. Many years ago we pledged all our love, a covenant neither of us could ever break. Our love has sustained us through sunshine and rain, good times and bad. Emmitt has given me enough love to last a lifetime. He has been my best friend, protector and soul mate. I can never thank God enough for giving me this precious gift, a man who has filled my life with love.

I have another friend. Jesus loves me even more than my husband does. He is preparing a place for me and is coming back for me. While I have a foretaste of heaven in my marriage, it is nothing compared to what heaven will be.

Think of the happiest occasion you have had on earth. Heaven will be happier. Think of the most beautiful thing you have ever seen. Heaven will be more beautiful.

My love for my husband is only surpassed by my love for the One who died on an old rugged cross for me.

Those in Jesus will have a heavenly marriage too!

Dear Lord, thank You for my earthly marriage, but most of all for my "Heavenly Marriage" and the "Marriage Supper of the Lamb." In my beautiful Bridegroom's name, Jesus. Amen.

July 31 Read Genesis 22:11-14

THE GOD WHO PROVIDES

Bible Thought: "But my God shall supply all your need according to his riches in glory by Christ Jesus" (Philippians 4:19).

Abraham performed one of the greatest acts of obedience of all time. He loved his son more than anything, but God held first place in his life. When told to sacrifice Isaac, Abraham would have been obedient but the angel of the Lord stayed his hand.

God provided a ram in the thicket instead. Abraham called that place "The Lord Will Provide."

Jehovah Jireh means "The Lord Will Provide." God stopped Abraham from sacrificing his son, yet God did not spare His own Son from dying on the cross. God spared us from eternal death and offers eternal life instead.

What a God! What a Savior! I cannot fathom so great a love. It goes beyond my understanding. I cannot grasp the height, breadth and depth of God's great love for me.

God loves you and me. He makes every provision for our well being. He is the Great Provider. He supplies all needs, so why should anyone worry?

Let's be joyful. Let's pray without ceasing. Let's be thankful. We have a God who loves us with an everlasting love.

Dear Lord, You are Mighty, Glorious, Beautiful, Holy. We praise You today for who You are. We give all glory and praise to our God. In our Savior's precious name. That name is Jesus. Amen.

AUGUST

August 1 Read Romans 8:35-39

GOD'S LOVE NEVER ENDS

Bible Thought: "For this God *is* our God for ever and ever: he will be our guide *even* unto death" (Psalm 48:14).

"I vowed to love and cherish her until death us do part," our friend remarked and it touched our hearts.

For many years now he has taken care of his beloved with little outside help. He bathes her, dresses her, feeds her and takes her riding. She doesn't know him now, but he knows her and loves her with an undying love. I see Jesus in this compassionate loving man. His sacrificial lifestyle is rare.

He has no complaints, no gloomy outlook for the future while living and loving one day at a time. He is grateful for every day of their fifty plus years. I see God's love shed abroad in this man.

God's wondrous love is a love unfathomed. In this temporary journey of life we face trials and problems, yet like our friend, we are more than a conqueror because "Greater is He" who lives in every one of us. That makes all things possible.

God's love sustains and His love never ends.

Dear precious Lord, thank You for Your incredible love…a love that lasts forever. "We praise You, adore You and fall down before You." Blessed be the name of Jesus. Amen.

August 2 Read Isaiah 54:10-13

HE WATCHES OVER THOSE HE LOVES

Bible Thought: "The LORD hath appeared of old unto me, *saying,* Yea, I have loved thee with an everlasting love: therefore with loving kindness have I drawn thee" (Jeremiah 31:3).

Remember the day you enclosed your tiny baby's hand into yours? Now Lance's big strong hands hold mind. My tears fell on Lance's feet as he held me in his arms and whispered, "Mom, a Christian never says goodbye for the last time."

Lance made sure we were at the right gate at the airport. He watched over us every minute.

On the plane I began to realize the impact of it all. You can love so much it hurts. That's what Jesus did. His love is stronger than anything. His love knows no end and He had you and me in mind when He endured the cross. Think of the anguish and pain He felt.

So I remind myself that a man came from Galilee to set me free. He suffered pain, He took my shame, paying a price…His sacrifice… securing agony for my destiny.

Lance lovingly watched over us. Jesus does that too.

Let Jesus watch over you today.

Dear precious Lord, we thank You today for Your hands of love that keep us in Your loving care. Thank You for those nail-scared hands that loved us enough to endure such agony. In ten thousand years we will have just begun to praise that name above all names. That name is Jesus. Amen.

August 3 Read Psalm 112:1-3

FAMILIES ARE FOREVER

Bible Thought: "Beloved, let us love one another: for love is of God; and every one that loveth is born of God, and knoweth God" (1 John 4:7).

Family gatherings are memory makers. Before you know it the time quickly comes to say goodbye. The backyard had become the perfect place for sons, daughters-in law and grandchildren to talk and play volley ball. We dined on barbeque, hotdogs and homemade ice cream. Most of all we kissed, loved and held the newest grandbaby.

Of course our house bulges at the seams when they are all at home, but we are all together…our family.

Families are God's design. A godly family is a family forever. Blessings come to the family who teaches and trains their children. I want my descendants to be blessed. It's a sobering thought to know the way I live my life today could affect those who come after me, even for a thousand generations.

Yes, trials and hardships come, but God is bigger and a strong faith is our refuge and fortress.

Let's pass down the commandments and blessings of the Lord to our children and grandchildren because families are forever.

Dear Lord, thank You for families. May we instill godly principles to others that they may have godly descendants. In Jesus' beautiful name. Amen.

August 4 Read Psalm 103-12-17

GOD'S GOOD THINGS ABOUND

Bible Thought: *"Oh* how great *is* thy goodness, which thou hast laid up for them that fear thee; *which* thou hast wrought for them that trust in thee before the sons of men!"

It seems bad news is presented every day. Seldom do we hear about things we love, enjoy and often take for granted. The next time you feel down about all the negatives think about the overwhelming positives surrounding us:"

Attending the church of my choice
Voting at the polls and having a voice
God's Word, the Bible to me so dear
My loving Savior who is always near
God's holy hush, putting nature to bed
The warm soft feeling after prayers are said
An older couple with a haltering stride
Reading the Bible for a lifetime guide
Forgiving those who trespass against me
My ancestors and the family tree
Giving a smile to everyone I meet
People praying for others, sacrificing their time
Not holding grudges nor deceit in mind
Righting the wrongs wherever you can
Living in peace with your fellow man.
What's right with our country
What is its great might
It's God-fearing people who try to do right

Dear God, thank You for giving an abundance of life. May we be always mindful for Your many blessings, especially the greatest blessing of all. His name is Jesus and it is in His wonderful name. Amen.

August 5 Read Psalm 91:7-11

WITH GOD YOU ARE NEVER ALONE

Bible Thought: "And they that know thy name will put their trust in thee: for thou, LORD, has not forsaken them that seek thee" (Psalm 9:10).

I realized something was terribly wrong. The deluge of rain pouring down made visibility zero as my husband drove frantically to the hospital. Once in the emergency room the attendants recognized the symptoms. A severe allergy to an antibiotic had practically paralyzed me. Needles and shots brought me back to normalcy and I am forever grateful. I felt in those four hours tender care that angels had surrounded me.

In the midst of everything going wrong in my body, something else took priority. In the core of my inner being, there was peace. That peace took precedence over my physical condition. It is a peace that surpasses all understanding. I call it a "secret place." It's one that tells me I am never alone. In the storms of life, there is a refuge, a hiding place. Whatever the circumstance God is there.

There is a God in heaven that never abandons His child. In the darkest hour, He is on the front line. He will not fail you. He is a refuge for you and me.

Trust Him today.

You are never alone.

Dear Lord, thank You for Your great love. May we always remember You will never forsake us. You are there for us and we give You our highest thanksgiving and praise.

In that beautiful name of Jesus. Amen.

August 6 Read Song Of Solomon:1-4

BLESSED MARRIAGES

Bible Thought: "Live joyfully with the wife whom thou lovest all the days of the life of thy vanity, which he hath given thee under the sun, all the days of thy vanity: for that is thy portion in *this*, life and in thy labour which thou takest under the sun" (Ecclesiastes 9:9).

I was 19 and he was 21. High school sweethearts so in love and after many years even more.

What keeps a couple together after many years? I believe a number of things. Praying out loud together reveals hearts. Humility in prayer cements a marriage as nothing else can. A verbal prayer of the wife touches the husband's heart and he realizes the importance of his prayers not being hindered. (1 Peter 3:7) A heartfelt prayer for guidance, wisdom and strength enables faith to grow into spiritual maturity. (2 Peter 3:18).

Going the extra mile for each other and never taking each other for granted is explained in 1 Corinthians 13.

A couple's gratitude for a world filled with wondrous things binds their hearts together. After all is said "trusting in God makes all the difference." Understanding God's love serves as a reminder to you and your mate that love is willing to sacrifice.

With Jesus your marriage is blessed!

Dear Lord thank You for Your plan for the family. A husband, a wife and children make a happy home. May we be quick to love and obey Your commandments. In Jesus' beautiful name. Amen.

August 7 Read Psalm 71:22-24

LESSON FROM CHILDREN

Bible Thought: "O God, thou hast taught me from my youth: and hitherto have I declared thy wondrous works" (Psalm71:17).

Telling my students "goodbye" at the end of each school year brought many hugs and tears.

When our last son left the nest my tears fell on his feet, yet in my heart I had to let go.

A student and his father came to my room one morning with a beautiful cake they had made. "We wanted to bless you with a cake." Their encouragement and comfort came back to me in many ways as I faced the death of my mom.

Nothing done for God is ever wasted. The seemingly little things in life become monumental to those who are ministered to. What seems so small to you becomes great in the eyes of a hurting soul.

"It's what's on the inside that counts," a student said during a Social Studies lesson. What a profound quote from a second grader. When I am faced with troubling situations, I look deeper to find the good in others and I find peace.

Expressing love is like "hugs" from God. While walking down the hall one day, I overheard a third grader say, "That's my teacher from last year. She loves me." If a child's affection fills my heart with delight, how much more does my delight in God fill His heart. I want to hear Him say, "That's my child down there. She loves me!"

Dear precious Lord, thank You for children. May their unconditional love and faith return to us as we travel down life's journey. In Jesus' beautiful name. Amen.

August 8 Read 1 John 3:1-3

A FATHER'S LOVE

Bible Thought: "Even so it is not the will of your Father which is in heaven, that one of these little ones should perish" (Matthew 18:14).

The playing of "Blind Man's Bluff" in our backyard brought squeals of laughter from our two sons. Then I heard Lane's piercing screams. Being blindfolded, he had stumbled and fallen on a huge rock. His daddy picked him up and we rushed to the hospital.

"He's all right," the ER physician remarked. "It's a head wound but we can fix it. We'll clean the wound and you can take him home."

What a relief. Driving into our driveway it hit me. "We forgot about Lance. We didn't mean to leave him alone. How must he feel about all of this?"

We found a note by the door: "Dear Dad, I cause too much trouble. I've run away. Bye. Lance."

We searched the house. Emmitt drove around, up and down the block looking for his son. I picked up the phone to call the police when I noticed "Blacky's tail wagging behind the butane tank. Emmitt ran to Lance and swooped him up in his arms "If you run away, we have to go too because we can't do without you."

That picture of God's love, a father to his son, brought tears.

Dear God, thank You for Your amazing love. Thank You for Your only Son to be saved for all of us. In His name, Jesus. Amen.

August 9 Read Revelation 21:4-6

GOD'S CHILD NEVER SAYS GOODBYE

Bible Thought: "The LORD is nigh unto them that are of a broken heart; and saveth such as be of a contrite spirit" (Psalm 34:18).

Losing a loved one is one of life's hardest experiences. Shock, pain and grief deals a cruel blow. The emptiness and loneliness can be overwhelming.

To those who have lost loved ones I pray God's Word ministers to you knowing Jesus is coming back for us.

If God watches over the sparrow, and He does then He certainly is not going to abandon us. At best this life is temporary. Those who believe look forward to an eternity of peace where there will never be a separation from loved ones.

I tell this story again about a little girl crossing the ocean for the first time on an airliner. Her father was the pilot. In the night the little girl awakened to lightning and thunder. "Is my daddy at the controls?" "Yes," the attendant responded. The little girl smiled, closed her eyes and went peacefully back to sleep.

If God is piloting your life, He will give you peace and strength in the midst of the storm.

God's child never says goodbye for the last time.

Dear Lord we praise You today for the blessed hope of heaven where You will wipe away all tears and sorrow shall be no more on that beautiful shore. Blessed be the name above all names…Jesus. Amen.

August 10 Read Psalm 1:1-4

JESUS WHISPERS "HOLD STEADY"

Bible Thought: "Keep yourselves in the love of God, looking for the mercy of our Lord Jesus Christ unto eternal life" (Jude 1:21).

A life lived for God brings a beautiful harvest at life's end. During life's journey times of drought prevail. Hope seems to fade and shadows try to block the sunshine in the garden of our hearts. Yet God's Word hidden in the heart brings great dividends. Each one of us can reflect back over our lives and see God's faithfulness.

So we do not lose heart. My great-grandparents, my grandparents and my parents endured many conflicts but their conquering faith resulted in triumph. They had a cutting edge for successful living as they "held steady" and relied on God's promises.

"Life has problems we cannot deny. For trials, we are never ready.
We have an answer we can live by. Jesus whispers 'Hold steady.'
Our lives are sown with patterns cut. Our needles become unsteady.
We tie a knot and try to hang on but Jesus whispers, 'Hold Steady.'
Of all the appointments I have to keep, for one I want to be ready.
When I lay me down to sleep, Jesus whispers 'Hold Steady.'"

Dear God, we come to You today with hope and trust. Empower us to have more increasing faith and more patience in trials knowing You will never leave us. We thank and praise You for the wondrous blessings You bestow on our lives.

We can't thank You enough for Jesus. In His wonderful name… Jesus. Amen

August 11 Read Psalm 21:1-5

BLESSINGS ABOUND

Bible Thought: "He shall receive the blessing from the LORD, and righteousness from the God of his salvation" (Psalm 24:5).

On any ordinary day, blessings abound. If I ignore, take for granted or pass them by, I forfeit and cheat myself out of a wonderful day. I have found that one of the secrets of receiving blessings is to acknowledge them with gratitude.

Rain in our dry climate is always a blessing. Those big white thunderheads are beautiful against our summer sky.

I am blessed with loving neighbors up and down our street. Sometimes at night I pray prayers across the street and down the block as far as I can remember the names. I am rewarded the next morning when I see their happy faces saying, "Hello."

I love to be outside and hear the happy shouts of children at play. It brings back thirty-one years of my classroom memories.

The chimes of church bells bless me as I recognize the hymns and sing along in praise.

One night I came to bed singing. When I finally finished my husband led us in a beautiful prayer. The atmosphere of sweetness remained with us throughout the night and gave us pleasant sleep.

It seems the more I discover blessings the more they return back to me. Excuse me, I just found another blessing!

Dear precious Lord, words cannot express our gratitude of joy. We are so glad You are our God. It keeps us singing all day long. Thank You for Jesus. In His beautiful name. Amen.

August 12 Read Isaiah 41:10-13

UPHELD AND LIFTED

Bible Thought: "The LORD upholds all that fall, and raiseth up all *those that be* bowed down" (Psalm 145:14).

Life has a way of inflicting wounds and burdens that we cannot bear on our own.

How can you bear the loss of a lifetime mate? How do you stand the agony of soul over the loss of a child, and what do you do in the still small hours of dawn when the pain pierces your very existence?

All of us have experienced pain and heartache, but those missionaries on foreign fields are especially vulnerable. They give their lives in spreading the Gospel. They sacrifice security, comfort, family and for some, even their lives.

We need to be reminded of God's special plan and purpose for all of our lives

God's greatness is mighty across generations. He is of glorious splendor and majesty. God rules and reigns. He is faithful and true. He is steadfast and hears the cries of His children.

If you are bearing a burden today let God lift you up. God's great big shoulders can carry our burdens.

Loving God, we come to You today with burdens and we give them to You. Thank You for taking them. Wherever Your servants are, we also pray for their peace. Amen.

August 13 Read Psalm 127:3-5

FAMILY BLESSINGS

Bible Thought: "Thy wife *shall* be as a fruitful vine by the sides of thine house: thy children like olive plants round about thy table" (Psalm 128:3).

"Mawmaw, I am so blessed to have a family that loves me. My mommy, daddy and sister make me feel so special. I know lots of kids that don't have the kind of love I have and I feel so sorry for them. I thank God for my family."

What mature insight from my eleven-year old granddaughter. Kallie's love for life is exceeded only by her love for God and family.

Thirty-one years of teaching instilled in me the importance of love. Children who are loved and nurtured by godly parents are happy, secure and successful. Many of my students were from broken homes. Some had been placed in children's homes.

Children are gifts from God. They are treasures to be cherished. A child who is truly loved can achieve the impossible. Behind every successful child you will find loving, caring parents who have sacrificial love. That kind of love comes from a heavenly Father who knows all about sacrifice.

A godly family builds a godly nation that would solve a lot of problems on planet earth.

Dear Lord, thank You for children. We pray for wisdom in guiding them in Your ways.

Thank You for the family of God. Most of all, thank You for Your precious Son. In His name, that name above all names…Jesus. Amen.

August 14 Read 1 Peter 1:3-6

LET THE LOVE OF JESUS BE IN YOU

Bible Thought: "My sheep hear my voice, and I know them, and they follow me" (John 11:27).

Have you ever thought about how this world would be had Jesus not been born? I shudder to think about it. Imagine a world of no absolutes, without any standards of right or wrong.

Mankind has always had a sin problem, but we do have a choice to do right. A wrong choice brings bondage, imprisoning the human soul. It's not just for a lifetime, but for eternity. At the point of death, the dye is cast. There are no second chances, no "do-overs."

The "Good News" is that Jesus did come. It's what the resurrection is all about. It brings hope for the hopeless and strength for the weak. The only way any of us will ever get out of this life alive is through Jesus.

The Bible cannot be rewritten for compromising situations and rationalizing actions. The truth remains. God's Word is still God's Word and it is the truth of the ages.

Let the love of Jesus be in you today and every day.

Dear Lord, we praise You. Words cannot express our gratitude for the agony and pain

Jesus bore for us. It is more than we could ever thank You enough. What a Savior. In His beautiful name. Amen.

August 15 Read Deuteronomy 1:42-45

STAY IN THE FIGHT

Bible Thought: "For by thee I have run through a troop: by my God have I leaped over a wall" (2 Samuel 22:30).

Have you ever had a day when nothing seemed to go right? In the midst of a desperate situation :throwing in the towel" seems tempting.

We have a choice of our thoughts, positive or negative. "For as he thinketh in his heart, so is he: Eat and drink, saith he to thee; but his heart is not with thee" (Proverbs 23:7).

Losers see only an ongoing battle. Winners see the end result, because they have read the "last page." One reason the enemy fights so hard is because just around the corner victory is waiting. Through Jesus, we "are more than conquerors." (Romans 8:37).

You are champions and champions get up coming out swinging. So stay in the fight. Encourage yourself in the lord. "The LORD will give strength unto his people; the LORD will bless his people with peace" (Psalm 29:11).

Losers focus on the war. Winners focus on the victory. Be the winner God created you to be. Put on those boxing gloves and plough right through troubling obstacles. Show the world the stuff you're made of.

With God on your side, you will prevail.

Life just doesn't get any better than that.

Dear precious Lord, thank You for being our Champion. Through Jesus we win! In His wonderful name. Amen.

August 16 Read Leviticus 26:6-9

FIND FREEDOM IN GOD

Bible Thought: "If the Son therefore shall make you free, ye shall be free indeed" (John 8:36).

Imagine my surprise when I saw a fluffy fat white rabbit in my flower garden. His long pink ears and twitchy nose looked like a mechanical toy. He hopped along happily as if to say "Look! I'm doing my own thing."

Later that day a neighbor and I were visiting. "Could I give you a white rabbit?" I asked not knowing it belonged to her children.

"My rabbit is here? We've been looking everywhere for him."

The children finally caught him and I began to think about it. The rabbit had enjoyed freedom but sooner or later that freedom would have led to destruction. We live on a busy street. Since we live at the edge of town hungry stray dogs appear from time to time. Yes, the rabbit was free but far from the safety his owner had provided.

The same thing can happen to us. If we go beyond God's boundaries and do our own thing trouble begins.

We are not our own. Our owner paid an inestimable price for you and me.

Let's make right choices and find freedom in God.

Dear Lord, thank You for Your commandments. They are a "lamp unto my feet and a light unto our pathway." In Jesus' beautiful name. Amen.

August 17 Read Isaiah 61:10-11

LOSE YOURSELF IN GOD

Bible Thought: "This is the day which the LORD will rejoice and be glad in it" (Psalm 118:24).

Today is a brand new day. Make it sparkle. Put on gladness. Let the celebration of the gift of life begin in you. Enjoy God's colorful world. Clap with the trees of the field. Count the many blessings in your life.

Negative living doesn't work. Every day we see the effects of cynicism and criticism. So what do you have to lose?

Lose your self in God. Make Him glad He created you. Love Him. Praise Him. You can never be lost to His Spirit. Start each morning pledging your life to Him. What a way to start the day.

God has a plan for you and me. Let's honor Him, glorify and serve Him. He watches over and guides our every step. With such an awesome God, we cannot help but sing. Open the gift of life today with joy. Share it with everyone you meet.

My husband waves to everyone when he is driving. "Do you know everyone in town?" I asked one day.

"Yes, because Jesus rides in my pickup with me and that makes my day!"

Jesus can make your day too.

Dear Lord, thank You for the time we have had to live and to love You. Thank You for our beautiful Bridegroom who is coming back for us. Blessed be the name of Jesus.

Amen.

August 18 Read 1 Peter 1:36

MY TIME TO LIVE

Bible Thought: "Who satisfieth thy mouth with good *things*; *so that* thy youth is renewed like the eagle's" (Psalm 103:5).

What if God said you could choose not to be born? Would you go or stay? The choice would be yours. If you chose not to come to earth, how would you experience the heights of heaven? If you had never experienced pain, rejection, troubles and sorrow, would you take heaven for granted?

I firmly believe God has a purpose for every person born on this earth. I also believe the highest form of selfishness and immaturity is to say, "I wish I had never been born."

To be given a chance at life is the highest form of love. If the Lord had given me a choice to be born or not, I would exuberantly say,

"Yes Lord, I will go to earth. I will seek forgiveness. I will overlook offenses. I will trust in Your plan for me and I will pray to be led by Your Spirit. I will fight the good fight of faith. I will return to You a different person than I was before."

Meanwhile, until my heavenly flight, I thank the Lord for my time to live on earth.

I wouldn't have missed it for the world!

Dear God, thank You for forgiving us, loving us and most of all sending Your Son to die for us that we may live with You throughout eternity. In the precious name of Jesus. Amen.

August 19 Read 1 Corinthians 9:24-7

WIN THE PRIZE

Bible Thought: "I press toward the mark for the prize of the high calling of God in Christ Jesus" (Philippians 3:14).

The desire for money and "things" are really desires for filling empty places of the heart. Only Jesus can fill those places in the human heart. Here are some of them:

An overflowing joy

A soul that never dies

A love that never ends

A light that shines forever

A life of purpose and success

A hope that is never disappointed

A wisdom that can never be erased

A peace that passes all understanding

These golden nuggets enable God's child to run the race of life with patience, knowing a loving God is guiding steps along the way. He watches over His Word to perform it. He is waiting for those who run to win.

WIN THE PRIZE!

Dear wonderful Lord, we will win the prize. We will press on toward the mark, resisting the enemy and conquering every foe because Jesus lives mightily in us. Thank You Lord for Your Son and His sacrifice. In His beautiful name. Amen.

August 20 Read Ezekiel 34: 28-31

THE GOOD SHEPHERD

Bible Thought: "He shall feed his flock like a shepherd: he shall gather the lambs with his arm, and carry *them* in his bosom, and shall gently lead those that are with young" (Isaiah 40:11).

Our youngest son came home from the first day of first grade puzzled about Mary's lamb. "I thought fleas were brown."

"They are," I assured him. "But we sang a song about a lost sheep and its fleas were white as snow."

Lane's innocence reminds me of Jesus whose blood washes our blackest sin away and makes us white as snow.

I thank God for the innocent "Lamb of God," whose sacrifice, once and for all died a cruel death for you and me. His precious blood redeems and restores the repentant soul.

His commandments are not grievous, but are given for our peace and protection. Those who live in God's ways are the real "successes in life." Those who are obedient have no regrets on that final day.

Meanwhile I will lie down on God's "green pastures" and follow His leading beside the "still waters."

All sheep are in great danger without a shepherd.

Without "The Good Shepherd" so am I.

Dear Lord, we will spend eternity thanking You for our Savior. In His beautiful name. Amen.

August 21 Read Psalm 100:1-5

LIFE IS DELICIOUS

Bible Thought: "Every good gift and every perfect gift is from above, and cometh down from the Father of lights, with whom is no variableness, neither shadow of turning" (James 1:17).

Today is all you have. Make the most of it. Say, "I love you" to someone dear. Today is now. The past is past. The future is not here yet.

I call life "delicious." If I had never been born, I would have missed everything. I'm so glad to be alive aren't you? Every day I thank the Lord for my time to live and the time I've had to love others.

Think of the happiest time you have ever experienced on earth. Heaven will be indescribably better.

Delight yourself in the Lord. We are His delight and He even sings over us. (Zephaniah 3:17) Did you know we are married to Him? Reading that marriage license makes me happy. (Jeremiah 3:14).

Check your spiritual joy level. Make a list of all of your blessings. You will run out of paper. Joy comes from gratitude. Joy comes from unselfishness. Joy comes from serving. Joy comes from Jesus. Let Him give you joy.

Everyone has two choices. One leads to life everlasting. Choose that one.

Let's make happy days because life is delicious.

Dear Lord, thank You for this day. Thank You for filling us with overflowing joy. In that beautiful name of Jesus. Amen.

August 22 Read Hebrews 12:12-13

NEVER GIVE UP

Bible Thought: "But exhort one another daily, while it is called To-day; lest any of you be hardened through the deceitfulness of sin" (Hebrews 3:13).

Our friend Steve recently had a brain tumor removed. We rejoiced that it was benign. His scar goes around the top of his head and he has a steel plate under his hair line. Yet he is the happiest man I know. He has had no pain and was back to work in a month. His faith is contagious. He says, "Either way I win!"

Another friend at 83 works as a carpenter. He has fallen off a house, had bypass heart surgery, broken his foot and has had a light stroke. Yet he goes to the rest home every Sunday and leads singing. He teaches a Bible class at church. He visits the sick and is a handyman to those who cannot pay for repairs. He says, "Helping folks keeps me alive."

Whenever I have problems I think of those who have giant faith and go through adversity with overcoming victory. They never give up.

What an encouragement they are to me.

We can be winners too.

As Steve says, "Either way, we win!"

Dear God, may we have ever increasing faith and never give up! In Jesus wonderful name. Amen.

August 23 Read Psalm 36:5-8

THE ABUNDANT LIFE

Bible Thought: "The thief cometh not, but for to steal, and to kill, and to destroy: I am come that they might have life, and that they might have it more abundantly" (John 10:10).

Life is a great adventure. It is filled with turns, detour surprises, excitement and most of all...love. In all of this we have a God who never leaves nor forsakes His children.

How many of us meander across life giving up and becoming a murmuring negative soul? That kind of life weakens the immune system, brings on insomnia, heart palpitations and the list goes on.

I say, "Give life a chance!" God is on our side. We have abundance here and an eternal life in the hereafter. We serve a Mighty God. I challenge you to take a big dose of enthusiasm. Spread it around to everyone you meet. Get excited about life. Isn't it rather selfish to spread negativity?

Falling in love with life is like falling in love with that one and only sweetheart. God is that sweetheart of life. You are a unique person with a special purpose in life. Love, peace and joy come with the package.

Each day is an opportunity to spread God's love to everyone you meet.

It's an abundant life. Try it. You will never be the same.

Dear God, thank You for the gift of life. Thank You for our "Sweetheart" of all time. His name is Jesus. It is in His wonderful name we pray. Amen.

August 24 Read Psalm 138:5-8

THE SAFE PLACE TO BE

Bible Thought: "My flesh and my heart faileth: *but* God *is* the strength of my heart, and my portion for ever" (Psalm 73: 26).

This world is a dangerous place. Nature's catastrophes coupled with wars, terrorists, accidents and illnesses could make you depressed. Throughout history mankind has struggled for survival against unspeakable odds, with one exception. The Bible reveals a "safe place" for those who loved God and followed through with obedience.

Yes they had hard times but undaunted faith led them to overcoming victories. Think of the parting Red Sea and Moses, Shadrach, Meshach and Abednego in the fiery furnace, Daniel in the lion's den and Elijah raising the widow' son. They all had a safe place because they honored and obeyed God. A child of God has the blessed hope.

The only safe place to be is in the arms of Jesus. Let's abide in the "secret place" under the shadow of the "Almighty."

You can have a safe place too!

Dear precious Lord, thank You for our safe place. Our total existence depends on You and we treasure that intimate place where You dwell with us. We honor and glorify You today and every day. In the name of Jesus. Amen.

August 25 Read Numbers 14:21-24

A DIFFERENT SPIRIT

Bible Thought: "And Caleb stilled the people before Moses, and said, Let us go up at once and possess it; for we are well able to overcome it" (Numbers 13:30).

The story of Caleb in the Bible impresses me. The Israelites paid a high price murmuring and complaining, but Caleb had a different spirit.

Caleb's descendants, because of his obedience, not only were blessed but eventually inherited the land.

I yearn to be like Caleb. He did not see with his natural eyes, but he saw difficult circumstances through the eyes of faith. He knew his God.

In the midst of trials we look to the Lord. Casting your burdens and trusting in Him is the only way to live for a life of rest and peace.

For "patience to have its perfect work," one must develop spiritual muscles. God is not in a hurry. Through Jesus, we can be "overcomers."

All of us can have a different spirit, a godly one.

Let's all be a Caleb!

Lord Jesus, we ask for courage and patience today. We seek courage to fight the good fight and patience to run the race, giving You all the glory every step of the way. In the mighty name of Jesus. Amen.

August 26 Read Jeremiah 31:1-4

GOD'S GREAT LOVE

Bible Thought: "As the Father hath loved me, so have I loved you: continue ye in my love" (John 15:9).

I wonder if we can ever understand how great God's love is for each one of us. God's thoughts are always on you and me. While we were yet sinners His love compelled Him to die for us. God longs for us. He yearns for us.

The prodigal son's father spent countless hours looking for his wayward son. This is a picture of God's attitude toward us when we walk away from Him.

God's love is gracious love. We cannot earn it. Yet His love is focused on us continually. Who would not want His incredible love?

Invite Jesus to make His home in your heart. Repent of all sin. Live for Him all the days of your life. Keep Him in your thoughts today. Focus on Him. Tell Him of your love and thank Him too.

It's all about God's great love for you.
Of all the riches in this world
Nothing can compare
To the One who died for me.
It's Jesus I must share.

He came to save my soul.
He washed my sins away.
How I love that Lamb of God.
I love Him more each day.

Dear Lord, we are overwhelmed by Your great love for us. May we awaken each morning saying, I love you Lord. In that beautiful name of Jesus. Amen.

August 27 Read 2 Chronicles 15:10-14

FOLLOW THE LORD WHOLEHEARTEDLY

Bible Thought: "Blessed *are* they that keep his testimonies, *and that* seek him with the whole heart" (Psalm 119:2).

Asa and his people wholeheartedly committed themselves to God. In fact they were so jubilant about it, they shouted and blew trumpets. I thrill to their eagerness in seeking and committing to Him. The result? The Lord gave them rest on every side. The nation had peace for many years.

I love to be around people who get excited about Jesus. Their joy is contagious. When they realize what Jesus has done for them, they cannot help but be joyful.

I have been accused as "coming on too strong," or "just a little far out," but I cannot apologize. It is the greatest news in the world. Jesus saves. He is King of kings and Lord of lords.

Jesus extends to us daily. His sacrifice paid for our sins. He is preparing a place for us so wonderful our minds can't contain it.

What beautiful news.

Oh happy day!

Somebody shout.

Somebody blow the trumpets!

Dear Lord, You are so beautiful. We commit to follow You with our whole being. Thank You for the joy that rises up within us. In Jesus' lovely name. Amen.

August 28 Read Isaiah 51:1-3

LIFE FOR TODAY

Bible Thought: "For a day in thy courts *is* better than thousand. I had rather be a doorkeeper in the house of my God, than to dwell in the tents of wickedness" (Psalm 84:10).

Enjoy today. It is a present from God. You cannot save, loan or borrow it. All you can do is live it and life is meant to live, not survive.

Love your children. They are growing older each day.

Memorize your spouse's face and never take his or her love for granted.

Find happiness in simple pleasures.

Appreciate a sunset.

Wonder at a rainbow.

Smell new mown hay. Not a blade of grass grows without God's permission.

Express gratitude to someone you have long admired.

Realize where there is life, there is hope.

Be positive and optimistic.

Look for the good in every situation.

Expect the best and know God is always with you.

Open your heart to the Holy Spirit and let God's love flow.

I am comforted by the fact that evil will never overcome the Light. Jesus is the "Light," and He is life for today and every day.

Dear Lord may we live one day at a time being thankful for Jesus. In His wonderful name. Amen.

August 29 Read Psalm 139:1-6

GOD IS EVERYWHERE

Bible Thought" "Who laid the foundations of the earth, *that* it should not be removed for ever" (Psalm 104:6).

One by one my children left home. Each departure gave an ache in my heart but they took God with them knowing God is everywhere.

I am just a tiny speck in God's vast universe but God knows every hair on my head. He even knows every time a sparrow falls.

If God is this big is He not mindful of you? You are never alone. He knows your every heartbeat. He is aware of you and your needs. He works everything for your good according to His purposes. You can never be lost to His Spirit. Wherever you are, He is. Nothing escapes His attention.

God is with you in every circumstance, situation, crisis or problem. His love is always reaching out to you, surrounding and protecting you.

God gave His only Son to die for you.

Open your heart to God's love.

God is everywhere!

He shed His blood upon a tree.

The precious Lamb who died for me.

He took my place to set me free,

In my heart He does abide.

He is always by my side.

His love for me is deep and wide.

Dear precious Lord, thank You for Your incredible love. May our hearts overflow with gratitude. In Jesus' beautiful name. Amen.

August 30 Read Psalm 25:7

YOUR TEACHER LOVES YOU

Bible Thought: "Make thy face to shine upon thy servant; and teach me thy statutes" (Psalm 119:135).

That's my teacher from last year. She loves me," the third grade student said to her teacher as I passed them in the hall.

Humbled, but grateful, I had not realized that she felt that way. As I performed my teacher duties the best I could, I often worried if I had done my best, especially after a hard day. Maybe we don't know all the good we do, but we keep on keeping. Each day brings challenges, yet we must keep the faith with persistence.

All of us are in God's classroom. He has demonstrated His love for us. I believe

life's school is a training ground to see if we can learn to love and forgive.

At the end of school a student said, "I don't want to leave you Mrs. Clayton, but I am growing up and have to go third grade."

I have a teacher too. His name is Jesus. Like I taught my students He shows me how to grow up in faith and maturity.

My Teacher loves me.

He loves you too.

Trust in the Lord and acknowledge Him.

Trust in the Lord no matter what you see

Living by faith is the only way

To live in victory.

Dear Lord, we are so glad to be in Your "school." Thank You for Your great love. On that great day may our diplomas read, "Well done, good and faithful servant." In that name above all names. His name is Jesus. Amen.

August 31 Read Deuteronomy 29:1-4

REMEMBER GOD'S FAITHFULNESS

Bible Thought: "And thou shalt remember all the way which the LORD thy God led thee these forty years in the wilderness, to humble thee *and* to prove thee, to know what *was* in thine heart, whether thou wouldest keep his commandments, or no" (Deuteronomy 8:2).

It is hard for me to understand how the Israelites witnessed so many miracles and yet spent forty years wandering and complaining. When I read about their disobedience I shudder. How much more do I need to remember God's goodness in my life.

I well remember many problems. God was there through my husband's major surgeries, our sons' illnesses and accidents, the care of elderly relatives. He certainly gave me wisdom and guidance in my thirty-one years teaching career. God has never left me, nor will He leave you.

Aunt Opal's Bible now belongs to me and her favorite scripture is now mine: "For this God *is* our God for ever and ever: He will be our guide *even* unto death" (Psalm 48:14).

When I think of all the things the Lord has brought me through I can't help but be thankful To me, eternity is not long enough to thank Him.

Praise Him today for His mighty works.

Dear precious Lord, we praise You with all of our might. That You should love us so much is beyond our understanding, and we love You with all of our being, In that beautiful name. That name is Jesus. Amen.

SEPTEMBER

September 1 Read Psalm 27:4-6

MAKE TODAY THE BEST DAY OF YOUR LIVE

Bible Thought: "To shew forth thy lovingkindness in the morning, and thy faithfulness every night" (Psalm 92:2).

I had never fully realized the breathtaking beauty of a sunrise until seasons changed in New Mexico. Arising while it is still dark doesn't appeal to me but I have discovered an amazing production of grandeur at daybreak.

Shafts of light come tiptoeing through my bedroom window wearing hues of pink attached to ribbons of sunbeams. A mockingbird's overture begins. He bows with enthusiasm before nature's audience. Earth waits with bated breath for the dawn of a new day. Lilies of the field begin to sway with the "Hallelujah" chorus.

The moment arrives. Glorious light appears dressing the world with awesome wonder. The crescendo mounts. The trees of the field clap their hands and my heart's melody beats with reverence.

"Good Morning, my child." I rejoice over you with singing." (Zephaniah 3:17).

I bask in the "Son's rays," bursting with delight.

Starting and ending a day with God makes everything better. We can never say "Thank You" enough to our loving Father. Early morning prayers give strength for the day and joy for the moments. It all starts with the "Son."

Dear precious Lord, You are Light, You are Beauty, You are love. With You everyday is a masterpiece. Thank You for our time to live, to love and to appreciate each day.

In Jesus marvelous name. Amen.

September 2 Read Proverbs 4:20-23

LIGHT BRINGS LIFE

Bible Thought: "This then is the message which we have heard of him, and declare unto you, that God is light, and in him is no darkness at all" (1 John 1:5).

Almost any thing that grows need light, even you and me. Isn't it just wonderful God knows what we need? Living things need light to live.

We also need "spiritual light" to live. Walking in the light of Jesus enables the believer to see by faith and that leads to a victorious life.

"But if we walk in the light as he is in the light, we have fellowship with one another, and the blood of Jesus, his Son, purifies us from all sin" (1 John 1:7).

On the contrary, sin breeds in darkness. Yet when we confess our sins they are exposed in the "light" of God's forgiveness and mercy. They are dispelled in the light of God's love.

The light of God sustains life. Without it mankind has no hope. Darkness can never overcome the light.

I've been delivered from darkness.

You can be too!

Dear Lord, You are "A lamp unto our feet and a light unto our path." May we follow that light to life's end and then we will burst into Your "Light." Thank You for Jesus, the "Light" of the world. In His beautiful name. Amen.

September 3 Read Psalm 78:1-4

TELL THE CHILDREN

Bible Thought: "A seed shall serve him; it shall be accounted to the Lord for a generation" (Psalm 22:30).

A feeling of lack of love and apathy seems to characterize the children of today. I learned a lot about children in my teaching career. Unloved and untrained children react one of two ways. One is extremely aggressive and the other extremely withdrawn.

Many children come from broken homes. A lack of love and a lack of training in God's commandments fill many prisons. We seem to forget that children are the leaders of tomorrow.

Training children right begins before they are born, beginning with righteous ancestors. Children who have not known love from an earthly father find it difficult to know the love of a heavenly Father.

Sin goes back generations in a family. How we live today affects generations to come. I want to leave godly principles to all of my descendants. What a terrible thing to sin and pass it on to those in my genealogy.

Let's tell our children about God when we walk in the way, sit at the table, at bedtime and all the time. It is the only hope for the future.

A loved and godly child makes a well-adjusted adult. A well-adjusted adult makes a law-abiding citizen. Law-abiding citizens build a nation.

Dear Lord, may we break the chain of evil in our generation. In Jesus' mighty name. Amen.

September 4 Read Psalm 145:4-7

GODLY GRANDPARENTS

Bible Thought: "When I call to remembrance the unfeigned faith that is in thee, which dwelt first in thy grandmother Lois, and thy mother Eunice; and I am persuaded that in thee also" (1 Timothy 1:5).

The influence of my godly grandparents is still with me today. The importance of grandparents in grandchildren's lives cannot be overstated. Godly families build a strong nation.

To me, living without lasting values is a wasted life. I want my grandchildren to have the blessing of a grandmother and grandfather's faith. My grandparents along with Joshua of old, marked their ancestors with "as for me and my house, we will serve the Lord."

Granny's songs are permanently stamped in my special book of memories. Her singing filled every facet of her life. Sometimes she cried while singing but that didn't stop her. I seldom have to look at a hymn. I know most the songs by heart because I learned them on granny's knees.

Granny made her heavenly flight many years ago. The Bible, so close to her heart, reached out to her family with words of comfort and songs of faith. At age ninety-two she went to heaven with a song in her heart.

Sing and talk about Jesus today with your grandchildren. It lasts a lifetime.

Dear precious Lord, thank You for godly grandparents. May we pass on our godly inheritance to others. Thank You for our beautiful Savior. His name is Jesus. Amen.

September 5 Read Psalm 46:1-5

THE GOODNESS OF GOD

Bible Thought: "O give thanks unto the LORD, for *he* is good: for his mercy *endureth* for ever" (Psalm 107:1).

Being grateful to God and praising Him changes my outlook and I want to thank Him for so many things. Even little things make me happy like glistening snow in a silvery moon light and the glow of my fireplace on a cold winter's night.

Here are some more blessings: Laughter of children as they run and play. My husband's "I love you," at the end of the day.

The life-giving force that flows through me, with ears to hear and eyes that see.

The dove's soft cooing as he sings to his mate, the roses growing by my garden gate.

For friends and neighbors with a loving touch, for God's Word, the Book I love so much.

For His lifting me up to a higher place and I fall asleep in His embrace.

Morning breaks with enthusiasm and all nature acknowledges God's gift of life.

Dewdrops of God's love sprinkles the earth with the promise of a new day.

This is the day to rejoice and I am thankful. I "walk upon the high places of the earth because He has "made my feet like hinds' feet."

It's the goodness of God.

Dear precious Lord, You are our song in the night, our everlasting light and we love You with all our might. In Jesus' beautiful, wonderful name. Amen.

September 6 Read 1 Samuel 25:29:31

WORDS HAVE POWER

Bible Thought: "A soft answer turneth away wrath: but grievous words stir up anger" (Proverbs 15:1).

I have discovered flaws that I see in myself. I need to look within myself instead of criticizing others. Looking at my own faults motivates me to forgive others and to overlook their offenses. If I send out criticism it returns to me. "If I give it, I receive it."

Critical words can follow a path to peace or a continual path of strife. The wrong kind of words take away our joy and zest for living, leading to depression and anxiety.

Critical comments can be dangerous. Miriam complained about Moses' wife and was stricken with leprosy. (Numbers 12:10) Korah and his followers led the people to rebel against God and as a result the earth swallowed them and their families. (Numbers (16:32) Michal remained childless because she despised David's dancing before the Lord. (1 Chronicles 15:29). Some boys came out of the city and made fun of Elisha and "two mother bears came out of the woods and tore forty-two of the boys to pieces" 2 Kings 2:24).

When negative critical comments come your way do what is right anyway. God's love enables you and me to see the good in others.

We can overcome critical remarks because words have power.

Dear Lord, we repent for wrong words spoken. Guide us and fill us with Your loving kindness. May we always look for the good in others. In that beautiful name. His name is Jesus. Amen.

September 7 Read Psalm 127 18:3-5

THE HEART OF A CHILD

Bible Thought: "Verily I say unto ye, Except ye be converted, and become as little children, ye shall not enter into the kingdom of heaven" (Matthew 18:3).

It was Lane's time to serve communion to the ones who couldn't make it to the church service. Little Kallie and her doll always went with her daddy.

The first person on their list was a kindly gentleman named George. He was so glad to see company. Kallie felt sorry for him and gave him a big hug.

Lane asked him if he had any family and he said no. Lane glanced at Kallie and could see the sympathy in her eyes.

After they served him communion and turned to go, Kallie hugged George and told him goodbye as she held up her doll.

"You can have her," Kallie said as she handed George her doll. Lane wanted to leap forward and say, "No...you don't have to..." but he was frozen in his tracks and didn't move. George bent down and took the doll with a smile.

What a life-lesson that was. Lane knew how Kallie loved that doll. As they drove away and with watery eyes Lane told Kallie how much he loved her, how proud he was of her and how she had just made God smile.

Dear Lord, thank You for children and their wonderful compassion. May we become as little children in our faith and in our hearts. In that beautiful name above all names. His name is Jesus. Amen.

September 8 Read Psalm 16:1-3

TEACHERS AND STUDENTS... FOREVER FRIENDS

Bible Thought: "Lo, children *are* an heritage of the LORD: *and* the fruit of the womb *is his* reward" (Psalm 127:3).

One of the many blessings in my life comes from former students. A special bond between teacher and student lasts forever. It thrills my soul for them to recognize me with a greeting and a big hug.

No matter how many years have come and gone, I still see my grownup students as those little trusting children who gave me love notes.

God has written me many love notes through His Word, the Bible. I am His child. He doesn't have to stop to remember who I am. He tells me in Isaiah 49:16: "Behold, I have graven thee upon the palms of *my* hands; thy walls *are* continually before me."

I am still learning in my "Teacher's Classroom." Some of the lessons are hard, but My Teacher is gentle and kind. When I do not understand, I go to Him for help and He patiently shows me the way.

Like my "little people" wrote love notes to me, I now write love notes to my "Teacher."

My Teacher and I are forever friends!

Dear precious Lord, thank You for Jesus, the greatest gift for all mankind. May we express our love and thankfulness with every heartbeat. In His wonderful name. Amen.

September 9 Read Psalm 24:1-5

A WONDERFUL PLACE CALLED HOME

Bible Thought: "Lift up your heads, O ye gates; and be ye lift up, ye everlasting doors; and the King of glory shall come in" (Psalm 24:9).

God's house shall stand for all eternity. Light illuminates this house for God's Word is honored here. It is hidden in the hearts of those who love Him. That Word profits those who listen. Those who hear pass through this house marked for the eternal Kingdom.

This house is covered with immeasurable love. This house is shielded and protected from the outside fiery darts of the enemy because the "King of Glory" reigns here.

This house is filled with sunshine for the light of the "Son" continually brightens those who love Him. This house has doors that open into arms of love. Other houses may crumble but this house stands firm and secure.

If you do not live in this house you are welcome. Just knock on the door of your heart and invite the special guest. His name is Jesus.

Dear God, may we live one day at a time. Help us to be quick to express our love to others. Help us to never take Your love for granted. Guide us to find happiness in simple pleasures. Teach us to number our days, making every moment count. May we make our home in our hearts. May our earthly temple be cleansed daily with the precious blood of the Lamb. In Jesus beautiful name. Amen.

September 10 Read 1 Samuel 15:19-22

LISTEN TO YOUR HEART TODAY

Bible Thought: "And Joshua said unto all the people, Behold, this stone shall be a witness unto us; for it hath heard all the words of the LORD which he spake unto us: it shall be therefore a witness unto you, lest ye deny your God" (Joshua 24:27).

Benny's job for the week included being a special friend to new students. This meant he would hardly have time to participate in "Play Day." The longing in Benny's eyes compelled me to appoint a substitute for that day. Benny competed in every event and won many ribbons. At the end of the day, Benny hugged me tight and ran to the school bus. Once on the bus, he waved from an open window: "Mrs. Clayton, you're the best teacher in the whole world…" his voice fading as the bus turned the corner. I watched the bus disappear through a blur of tears, thankful that I had seen and listened with my heart.

I have learned through the years people are different, yet alike. Everyone, young or old need a heart felt touch of understanding.

Do we really listen to those around us? Unspoken words reveal pain and hurt. Being sensitive to others is a virtue and solves many problems.

Listening requires patience to hear what is said between the lines.

Listen with your heart today.

You will be blessed.

Dear precious Lord, help us to listen with our hearts today. May we be quick to love and slow to judge. Grant us patience in all of our relationships. We ask these blessings in that wonderful name of Jesus. Amen.

September 11 Read Psalm 37:1-8

STRESS FREE LIVING

Bible Thought: "And which of you with taking thought can add to his stature one cubit?" (Luke12-25).

Stress free living seems impossible in a world of duties, obligations and responsibilities. Any number of circumstances can bring on stress...a loved one's illness, a financial crisis, misunderstandings, overdue bills and the list goes on.

The stress level is determined by a person's reaction to a situation. Stress increases when he or she cannot decide what to do or how to respond.

Stress steals the joy of today for you and me.

Stress causes harsh words and hurt feelings.

So how do we react in stressful times in coping with difficult circumstances? We do have a choice. Making the right choice results in better health in daily living. God's Word is the guide. Face life with God's promises.

"Pray without ceasing" (1 Thessalonians 5:17).

"Trust in him at all times; ye people, pour out your heart before him: God *is* a refuge for us. Selah" (Psalm 62:8).

Be able to say at night, "Lord, I did better today and will have a better tomorrow."

Dear precious Lord, we repent today and confess our sin of allowing the world's stress to spoil our day. May we rest in Your love and peace in any stressful situation realizing that we can do nothing without You. In Jesus' beautiful name. Amen.

September 12 Read 1 John 1:4-7

LET THE LIGHT IN

Bible Thought: "Then spake Jesus again unto them, saying, 'I am the light of the world: he that followeth me shall not walk in darkness, but shall have the light of life" (John 8:12).

Have you ever walked into a room at night in the dark? It's hard to see. When I arise every morning I open the shutters of my windows. I want the "light" in. I surely don't want to be in a darkened house all day. It's something about sunshine that cheers me up…the gift of another day.

God's Word is filled with "light and sunshine." Walking in "His Light" paves the way for a happy life. Without His "Light" I would stumble and fall, touching those around me who are looking for an example to follow.

God's sunshine is for everyone. He has left His "Book of Life" for us to find our way. I like the acrostic:

B…Bible…I…Instructions…B…Before…L…Leaving…E… Earth.

You will find answers in the "Good Book" for any problem you will ever encounter in life. You will find forgiveness, love, hope and salvation. You will find grace from a loving God and you will find "peace that passes all understanding."

The Bible is the blueprint on the way to your destination. Walk every day with God. Read His Word and let the "Light" in your life.

Dear Lord, thank You for sending the "Light of the World." His name is Jesus. Amen.

September 13 Read Numbers 14:6-9

TAKE COURAGE AND OVERCOME

Bible Thought: "But my servant Caleb, because he had another spirit with him, and hath followed me fully, him will I bring into the land whereinto he went; and his seed shall possess it" (Numbers 14:24).

We have a dear friend who is eighty-one. He doesn't know the meaning of "retire." He works every day with vigor and enthusiasm. His positive attitude and his love for the Lord gives him strength for hard work. He patiently helps others and always has an encouraging word. I think he's like Caleb in the Bible.

Caleb encourages me to go with full speed ahead in life with trust and faith. His example inspires me to have hope because faith always has a future while fear is destruction.

We can be "Calebs" in this life or we can be those murmuring, whining, complaining poor souls who spent the best time of their lives in the desert.

God gives us the gift of life. The way we live is up to us. As for me, I find life exciting and "delicious."

With Jesus on your side, nothing is impossible to you. You can be bitter or better. Be better.

Through Jesus you and I are overcomers. If Caleb can, you and I can.

Dear precious Lord, thank You for those who have gone before us in victory. Most of all we thank You for our Champion. His name is Jesus. Amen.

September 14 Read Psalm 146:1-5

WITH JESUS THERE'S HAPPINESS

Bible Thought: "Happy *is that* people, that is in such a case: *yea,* happy is *that* people, whose God is the LORD" (Psalm 144:15).

Who of us have not made mistakes? Once we have confessed our transgressions to our loving God we are forgiven.

We thank God for His mercy. We do not look back. We look forward to each new day and its wonderful surprises. We are happy with Jesus.

Age is not a factor. We are thankful for whatever age we are. Each day is one more day closer to heaven. So let's make each day an adventure with Jesus.

I happened to be in a printing office when an elder happy man came in. "What a great smile," he said to me.

"You have one too," I answered.

"I've been in the darkness but now I'm walking in the light. It's because of Jesus." Then he shook my hand as he left. He had Jesus and I had the blessing.

Let's not be ashamed of our imperfections. A cracked and broken pot allows light to shine through.

Be a vessel for God by allowing His love and His light to shine through to others.

With Jesus there's happiness!

Dear Lord, thank You for the enthusiasm and encouragement you give us. We are so happy with You and we want to tell others. In Jesus' wonderful name. Amen.

September 15 Read Psalm 112:1-4

CELEBRATE GOD'S BLESSINGS

Bible Thought: "Every good gift and every perfect gift is from above, and cometh down from the Father of lights, with whom is no variableness, neither shadow of turning" (James 1:17).

It is easy to rationalize the blessings in our lives or to let them go by as mere "coincidences." I believe both great and small miracles happen every day and we let them go unnoticed while never expressing gratitude.

To celebrate God's many blessings I want to recognize the touch of my Master's hand. Knowing that I can relax because Jesus loves me and will never leave me.

Scars are evidence of great love. It hurts to love. Who knows that more than Jesus? Those nail-scarred hands and feet are evidences of His great love. The next time you go through a trial remember the price Jesus paid.

Even the little things are blessings. I must realize that nuisances can be blessings in disguise. Birds outside my bedroom awaken me early each morning. They irritated me until a severe sinus infection caused a terrific roar in my ears. I couldn't hear anything. After many trips to the doctor I regained my normal hearing and realized what a blessing it is to hear…even from birds.

God blesses with wonderful surprises every day.

Be enthusiastic in expressing your gratitude to God for every thing.

What a wonderful way to celebrate life.

Dear precious Lord, we celebrate today and we enter Your courts with praise. Our hearts are filled with praise and thanksgiving for the gift of Your Son. In His beautiful name. Amen.

September 16 Read Proverbs 23:9-12

FREEDOM IN GOD

Bible Thought: "Stand fast therefore in the liberty wherewith Christ hath made us free, and be not entangled again with the yoke of bondage" (Galatians 5:1).

"Breezy," our new horse, checked out the boundaries in his pasture. He wanted to know the limits of his new home. I like to think he also wanted to know that he was safely enclosed in his space. He looked around until he felt secure.

I need boundaries too. God's rules are for safety. His way gives freedom, protection and a sense of well being. If I step beyond God's boundaries in life, I am away from His safety. Then I would suffer the consequences.

I am not my own. My owner paid an inestimable price for me. Right choices make freedom. If I go out of God's boundaries I am in extreme danger. I don't have the wisdom to know what is best for me Yet God knows and that makes me free.

My freedom is in God.

Heaven Bound
The just shall live by faith.
They are not their own.
For in them the Greater One
Reigns upon the throne.

Blessed are those who know Him.
They will never be alone.
God will guide them through this life
To reach their heavenly home.

Dear precious Lord, thank You for Your Word that sets boundaries in our lives, giving us freedom, protection and safety. In Jesus' wonderful name. Amen.

September 17 Read Psalm 84:9-12

THANK GOD FOR THE GIFT OF LIFE

Bible Thought: "These things have I spoken unto you, that my joy might remain in you, and *that* your joy might be full" (John 15:11).

Do you like to be around enthusiastic people? I do! I think life is exciting. It's an adventure and a treasure. Life is a gift from a loving God who loves His children and wants the very best for each one.

I think it's an affront to God to be miserable when we have so many blessings all around us. I am convinced that what we give to life returns with blessings galore.

I like to see how many people will smile back at me. A surprise phone call from a caring friend makes me happy. I feel love and joy when my husband whispers, "I love you." I am filled with enthusiasm when a former student recognizes me. I get excited about writing this devotional and I am grateful for the opportunity.

I just can't keep enough praising and thanking God for the gift of life. I wouldn't have missed it for the world!

For a blessed life think big with faith in your heart and you will enter a new life of hope. Embrace those heavenly special moments and more will come to you with memorable blessings.

Your faith and belief in God are the greatest things you can ever have and that is something to be excited about.

Dear God, thank You for the joy You give. It becomes our strength and we sing with melodious happy hearts. We praise You with joy and thanksgiving. In Jesus' wonderful name. Amen.

September 18 Read Romans: 8:36-39

GOD'S SCHOOL OF LIFE

Bible Thought: "Wherefore seeing we are compassed about with so great a cloud of witnesses, let us lay aside every weight, and the sin which doth so easily beset *us*, and let us run with patience the race that is set before us" (Hebrews 12:1).

We may have difficult challenges in life's school, but we bounce back because no one can cripple our love, corrode our faith, take away our peace, silence our courage, quench our spirit, destroy our confidence, erase God's promises, steal our happy memories, shatter the hope of heaven or lessen the power of the resurrection.

So we stay in the fight. We run the race to win. Be glad you're in the Lord's classroom. Be thankful your Teacher is on your side teaching you and me how to overcome hurdles in life. Be grateful for His Spirit who stays with us in the "recesses" of our lives. He helps and tutors the things we need to learn.

What a way to live. I love this "School of Life." Every day with Jesus is a day of adventure and excitement. The cycle of life is a wondrous thing.

When that final "bell" rings and time in life's school is over we want to receive a diploma with our names written in the "Lamb's Book of Life."

For the child of God, the end is not the end but only the beginning.

Dear Lord, thank You that nothing can ever separate us from You. Your love is forever and we are forever grateful. We praise You today and every day in that wonderful name of Jesus. Amen.

September 19 Read Mark 4:38-41

THE "HEART" OF THE MATTER

Bible Thought: "The righteous shall be glad in the LORD, and shall trust in him; and all the upright in heart shall glory" (Psalm 64:10).

I have learned through the years people are different yet alike. Everyone needs understanding. If I make the first step most respond with friendliness. Something unique about each person is different and it comes from the heart. Many ways of individuals express themselves. Listening requires patience to hear what is said between the lines.

What seems paradoxical to me is spending a lifetime gaining wealth and then spending the wealth to regain the health. In the pursuit of life the really important things are neglected.

Some relics my husband brought home from his pasture reminds me to prioritize what is really important. Just an old rusty cream can, broken old silverware, and a plow remained. Where once a house stood had evidence of someone's life. I wondered about the storms of their lives.

Today's Bible reading tells of the disciples fearing for their lives upon the troubled sea. Jesus rebuked the storm and it became calm.

What about the storms in our lives? There is One, the only One, who can calm our troubled sea. His name is Jesus.

That gets to the "heart" of the matter.

Thank You Lord for Your anchor in the storms of life. Empower us to keep our priorities straight, setting our goal on our heavenly home. How we praise and thank You for Jesus. In His beautiful name. Amen.

September 20 Read Exodus 17:11-14

HONOR GOD'S ANOINTED

Bible Thought: "The liberal soul shall be made fat: and he that watereth shall be watered also himself" (Proverbs 11:25).

Ministers who respond to God's call are special people. These spiritual leaders are God's gift to all of us.

Pastors and their families live in a world that never stops. Their workload is large and tedious. There's always another Bible study, a sermon to prepare, a funeral, hospital visits or whatever needs the congregation requires.

Encourage your pastor. Everyone wants to know he and his wife are appreciated.

Pray for your pastor and include those in other areas of the church ministry. Take time to applaud and affirm those servants of God who are entrusted with your spiritual growth. Applaud the magazines that bring God's light to a dark world.

Ministers are human beings with needs. Treat them generously in every way. Stand by them. Value them.

They are God's anointed and our national treasures.

Dear Lord we thank You today for godly leaders. Bless them and keep them in Your care. We thank You for Jesus. In His wonderful name. Amen.

September 21 Read 103:1-4

FORGIVING TODAY TAKES CARE OF TOMORROW

Bible Thought: "I have blotted out, as a thick cloud, thy sins: return unto me, for I have redeemed thee" (Isaiah 44:22).

Do you live in the yesterdays of regrets? Do you ever wish you could go back and remove that hasty remark and the loss of temper? I have and I've had to ask forgiveness again and again.

One day one of our sons said to me, "Mom, there is nothing you could ever say or do that would make me not love you." That is true forgiveness.

Mistakes require repentance and forgiveness. I find after I ask forgiveness I have to forgive myself and go on with life. All of us have had hurt and pain. Yet we don't have to allow the past to rob us of today or tomorrow. It is a new day. God gives us one day at a time. Forgiving others removes the worry and anxiety of the situation.

I'm so glad God forgives us and drops our sins in the sea of forgetfulness. What an awesome God we serve.

Do you need to forgive someone today? Forgive. Then you will be happy and that takes care of tomorrow.

Dear Lord, may we be quick to forgive others. May we repent any sin that is hidden in our hearts. Thank You for sending Your beautiful Son. His name is Jesus. Amen.

September 22 Read Proverbs 31:25-29

SEEING WITH THE HEART

Bible Thought: "For our heart shall rejoice in him, because we have trusted his holy name" (Psalm 33:21).

Aunt Mary endeared herself to all of us but to me she held "angel's status" from the earliest time of my childhood. At the ripe old age in her nineties she made lap robes for rest homes. Though legally blind and living alone Aunt Mary amazingly found all kinds of ingenious ways to maintain her independence.

Many times we brought Aunt Mary home with us for weekend visits. Treasured memories still linger lovingly in my mind. On one occasion we took her for a ride. When we came back home and as my husband helped her out of our car something unexplainable happened. She took a deep breath. "Just smell the fall air. Isn't it delicious? And look at that tree over there. It is beautiful!"

"Aunt Mary," I gasped. "Can you see that tree?"

"No, but I can feel it. Somehow I know it's there. Maybe I can smell it. It's just such a beautiful day and everything seems so right. It's kind of like I feel it in my heart."

I learned a lot from Aunt Mary that wonderful autumn day. I discovered something.

"Seeing with the heart is the best sight of all!"

Dear heavenly Father, thank You for the beautiful seasons. Thank You for loved ones and the many blessings You bestow. In Jesus wonderful name. Amen.

September 23 Read Proverbs 4:4-7

FOCUS ON JESUS

Bible: "Hear instruction, and be wise, and refuse it not" (Proverbs 8:33).

I didn't realize my knee had leaned on the rung of the stepladder. The pressure against one rung helped me keep my balance. It didn't hurt at the time but the next day paid for it. The swelling and soreness made me wish I had not painted anything. How easy it is to get into difficult circumstances. I've learned many lessons from that. I had missed reading my devotion that morning and nothing seemed to work right.

I must keep my thoughts on Jesus. Focusing on Him brings clarity and well being. If I miss my daily quiet time my day doesn't go well. I need to guard my words and deeds. I want to do my best and trust Him in every circumstance. Keeping my thought life on God's Word will help me to be alert. Then I will have peace.

Though you are impatient
And anxious in life's cares
Just renew God's promises
For He is always there.
So if you are discouraged

When troubles come your way,
Thank God for His promises
And you will be okay!

Dear Lord, help us to think by concentrating on Your Word. May we be "transformed by the renewing of our minds." Please keep us in Your loving care and keep us from all danger and harm. In Jesus' precious name. Amen.

September 24 Read 1 Corinthians 15:41-44

NEW BODIES

Bible Thought: "For this God *is* our God for ever and ever: he will be our guide *even* unto death" (Psalm 48:14).

Living in the same house for many years has called for a lot of repairs and up keep. I'm convinced a house has to be maintained or it will fall apart.

So who wants an old house? I do! It's home. It's a house filled with memories. It's a house where three boys wrote their names in cement and on my heart. It is where Lance ran away from home and hid behind the butane tank. It is where the boys' daddy wrestled all three at once and ended up in the emergency room with a broken rib.

If our house could talk, it would talk about a lot of happy times, crises, tears and most of all, love. It would tell of pain, forgiveness, repentance and shelter for imperfect people straining to embrace the good.

Our older house reminds me of our earthly bodies. If one refuses to acknowledge Jesus as Lord and Savior, they are refusing the new heavenly body that is awaiting the child of God.

Those who are in Christ Jesus will exchange an old body for a new body just as you would an old house for a new house…a house that will never need repair.

Dear precious Lord, we thank You for our time to live in these earthly bodies. We thank You even more for our heavenly bodies that will live with You forever. What a loving wonderful God You are. It's all because of Jesus. In His beautiful name. Amen.

September 25 Read Galatians 3:11-14

FAITH CONQUERS

Bible Thought: "Behold, his soul which is lifted up is not upright in him: but the just shall live by his faith" (Habakkuk 2:4).

Every day you and I are faced with choices. We believe "God works all things for our good" (Romans 8:28), or we react to hard circumstances with self-pity and depression. It is a matter of faith.

In that great "hall of faith" believers in Hebrews 11, we are told of people with giant faith. Noah, Abraham, Joseph, Moses and David are just a few among those faithful "Who's Who" of the Bible. Their faith moved mountains and overcame enemies. They simply believed God. No matter what happened they knew they were in God's hands.

How does this apply to us today? Without faith it is impossible to please God. Without faith we would be walking in darkness. So we must be persistent and stubborn in our faith. With God on our side, how can we lose?

We believe our God. We are justified by our faith. That makes us more than conquerors.

Faith is the victory!

Dear Lord, grant us the faith that moves mountains. May we boldly declare our faith to others. Thank You for Jesus. In His wonderful name. Amen.

September 26 Read Daniel 6:24-27

BLESSINGS FOLLOW THE GODLY

Bible Thought: "And all nations shall call you blessed: for ye shall be a delightsome land, saith the LORD of hosts" (Malachi 3:12).

As a former teacher, I saw first hand the effects of ungodly parents upon their children. I had many students in foster care because of abuse and neglect. My heart went out to these children. Their typical response was either lashing out and fighting back for survival or becoming withdrawn so much they could hardly be reached.

The men who had accused Daniel were thrown into the lion's den along with their children and wives. These ungodly men took their wives and children down with them.

The concept of "doing one's own thing" is a most selfish one. Sin always hurts someone else. Sin is never committed in isolation.

Jesus voluntarily gives His life to those who accept Him. Think of it. The way we live our lives today can affect our descendants for generations to come.

Surely everyone wants children and grandchildren blessed.

Blessings follow the godly.

Dear precious Lord, we want to be the ones who break the chain of evil in our generation. Thank You for Your faithfulness and thank You for Jesus, our beautiful Savior. In His name. Amen.

September 27 Read Matthew 15:17-20

PUNCH HOLES IN THE DARKNESS

Bible Thought: "In him was life; and the life was the light of men" (John 1:4).

Every day the world walks in darkness without the light of God. The world cannot offer joy or peace of mind although it tries with various and sundry means. At best, they are pathetic substitutes. Without God, there is nothing. "Sin for a season" eventually gives way to despair and hopelessness.

God's children walk in light and punch holes in the darkness. My mother was one of those. She sacrificed her desires to serve others and she touched many souls in need.

Mother never bought herself a new dress but I can remember numerous dresses she bought for me. She befriended the friendless, gave hope to the hopeless and cooked for the hungry. She punched holes in the darkness.

Take an uncompromising stand for righteousness when it is sin. Vote for a leader who stands for biblical principles. Pave the way for others to follow.

Punching holes in the darkness is not hard. All that is required is a determination to be obedient by walking in the light and sharing that light with others.

Dear Lord, thank You for Jesus, the Light for all mankind. Empower us with boldness to declare to others the wonderful news of the gospel. In that name above all names. His name is Jesus. Amen.

September 28 Read 2 Peter 3:10-14

SPIRITUAL DETERIORATION

Bible Thought: "And every man that hath this hope in purifieth himself, even as he is pure" (1 John 3:3).

Taking care of our physical bodies is vital for good health. Abusing these bodies hastens disease and death. Have you seen signs in a doctor's office or magazines about the signs of physical cancer? These signs tell of warning signals.

It is the same for spiritual health. If we are no longer moved by the story of the cross, we are heading toward spiritual deterioration.

Disobedience and unconcern are warning signs of the beginning of spiritual malignancy. Pleasing ourselves instead of God sets the stage.

Yet there is hope dear reader. We can keep our spiritual health vibrant by having a passion for Jesus. Seeking and loving Him with all our hearts eliminates spiritual deterioration.

Jesus has promised: "And I say unto you, Ask, and it shall be given you; seek, and ye shall find; knock, and it shall be opened unto you" (Luke 11:9).

Seek and knock.

It's a great life!.

Dear precious Lord, we repent today. Forgive us for being lukewarm and apathetic. We want You. We need You. We love You. In Jesus' beautiful name. Amen

September 29 Read 2 Kings 17:32-35

THE DANGER OF IDOLATRY

Bible Thought: "Therefore say unto the house of Israel, Thus saith the Lord God; Repent and turn yourselves from your idols and turn away you faces from all your abominations" (Ezekiel 14:6).

An idol is anything that stands between God and His people. In Bible times God's people kept getting into trouble. They made idols to worship which stood for all the evil qualities the idols represented.

Idols are still around today. Some trust in horoscopes. "It's just for fun," I hear some say, but God is very specific about it. (Isaiah 47:13)

Some trust in material possessions or money, neither of which will get one to heaven. (Luke 18:24) Keeping up with "The Jones" is an idolatrous condition of self-glory. To have bigger and better causes the overworked husband to strive even harder to pay for the demanding lifestyle. Many times it destroys health in the process. Trusting in position or a place of authority can be short lived. Jesus in the only One that never changes.

Jesus loves His children with an everlasting love. As Christians we have one focus. We look to Jesus, the author and finisher of our faith.

Let's guard ourselves against idols.

Dear Lord, we lay down every idol in our lives. May we daily seek to keep our priorities upon You and You alone. In His wonderful name...Jesus. Amen.

September 30 Read 1 Chronicles 16:23-28

PRAISE HIM

Bible Thought: "Let the people praise thee, O God; let all the people praise thee" (Psalm 67:5).

My favorite childhood memories are those of listening to my grandmother sing those grand old hymns of praise. As she went about her daily chores, her voice continually praised God. Because of that I rarely need a songbook to sing. Those hymns are deeply planted in my heart. Those songs shaped my life at an early age.

Granny's daily praises to her God reached out to those around her including her grandchildren. She produced a generation of God's love that made honorable adults.

Granny's face seemed to glow when she sang about her Savior. Looking back I realize she transformed from one degree of glory to another and she took God with her everywhere she went.

Living a daily life of worship influences others and changes our world.

Praise and worship is the breath and life of God.

Sing yourself to Jesus!

"I will love Him joyfully
And daily give Him praise
'Til He comes to take me home
I'll sing to Him each day!"

Dear wonderful Lord, thank You for the joy You bring to our lives. May that joy bubble up and spill on to others. In Jesus' beautiful name. Amen.

OCTOBER

October 1 Read Psalm 1-6

THIS GAME OF LIFE

Bible Thought: "Blessed *are* they that do his commandments, that they may have right to the tree of life, and may enter in through the gates into the city" (Revelation 22:14).

The men of my household like to tape football games. They enjoy replaying tapes for friends who missed certain plays. Even though my grandsons have seen the actual game they like to see the winner.

Life is like a football game. You may drop the ball. Problems may tackle you. You may have a ten-yard penalty now and then. There may be more month than money, unrest in marriages, misunderstandings or illness. The score may be "49 to "0" in the opponent's favor, but in all of these situations, you are "more than a conqueror." The "Almighty" lives in you and He knows the score at the end of the game. Our side wins!

So don't be moved by setbacks. Our guide is God's Word inside us, the shield of faith before us and the sword of the spirit upon us. We are armed and dangerous.

We like to see winners and we don't have to wait until we get to the finish line to cheer. Let's cheer now. It's great to be alive in this game of life and I like to see the winner. Tell someone today:

"We win! I've read the last page."

Dear Lord, thank You for Jesus who paved the way to victory in this game of life. Because of Him, we are on the winning side.

October 2 Read Psalm 104:1-5

GOD'S CREATION

Bible Thought: "To every *thing there is* a season, and a time to every purpose under the heaven" (Ecclesiastes 3:1).

God paints autumn with strokes of brilliant gold, hues of burnished brown, and flames of reddish orange. The leaves of summer now become breathtaking jewels, escaping from God's treasure box. The awesome magnificence of God's creativity is overwhelming and colors my world with beauty.

Listen to the crunching sound of leaves as you walk along the way. Be reminded that God is making way for new growth, not only in the physical but also in the spiritual realm of your life. Step out in faith and grow. God plants seeds of beauty, righteousness and kindness.

God's cycle of life is a wondrous thing. I'm so glad you and I were born. God makes no mistakes. He planned our lies and surrounds us with special, unique people to love. He also paints lives with beautiful "leaves" of memories to keep in our heart.

Enjoy the season. It is God's beauty. Appreciate God's indescribable work of art.

"Fall" with me for this lovely time of year.

Dear precious Lord, thank You for painting our lives with such beauty. You are so beautiful, "How beautiful heaven must be." Thank You for Jesus, the way, the truth and the beauty. In His wonderful name. Amen.

October 3 Read Psalm 34:1-4

HAVE PEACE IN A TROUBLED WORLD

Bible Thought: "Peace I leave with you, my peace I give unto you: not as the world giveth, give I unto you. Let not your heart be troubled, neither let it be afraid" (John 14:27).

In this world of economic meltdown we tend to lose our joy allowing anxiety, worry and depression to dominate circumstances. Yet we can cope in the midst of it. Thankful prayers for many blessings keep us joyful. It's a breath of fresh air to be around someone filled with praise. God is always willing to strengthen those who turn to Him.

Let's remember this world is not our permanent home. Be certain that God is in control and we can have peace even in turmoil.

Prayer changes things and is vital to our lives. Prayer warriors "build a hedge" and stand in the gap for others. These prayers require sacrifice and they are motivated by love, building walls of care and concern while promoting positive affirmations that enhance healing and well-being.

The greatest defense for our nation is "knee" praying power. All of us are in this journey of life together so let's help each other and go the second mile with our prayers.

Dear Lord, thank You for the "peace that passes all understanding." Thank You for answering our prayers even while we speak. We praise You today and every day. In that beautiful name of Jesus. Amen.

October 4 Read Isaiah 53:2-6

WHAT A SAVIOR!

Bible Thought: "Nor height, nor death, nor any other creature, shall be able to separate us from the love of God, which is in Christ Jesus our Lord" (Romans 8:39).

Jesus was willing to give His physical life to resurrect new life for mankind. Of course we are not perfect yet but we "strain toward the mark," and press on. We grow in faith and gratitude. We pray. We study. We meditate and "hide the Word in our hearts.

Jesus makes a home in our hearts because He loves us with a love that goes beyond our mortal understanding.

With Him, we live this life victoriously. Even in death we have victory. Death is only a shadow to walk right through. The grave is not the end. God sends His angels to escort His children into His presence. For the Christian, death is a reward. No more pain or sorrow…no more battles to fight…only blissful peace in a place of eternal "Light."

I grew up hearing my grandmother singing those grand old hymns about heaven. Many times in the night I awaken with those songs in my heart. I think God has been singing to me. (Zephaniah 3:17)

What a Savior!

Dear precious Lord, thank You for loving us, forgiving us and redeeming us. Thank You for the time we've had to live on earth and the future to live forever with You. In Jesus' beautiful name. Amen.

October 5 Read Psalm 84:9-12

THE BRIDGE TO HEAVEN

Bible Thought: "But there the glorious LORD *will be* unto us a place of broad rivers *and* streams; wherein shall go no galley with oars, neither shall gallant ship pass thereby" (Isaiah 33:21).

I have always wanted a garden bridge. Something beckons me to walk across a bridge. It's as if I'm walking over trials and difficulties that are under my feet. I find a different perspective and a new perspective on the other side.

To my joy, my husband asked a friend to make a bridge for me. Even though it is strictly ornamental each time I view it standing strong and sturdy, I am reminded of God's many promises. I like to think the Israelites walked over a "bridge" of dry ground with a "wall of water on their right and on their left." (Exodus 14:22).

When I awaken in the wee hours of the morning, I like to think of the "still waters" under my bridge. (Psalm 23)

We anchored our bridge close to a tall flourishing pine tree so I could be reminded, "my leaves will never fade nor wither." (Psalm 1)

Jesus is the bridge of safety, the "crossover" from trials and heartaches. I thank my Lord for the "bridges" in my life because He helps me to cross over.

Jesus is the bridge to the Heavenly Kingdom.

I love my "bridge."

Dear precious Lord, thank You for holding our hands while we walk over the bridge of problems in life. The greatest bridge of all is crossing over to heaven where we will praise You throughout all eternity. In Jesus, that name above all names. Amen.

October 6 Read Revelation 22:1-7

THE GREATEST HOMECOMING

Bible Thought: "But as it is written, Eye hath not seen, nor ear heard, neither have entered into the heart of man, the things which God hath prepared for them that love him" (1 Corinthians 2:9).

My University Homecoming brings many memories of beloved classmates and Professors. Some are no longer here. I honor their memory with gratitude. Their guidance enabled me to have a teaching career, a job I loved. My English instructors influenced me to embark on a writing career.

This collegiate Homecoming reminds me of another celebration. A greater one is awaiting the child of God. Because of Jesus, the best "Homecoming" of all is yet to be.

Can you imagine seeing Jesus face-to-face? What a day that will be. Think of a wonderful reunion with loved ones who have gone on before us. There will be no sickness, sorrow or heartaches. There will be no more death. We will have new bodies. We will be in that beautiful land of joy and peace. I can almost see loved ones waiting at heaven's gate to welcome us home.

We will see the Tree of Life and live forever. I will praise my Savior throughout all eternity.

It will be the greatest Homecoming of all.

You come too!

Dear Lord, thank You for the time we've had to love and live on this earth, but most of all for our heavenly home. It's all because of Jesus. In His beautiful name. Amen.

October 7 Read John 14:1-4

REPLACE FEAR WITH FAITH

Bible Thought: "Be not afraid of sudden fear, neither of the desolation of the wicked, when it cometh" (Proverbs 3:25).

Fear is the most destructive force I know. It is paralyzing and tormenting. Its grip literally drains life away. Fear robs one of sleep, peace and joy in daily living Anytime you are plagued with fear be assured it is not of God.

To overcome fear know God planned your life. You are wanted and loved by Him. He wants your highest good. He has an investment in you.

Live one day at a time and live it to the fullest. Yesterday is gone along with its mistakes. Look to today. Tomorrow will take care of its self. Realize nothing can happen to you that Jesus and you cannot handle.

Feed your faith by reading God's Word. His Word is full of hope and promise. Hiding the Word in your heart builds confidence and assurance.

Pray the answer, not the problem. Do you know God's telephone number? It is Jeremiah 33.3.

Trust in the Lord. Trust in Him cancels fear.

Fear tolerated is faith contaminated.

Replace fear with faith and celebrate life!

Dear precious Lord, what a mighty God You are! You love us, guide us and stay right beside us. We praise You today and everyday for the many blessings You bestow. In Jesus' wonderful name. Amen.

October 8 Read 2 Timothy 4:6-8

"LAST TIMES" ARE "FIRST TIMES"

Bible Thought: "And the Spirit and the bride say, Come. And let him that is athirst come. And whosoever will, let him take the water of life freely" (Revelation 22:17).

Even though it was our grandson's "last" college football game he looked forward to the "first" time pursuing his career and the next stage of life.

I cried when we had to place my aunt in a rest home. "This will be the last night she will spend in her own home," I moaned. "I guess there's a last time for everything."

"Or a first time," my husband added. "She may like the retirement home. I know she will enjoy the good food and the care. The 'last time' leads to a' best first time.' It all depends on how you look at it."

When our children left home for the last time it was hard for me to know they must pursue their "first time" in the world.

Such is the journey of life but for the child of God, the best is yet to be because it's the "first time" to burst into the "light." It's the "first time" to experience the joy of eternal bless free from pain and sorrow. It's like my husband said,

"It's all depends on how you look at it!"

Dear Lord, thank You for Your plan for our lives on earth. It will be our "last time" here but our "first time" to see You face to face. What a day that will be! In Jesus' beautiful name. Amen.

October 9 Read Psalm 17:5-8

HE IS YOUR HIDING PLACE

Bible Thought: "Thou *art* my hiding place; thou shalt preserve me from trouble; thou shalt compass me about with songs of deliverance. Selah.

Throughout history mankind has struggled for survival against unspeakable odds, with one exception. The Bible reveals the "hiding place" for those who love God and follow through in obedience.

The Red Sea, the widow's son, the fourth man in the fiery furnace, the closed mouths of lions in the lions" den and many more had a "hiding place" that enabled God's people to conquer every foe.

I ran to my hiding place when our oldest son was injured in a mowing accident. I remained in that hiding place when our middle son was severely burned in a butane explosion. I clung to my hiding place when a swamp cooler landed on our youngest son's head. I relied on that hiding place during my husband's five major surgeries. In all of these I found refuge, strength and comfort.

I love my hiding place. Jesus is waiting for me. I tell Him of my love and I share my deepest feelings with Him. He loves me and He loves you. Nothing can separate us from His love. (Romans 38:39)

I treasure my hiding place. He can be your hiding place too.

Dear Lord, only You alone can save us from all our troubles. We run to You for You are our Deliverer. In that wonderful name of Jesus. Amen.

October 10 Read Joshua 4:21-24

LEAVE NO REGRETS, BUT LOVING MEMORIES

Bible Thought: "The memory of the just *is* blessed: but the name of the wicked shall rot" (Proverbs 10:7).

Every day you and I are leaving memories and those we leave behind will remember, good or bad.

We are given just so many years with the gift of life. How you spend your life is immensely important. Have we taken up space or have we made our lives count for something? We may not be rich by the world's standards but we can give what we have. Everyone can have a smile, a caring attitude and compassion for a needy soul.

To leave good memories and have a life of victory follow Matthew 6:33 : "But seek first for his kingdom and his righteousness, and all these things will be given to you as well."

I have been blessed. My memories include my little school students' smiling faces, my husband's goodnight kiss, the "I love you mom "phone calls and the many words of encouragement I have received from so many.

"On the last day of life

What would you do?

Keep taking for granted

Those around you?

Make a loving memory today.

Dear precious Lord, every day is sweeter than the day before because of Jesus. Thank You for sending Him to earth to save us. May we have no regrets but loving memories.

Amen.

October 11 Read Psalm 145:1-7

CHERISH SPECIAL MOMENTS

Bible Thought: "The memory of the just *is* blessed but the name of the wicked shall rot" (Proverbs 10:7)

"Close your eyes and hold out your hands," the waitress said to me. I opened my eyes to find a pair of unique beautiful earrings. I thanked her for this beautiful gift. As we talked she shared her faith and the love for Jesus. What a blessing for my husband and me.

We learned weeks later she had died from a long-term disease. No one would have guessed this young joyful woman had only a few weeks to live. Touching lives and warming hearts had become a mission in her short life. Now when I wear those earrings I think of her and I thank God for sending her into my life. I will always remember her loving heart.

Good memories are photos in the camera of our hearts to be cherished. Yet there is love beyond our finite minds to grasp. It is God's love. His love never comes to an end for those who will receive it.

Let's spread God's love while we have time on earth and be thankful for special blessings.

Dear God, Thank You for Your love that never comes to an end. Help us to realize the only thing we get to keep is the love we have given away. In that precious name of Jesus.

Amen.

October 12 Read Philippians 4:4-8

WORRY...A TRAIN RIDE TO NOWHERE

Bible Thought: "Thou wilt keep *him* in perfect peace, *whose* mind is stayed *on thee:* because he trusteth in thee.

Whatever the situation, does worrying help? Does it give you comfort or peace?

I wonder how God feels when we stew and fret while waving around in doubt and unbelief?

God is still in control. We humans get caught up in daily deadlines bringing on stress and worry. We forget the many good things in life while looking for the "good life" that we already have. If we have God, family and friends we are rich beyond belief.

If we had only twenty-four hours to live how would you spend it? I believe you would want to make every second count.

I would want to feel my husband's arms around me and tell others what they mean to me. I would want to enjoy the fellowship of friends...to hear the laughter of children at play and the melodic song of birds at the break of day. If I lived my last twenty-four hours doing this, why wait? Why not do that now?

I cannot change anything by worrying, but I can change my world with my faith and attitude.

Because of Jesus, life is delicious and I wouldn't have missed it for the world.

Dear Lord, thank You for this day and may we live it to the fullest. Grant us every opportunity to spread Your love to others. In Jesus' name. Amen.

October 13 Read Song of Solomon 8:6-7

THE LOVING HEART

Bible Thought: "One *thing* have I desired of the LORD, that I will I seek after; that I may dwell in the house of the LORD all the days of my life, to behold the beauty of the LORD, and to inquire in his temple" (Psalm 27:4).

The Song of Solomon reminds me of my husband's love too. He has a heart filled with love, kindness, consideration, patience and joy.

It doesn't take long for someone to know one's heart. You can recognize it by actions, speech and behavior.

Through the years of my marriage I have learned the real reason that attracted me to the man of my dreams. A loving heart makes life happy.

I see Jesus when my husband sacrifices for our family and when he holds me in his arms to pray.

A loving heart goes beyond age, race or status. Love in the heart brings out the best in everyone.

Let God be in your heart because a heart lived for God is a beautiful heart.

"I'm in love with Jesus
And He's in love with me.
He walks daily by my side.
And I have victory!

You can have that too.
He's just a prayer away.
Give your heart to Jesus
And love Him every day!"

Dear God, thank You for the precious gift of Jesus and may all of us be testimonies of loving hearts. In Jesus' beautiful name. Amen.

October 14 Read Mark 8:34-37

BE A GIVER

Bible Thought: "He that handleth a matter wisely shall find good: and whoso trusteth in the LORD, happy is he" (Proverbs 16:20).

Life is difficult without kindness, unselfishness and most of all love for others. For many years I thought "hate" was the opposite of "love." I now realize the opposite of love is "selfishness." The one who is always thinking "What about me?" is bound to be unhappy.

Material things satisfy for a season but real joy comes from a loving God. Pursuing happiness is vain without knowing the secret of life.

Blessing someone else brings happiness to the giver. Giving without expecting in return brings joy to all concerned. Without givers there would be no harmony, success or peace. Givers are "lights" in a cold dark world. Their gift of "Good News" brings hope for tomorrow which we desperately need to hear.

Giving is a natural response of love. Jesus gave His life and that is love unequaled. Since Jesus gave once and for all the supreme sacrifice surely we can give in return to those around us.

Let's wrap ourselves in love and take the news and love of Jesus to a lost and dying world. It will bring joy to them and to you too.

It's the secret of a happy life!

Dear precious Lord, thank You for Jesus, the ultimate gift for mankind. May we reflect

Him in every thought, word and deed. In His wonderful name. Amen.

October 15 Read 1 King 18:27-30

LAUGHTER IS A GIFT

Bible Thought: "A merry heart doeth good *like* a medicine: but a broken spirit drieth the bones" (Proverbs 17:22).

I like Elijah's humor in today's Bible Reading. He challenged the people and proved that God is the one and only true God.

Medical science has said laughter is one of the healthiest things we can do. Laughing dispels anxiety. Finding things to laugh about breaks tension and sets a friendly tone. Even in hard situations a sense of humor lifts our spirits and conquers gloom. Laughter promotes optimism, clears the atmosphere and enables one to be on the winning side.

The gift of laughter makes everyday sparkle. It makes a happy face instead of a frown. I don't want to be remembered as a worrier, crier or miserable person feeling sorry for "poor little me."

I love this Irish Proverb: "Dance as if no one's watching, sing as if no one's listening and live everyday as if it were your last." To that I say, "Amen."

I want to live every day of my life with the "joy" of the Lord. Laughter in my heart reminds me of that joy.

The gift of laughter is one of God's gifts, a gift to share. Allow someone to "catch" your laughter. Today spread sunshine.

Keep laughter in your heart.

Dear Lord, thank You for the gift of laughter, but more than that thank You for the joy in Jesus. In His marvelous name. Amen.

October 16 Read Isaiah 37:1-4

LIFE IS NOT ALWAYS EASY

Bible Thought: "Peace I leave with you, my peace I give unto you: not as the world giveth, give I unto you. Let not your heart be troubled, neither let it be afraid" (John 14:27),

Someone has said, "If you never wanted to be hurt, move to a desert island and be a hermit." Maybe you would never be hurt, but think of the loneliness. Missing the joy and ecstasy of love would make life meaningless.

Life is not always easy. Problems and trials do occur. It's not easy to sit by a sick loved one. It's hard to have low finances with bills coming in and it's surely hard to have misunderstandings with others.

Yet hope springs eternal. The Creator of the universe has made provision for our peace, even in the midst of adversity. It's all about peace and hope.

Today's Bible Thought implies some action on our part and that action is "trust." Let us have a trust that is unshakable and unmovable with mountain moving faith.

I look into the faces of some of the older beautiful saints at church and I see the love of Jesus. I see pain in aging bodies and I have seen deep sorrow in the loss of loved ones. Yet they keep pressing on toward the mark for the prize of the "high calling in Christ Jesus." Their faith is an example for all of us.

When Jesus hung on that cruel cross He didn't look for a way out. He gave all of us the greatest love this world has ever known. It didn't come easy.

Dear Lord, may we grow in faith that increases day by day. Thank You for each day that brings us closer to heaven. In that beautiful name of Jesus. Amen.

October 17 Read Psalm 63: 1-4

JOY COMES FROM JESUS

Bible Thought: "And my tongue shall speak of thy righteousness *and* of thy praise all the day long" (Psalm 35:28).

"May I ask you something?" the receptionist asked. "Sure," I responded. "Why are you always so happy?" Immediately I heard myself say, "JESUS!" A patient waiting behind me said in a loud voice, "AMEN!"

I had expected the receptionist to ask about medical history, addresses, etc, but when she asked me the happy question the word "Jesus" automatically came out.

It's the joy of the Lord and some tell me I come on too strong. I remind them Jesus died for me and I am overwhelmingly thankful.

God is the "joy giver." Think of the happiest time you have ever experienced on planet earth. Heaven will be indescribably better.

The words joy, joys, joyful, rejoice, rejoices, rejoiced and rejoicing appear many times in God's Word. It's because the gospel is indeed "Good News." Make a list of all your blessings. You will find a lot about your spiritual joy level.

The Lord gives you and me a gift each day. It is wrapped with wondrous beauty and tied with ribbons of joy.

Open the gift and untie your ribbons of joy!

Dear precious Lord, may we be filled and overflowing with Your love so much that it will cause others to want it too. In Jesus' name. Amen.

October 18 Read Psalm 20:15-9

HIS BANNER OVER YOU IS LOVE

Bible Thought: "He brought me to the banqueting house, and his banner over me *was* love" (Song of Solomon 2:4).

I bought a birthday banner for our growing young sons. Little did I know I would be using it for many years, first for our sons and now our grandchildren. I taped my banner to the wall many times. Needless to say, the banner is frayed and faded but I just can't throw it away. It has become a tradition in our house and the occasion is not the same without it. The "Happy Birthday" banner is a symbol of love, leaving precious memories. To me it is the "banner" of our family and represents loyalty, unconditional love and strong faith. It is a symbol of faithfulness to me.

I have another banner that is not taped on my wall but is taped on my heart and I remember it each day. God's banner reminds me that nothing can separate me from His love and I am "engraved in the palm of his hands." (Isaiah 49:16).

Let God's banner wave proudly over you. His banner is wealth far more precious than jewels.

He brings you to the "banquet room and his banner over you is love!"

"Tell others about His love and
Wave your banner today.
He will come and save you too
And wash your sins away!"

Dear Lord, You are "Jehovah Nissi, The Lord our Banner" and we can't thank You enough. Your love is forever. His name is Jesus. Amen.

October 19 Read 1 Samuel 12:22-25

I AM PRAYING FOR YOU

Bible Thought: "I thank my God upon every remembrance of you" (Philippians 1:3).

I waited in the car while my husband had an errand to do. An elderly man walking on a cane could hardly walk to the door of a store. I secretly prayed for him. Another parked his pickup and had to lean on it a while before he could make his legs work. I secretly prayed for him too. I secretly prayed for my students as they came to my classroom each day.

As my husband came out of the bank I began to thank the Lord for the time we have to pray for others. I've found that silent prayers for others does make a difference. We can pray for anyone at anytime, anywhere about anything. It can happen in a doctor's waiting room, in line at the Post Office, or waiting for a streetlight to change.

Look at those around you. There are people made in God's image and a prayer for them brings blessings not only to your well being but for those you pray for. They may never know your prayer but that's all right because God knows. Who knows what your prayers can do?

…"The effectual fervent prayer of a righteous man availeth much." (James 5:16)

Dear precious Lord, our hearts are filled with love and gratitude for Jesus, our Savior. Thank You for loving us and forgiving us. May our hearts overflow with love. In Jesus' beautiful name. Amen.

October 20 Read Mark 2:18-28

THE SABBATH WAS MADE FOR MAN

Bible Thought: "And he said unto them, 'That the Son of man is Lord also of the Sabbath.'" (Luke 6:5).

My husband and I were going to church one Sunday when we saw a random kindness scene. A lady and her three little children were standing by her flat tire. A state policeman had taken off the flat tire and was putting on the spare. What a wonderful sight. Of course I didn't where they were going but they could not of gone anywhere with a flat tire and her little children. I know the mother was ever so thankful.

The Pharisees thought everything on the Sabbath had to be stopped. Fast, wineskins, heads of grain to eat and anything they could find that was on their mind. They even thought no one could be healed on that day.

I think Sunday is a day of rest and worship. Yet if there is something that has to be fixed that is another thing.

I'm so glad we have a God who loves us so much He made every commandment governed by love.

The Sabbath was made for all.

Dear Lord, we thank You for such love. You have given us everything we have ever needed. Thank You for The Sabbath. In Jesus name. Amen.

October 21 Read Psalm 119:17-32

BIBLE'S GUIDELINES

Bible Thought: "For thou *art* my rock and my fortress; therefore for thy name's sake lead me, and guide me" (Psalm 31:3).

A friend of mine worried about her salvation. "I repent nearly every moment. Am I going to heaven?"

We helped her to see how much Jesus loved her. "Read the Bible, study and grow. That will make you be happy. Through life's journey we grow. We study the scriptures and begin to understand God's commandments. By studying the Bible the more we grow but if we avoid God's commandments we will have a restless life with no purpose."

The Bible is like a map and it leads us to our destination. Each year we want to have grown spiritually with the Bible's guidelines.

My friend is so happy now. She understands her salvation and is growing.

You can do that too!
God reached down to you and me
Is more than we can see.
For such great love at Calvary
Removed our sins and set us free.
Forever grateful we'll always be
And live with Him eternally!

Dear Lord, Thank You for giving us grace and mercy when we worry. You lead us back to You and cover us with Your wings of love. In the name of Jesus'. Amen.

October 23 Read Numbers 16:41-50

COMPLAINING IS UNGRATEFUL

Bible Thought: "Do all things without murmurings and disputings" (Philippians 2:14).

A study was conducted of fifty people who had lived over 100 years and still enjoyed a happy life. They were asked about diets, exercise and lifestyle. When a common denominator could not be found they were asked about daily living and attitudes. The majority of those interviewed said they awoke each day being grateful for another day of life. They also stated life was too short to hold grudges or spend time complaining.

We can learn a lot from these centenarians. The gift of time is a wonderful gift. Each day presents an opportunity to make a happy day by praising God and thanking Him for our many blessings.

Happy days are obtained by making others happy. All it takes is a little act of kindness…a note, a smile, an encouraging word, a pat on the back and a loving heart.

Love is a priceless gift coming from a loving God. I don't want to grieve Him by murmuring or complaining. I want to thank Him for the gift of life and I will tell Him so!

I am not what I out to be
Yet I'm not what I used to be
I will strive more to be
That which I long to be…
Like Jesus, my Savior!

Dear precious Lord, You are the reason we live, love and have joy in our soul. Thank You for the most gift in the entire world. That gift is Jesus. In His wonderful name. Amen.

October 24 Read Psalm 119:1-8

DO THE BEST YOU CAN

Bible Thought: "Meditate upon these things; give thyself wholly to them; that thy profiting may appear to all" (1 Timothy 4:15).

"I'm so glad to be back in your class." Becky said with a hug. She had moved back to our school in the spring after an absence of several months.

I discovered she had missed many important math concepts. I felt amazed when Becky asked if she could have some practice papers to take home. She brought them back all perfectly done. When I expressed surprise she had mastered such difficult concepts so quickly, she replied, "I try to do the best I can, so I study and work hard."

What an astonishing concept for one so young. This seven-year-old had demonstrated a philosophy of life for people of any age.

My sweet little Becky became my teacher and I want to be like her. The attitude and willingness to do the extra mile touched my heart. Here am I in the "Master's Classroom" and how often do I tell Him, "Thank you?" How often do I tell Him I'm thankful He stays with me in the "recesses" of my life, to help me and teach me the things I need to learn.

Every spring reminds me of Becky. I wonder where she is. Yet I know she will make it because of her outlook on life and what she said to me, "I try to do the best I can, so I study and work hard!"

Dear Lord, thank You for children. May we become like children in faith and humility.

Empower us to do the best we can. Amen.

October 25 Read Psalm 134

DON'T FORGET YOUR MANY BLESSINGS

Bible Thought: "Praise ye the LORD, O give thanks unto the LORD; for *he is* good: for his mercy *endureth* for ever" (Psalm 106:1).

Daily you and I seem to be bombarded with bad news. One would think it's terrible to be alive. Seldom do we hear about the many good things in our lives.

Every day God showers us with His goodness. I am reminded of the ten lepers in Luke 17. Jesus healed them all but only one returned to say, "Thank You." Wouldn't you think the other nine would be overjoyed with thankfulness?

Find the blessings in each day. Thank God for your bed and a roof over your head. Every night count the blessings you received that day. You will fall asleep before you have gone through your list.

Appreciate God's beauty in nature. I think New Mexico has sunrises and sunsets that cannot be equaled. Birds greet the dawn with melodious praises to their Maker. The quiet in the country at twilight is spectacular to me. God puts nature to bed with a "Holy Hush."

Friends and family are precious jewels straight from the heart of God. Please don't forget your many blessings.

It's a wonderful life.

I wouldn't have missed it for the world.

Dear precious Lord, we bless You today and every day. Words cannot express our gratitude for our many, many blessings. Thank You for Jesus, the greatest blessing.

Blessed be His name and it is that name we pray today. Amen.

October 26 Read Psalm 56:10-13

OVERCOME FEAR WITH FAITH

Bible Thought: "Be careful for nothing; but in every thing by prayer and supplication with thanksgiving let your requests be made known unto God" (Philippians 4:6).

Fear is the most destructive force I know. It destroys peace of mind...fear of failure...illness...old age...death...accidents...financial loss...the list is endless.

Let's trade our fears for faith. Know that God has plans for your life. God has an investment in you. Live one day at a time and live it to the fullest.

Settle your eternal destiny. Know that nothing can happen to you today that Jesus and you cannot handle. Hide God's Word in your heart and trust in the Lord.

When fear comes knocking at your door, hang out a sign that says, "Wrong Address. Faith Lives Here." You will have won one more battle with the enemy.

Cling to God's promises and walk upon the high places of the earth.

Your faith conquers fear!

In the darkest night
He is still there.
Come what may
He hears our prayer.

Trust in God
And you will see
Through it all
Comes victory.

So keep the faith
His laws obey.
You'll have peace,
Strength for your day!

Dear precious Lord, thank You for ever increasing faith. We are far from oppression and fear does not come near us. It's all because of Jesus. Amen.

October 27 Read Psalm 91:1-6

LET JESUS MAKE YOUR DAY

Bible Thought: "Let the words of my mouth, and the meditation of my heart, be acceptable in thy sight, O LORD, my strength, and my redeemer" (Psalm 19:14).

If someone knocked on your door today and asked, "Could I sell you some misery today? We have all kinds for sale."

Would you buy it? Of course not, but many of us including me have bought it from time to time.

Negative living doesn't work for me. I refuse to let my day be ruined by pessimism. I'm not perfect by any means but I am determined to be happy.

This is a brand new day. I want it to sparkle with verbal sunshine. Life is too short to be miserable. I want the celebration gift of life to begin for you and me. Let's enjoy God's blessings. God cares about every aspect of our lives, each detail, large or small. He is our breath and our heartbeat. He is life in abundance. With Him nothing is just happenstance...IT IS EVERTHING!.

With so many blessings how can any of us be unhappy? Even in a crisis we can find something to be thankful for. Our purpose on earth is to love God, to honor Him, to glorify and serve Him.

Let us be the good with Jesus because that will make our day.

Dear Lord, we thank You for so many blessings...so many we can't begin to count them all. May today and every day find us praising You with all our hearts. In Jesus' name.

Amen.

October 28 Read Psalm 16:7-11

LIFE IS DELICIOUS

Bible Thought: "Wait on the LORD: be of good courage, and he shall strengthen thine heart: wait, I say, on the LORD" (Psalm 27:14).

Are we aware of God's wonderful blessings in the excitement of life?

Life is music. Do we hear it? To hear the music we must take time to allow God's many blessings to reign in our hearts. He is love. He is life. He is our breath and heartbeat.

Let's find enthusiasm for life. Peace and encouragement comes with it. Our lives are strengthened as we open today's gift.

We find new concepts and ideas as we bask in the joy God freely gives. Let's be a representative of God today and every day.

I hear the music. Life is delicious!

He is with me in the sunshine. He is there in the rain.

He is there when I'm weary and in the midst of pain.

He is there in the trials when shadows block my view.

He gives me daily blessings with a day that is brand new.

He is there when clouds of sadness try to dim my life.

He is there to remind me to refrain from any strife.

He is there to provide for everything I need.

He is there to protect me and on His Word I feed.

He is there to receive me as I reach my end of days.

He is there forever and I'll always give Him praise!

Dear Lord, thank You for Your extravagant love. May we ever be aware of the many blessings You bestow. In Jesus' name. Amen.

October 29 Read Psalm 104:14-19

CELEBRATE GOD'S BEAUTY

Bible Thought: "He hath made every *thing* beautiful in his time…" (Ecclesiastes 3:11).

I love the fall season. I find it intriguing when the leaves fall because they are even more beautiful as they cling to their final beauty. They are dazzling jewels escaping from God's treasure box. The scarlet leaves, golden grain, brilliant pumpkins and shiny red apples warm my soul. I thrill to the call of wild geese as they instinctively know where God wants them to be. Beauty of cottonwood leaves wear golden crowns looking up to heaven. Ornamental pear trees grace the landscape with deep red leaves. Farmers' fields display God's faithfulness. Colors of rich brown earth and golden grain bestow a harvest with God's artistic landscape.

Once again, seed has occurred, bringing the assurance of God's promises. (Genesis 8:22) The earth has provided its fruit in all of its beauty. What started as a seed has now grown to maturity bringing a hundred fold return.

I pray I will never take God's many blessings for granted. Each day and each season is a gift. God's beauty is all around. Celebrate Jesus. He made it all possible. Tell Him of your love and thank Him for His beautiful gifts.

Let's find a celebration of beauty in every day for God has made us glad!

Dear precious Lord, our hearts are filled with overflowing gratitude for Your many wonderful blessings. Thank You for the beauty of the earth and its fruit. May we be just as happy in our spirits. In that lovely name of Jesus. Amen.

October 30 Read Malachi 3:3-6

LIFE IS FULL OF CHANGES

Bible Thought: "Heaven and earth shall pass away: but my words shall not pass away" (Mark 13:33).

Have you ever returned to your childhood home and found it to be almost unrecognizable? The tree where Emmitt carved our names so many years ago is gone.

Every time we drive by my grandmother's house I can almost smell fresh baked gingerbread. I can almost hear her singing about the wondrous love of Jesus.

Life is a growth process. It is a natural occurrence and brings many changes. Since life is a series of adjustments the real "Good News" is there someone who never changes. "Jesus Christ the same yesterday, and to-day, and for ever" (Hebrews 13:8).

He is faithful and true. It is such a comfort for me to know the same God who guided Abraham, Isaac and Jacob centuries ago guides me today.

Although we cannot stop physical changes in or around us we do have the power to change our attitudes. We either allow problems to cut us down or bring us closer to God because He will never change and He will never abandon us.

God's children are not defeated and they will not quit. We are stubborn in our faith. We will not give up or shut up because one day we are "going up!"

Dear precious Lord, we're so glad You made us. You give life abundantly here and eternal life in heaven. Thank You for life's purpose. It is the joy of the ages! In Jesus' beautiful name. Amen.

October 31 Read Ephesians 5:6-11

MAKE A DIFFERENCE

Bible Thought: "Then spake Jesus again unto them, saying, I am the light of the world: he that followeth me shall not walk in darkness, but shall have the light of life" (John 8:12).

Recently I was asked to be a judge of Halloween costumes worn by children. I graciously declined, explaining I could not violate my conscience. I further explained I didn't want to impose my views on anyone but I had to stand by my convictions.

I know some Christian businessmen who lost money because they refused to sell profanity tapes.

I read where many citizens protested the sale of pornography in their small town and the pornography was removed.

What a difference people can make. One by one we can take a stand. We let our voice be heard. We make our vote count by voting for someone who honors God. We demand integrity from public officials. We object to questionable concepts in school programs. We call for accountability in leadership.

Little by little and one by one we make a difference in our world.

Make a difference today and help change the world.

Dear Lord, grant us the courage and boldness to take a stand for righteousness. May we stand strong in You and the power of Your might. In Jesus' mighty name. Amen.

NOVEMBER

November 1 Read 1 Corinthians 16:20-24

A KISS TOWARD GOD

Bible Thought: "For thou *art* great, and doest wondrous things: thou *art* God alone" (Psalm 86:10).

I had the privilege of witnessing an unusual baptism. When the lady came up out of the water she began to cry uncontrollably. The revelation and understanding of her commitment had touched her innermost being. To me, this personal tender moment became a kiss toward God.

I had a similar response one day while watching TV. A singer singing my favorite praise hymn touched my heart in a special way. Tears streamed down her face as she sang from the depths of her soul. I delighted in her song as spontaneous praise from both of us had drawn a kiss toward God.

We have special moments in our lives that move us to overwhelming joy. These heavenly moments bring a realization of God's beauty around us. That beauty yearns to be acknowledged.

God's lullaby of quiet's stillness tells nature "good-night." We tell our children "good-night." Let's give a prayer and kiss toward God too

Enjoying each day with gratitude is a kiss toward our Maker.

Give a kiss toward God today!

Dear precious Lord we just came to love You today. You are the greatest thing that ever happened to us and we honor and praise You. We want to stay in Your presence forever. In Jesus' beautiful name. Amen.

November 2 Read Ruth 4:13-17

THE BRIDEGROOM COMETH

Bible Thought: "Turn, O backsliding children, saith the LORD; for I am married unto you: and I will take you one of a city, and two of a family, and I will bring you to Zion"(Jeremiah 3:14).

Cody's beautiful bride walked down the aisle holding her father's arm. Tears of joy streamed down each face. More tears came when my husband gave a "Grandfather's Blessing."

Cody and Ashley's wedding, sealed and honored by God, brought blessings to all of us. The couple pledged a lifetime of devotion to God and to each other.

In a sense when we accept Jesus we do the same thing. We are faithful to Him throughout life's journey. God does not break His covenant. I think of it as His heavenly covenant marriage.

Making God the third partner in any marriage makes a happy home on earth and an eternal one hereafter. People in these kind of marriages are blessed for generations.

If you are planning to be married or if you are already married, devote to and delight in your marriage with Jesus.

When you meet Jesus in heaven you will attend "The Marriage Supper of the Lamb."

While on earth you will also have a happy marriage!

Dear Lord, thank You for Your plan of the family and the blessings that follow those who honor You. Most of all thank You for our heavenly wonderful bridegroom. His name is Jesus. Amen.

November 3 Read Psalm 92:12-15

LESSONS FROM MY TREE

Bible Thought: "In the midst of the street of it, and on either side of the river, *was there* the tree of life, which bare twelve *manner of* fruits, *and* yielded her fruit every month: and the leaves of the tree *were* for the healing of the nations" (Revelation 22:2).

It takes a long time for a tree to grow but only minutes to cut it down. I can do the same thing in my relationships with others using cutting remarks.

A tree requires care for its well-being. That's a lesson for me in my spiritual life. God's Word provides spiritual health and nourishment for my every day living.

A tree is known by its fruit. If I produce bad fruit I will bring grief and heartache to those I love. I must remember as long as I am growing I am fresh and green but if I stop growing I could become rotten. That lesson tells me no one wants bad fruit from others.

Ecclesiastes 11:3 states an unforgettable truth about trees: "If' the clouds be full of rain, they empty *themselves* upon the earth: and if the tree fall toward the south, or toward the north, in the place where the tree falleth, there it shall be" This tells me that at the point my life ends, I have forever sealed my destiny.

The most important tree of all is the "Tree of Life." Revelation 22 paints a beautiful picture of those who will live with God forever where there is no more death or decay, no tears or sorrow, no heartaches or pain.

I want to eat the fruit of the "Tree of Life" and live forever.

You come too!

Dear Lord, we thank You for the blessings of trees and their many uses on planet earth. Most of all we thank You for the "Tree of Life" and the eternal blessings it bestows. Amen.

November 4 Read 2 Timothy 4:6-8

THE MASTER PAINTER

Bible Thought: "Precious in the sight of the LORD *is* the death of his saints" (Psalm 116:15).

My art teacher made her heavenly flight today. For many she not only taught me to oil paint but taught me how to see with my heart.

She taught me something else. Her love and faith in the Lord made every painting session a delight. She was God's gift to me and I treasure the time we had together.

I went to Virginia's funeral with sadness but I came away with joy. The minister's message thrilled my heart. "Virginia is not dead. She is alive in the Kingdom of God."

A friend remarked to me, "Being an artist can you just imagine how she must be enjoying the beauty of heaven?"

Heaven is a beautiful place, reserved by God for those who love Him. We will have no more pain, no more sorrow or heartaches, no more trials…just joyful bliss that permeates the halls of heaven. It's a Kingdom of love, peace and beauty. We will see our Savior who died for you and me. I will not be able to praise Him enough, but I'm going to try.

Virginia is now with the Master Painter. Will you paint your life in such a way you can be with Him too?

Dear precious Lord, thank You for life beyond the grave. Teach us to number our days. May we live them wisely and have no regrets. Thank You for our risen Lord. In his beautiful wonderful name… JESUS. Amen.

November 5 Read James 1:16-19

REJOICE AND BE HAPPY

Bible Thought: "The LORD thy God in the midst of thee *is* mighty; he will save, he will rejoice over thee with joy; he will rest in his love, he will joy over thee with singing" (Zephaniah 3:17).

Have you ever noticed how many times the words "joy, joyful, rejoice and rejoicing" appear in the Bible? It's because the gospel is indeed "Good News."

Joy is a fruit of the spirit. Happiness depends on circumstances, but joy rises up in the believer even in adversity. It's easy to rejoice when all is well. The real test comes in rejoicing in the hard places. Joy does not come from worry, fretting and stewing around. The enemy would have us walk in defeat, depression, discouragement, misery and woe. Who could have joy in the midst of that?

Being joyful in every situation lowers blood pressure, cholesterol and friction of every kind. Joy reduces stress. Joy anticipates hope and optimism. Joy attracts others and displays faith.

To make your day arise each morning say, "This is the day that the LORD has made. Let us rejoice and be glad today." (Psalm 118:24).

Rejoice your way through life. You will be blessed and highly favored.

"The best is yet to be!"

Dear Lord, we rejoice today and every day for Your great love, for Jesus and salvation. May we bring the joy of Your love to everyone we meet today. In Jesus' beautiful name

Amen.

November 6 Read Psalm 37:23-26

THE BEAUTIFUL YEARS

Bible Thought: "Beautiful for situation, the joy of the whole earth, *is* mount Zion, *on* the sides of the north, the city of the great King" (Psalm 48:2).

I call the 60s, 70s, 80s, and even 90s "the beautiful years." What is more beautiful than a precious older saint whose life has been lived with loyalty, righteousness, courage and love?

Those saints having walked with God a lifetime with triumphs and victories have a way of mellowing. Their wisdom and past experiences speak volumes of God's faithfulness. They know who they are in Him and "the love of God is shed abroad in their hearts." (Romans 5:5).

Society puts a premium on youth, strength and abilities, but God sees a life lived for Him as precious and still bearing fruit.

With autumn and its beauty we begin to see the true colors of leaves. As the flames of scarlet and burnished gold leaves decorate the landscape, I am reminded of the true colors of life. Those who have followed the Lord are even more beautiful in older age. They have painted lives with colors of sacrifice and service. Their strokes of magnificence are imprinted upon our hearts.

Is it any wonder I call the later years, "The Beautiful Years?"

Dear wonderful God, thank You for the life You have given us to live and the time to live it. We would not have missed it for the world. May we realize as we grow older "the best is yet to be" because we will be with You forever. In that name above all names. His name is Jesus. Amen.

November 7 Read 2 Corinthians 4:15-18

GOODBYE HERE IS HELLO THERE

Bible Thought: "Therefore *we are* always confident, knowing that, whilst we are at home in the body, we are absent from the Lord" (2 Corinthians 5:6).

Someone is waiting for someone to leave or someone to arrive I thought. We were in an airport terminal. I looked around at the teary faces of people waiting to say their last goodbye. I also watched those happy expectant people waiting to hug a loved one and to say "hello." People arrived and departed. With apparent tears all revealed love from the heart.

When a child of God goes home it is a "goodbye" here but a "hello" there. Can you imagine the homecoming of God's child, because of Jesus it will be a glad reunion.

He is the Comforter, Savior, Redeemer, Protector, Healer, Friend and I could go on and on.

When our middle son said to me when he left home, "Don't cry Mom, a Christian never says goodbye for the last time." He is right.

What a day that will be saying "Goodbye" here and "Hello" there!

"That He should die for me
On a cross at Calvary,
For me to be forever free
To live with Him eternally!"

Dear precious Lord, thank You for our blessed hope of seeing Jesus face to face. Time will be no more but one eternal day. Our gratitude is so great we can hardly express it.

In Jesus' wonderful name. Amen.

November 8 Read Revelation 21:1-4

HEAVEN

Bible Thought: "But as it is written Eye hath not seen, nor ear heard, neither have entered into the heart of man, the things which God hath prepared for them that love him" (1 Corinthians 2:9).

Think of the happiest day of your life. Heaven will be better than that. Think of the most inspiring moment of your life. Heaven will be more than that. Think of the most beautiful sight you have ever seen. Heaven will be more beautiful. Think of your heart's desire. Heaven will fulfill that and even more.

For the Christian the best is yet to be. Whatever joy or ecstasy you have experienced in this life will not be compared to heaven.

Dear reader, if you have given God your life you can look forward to the best thing that could ever happen to you.

"Fill me with your Spirit Lord
And with your words of grace
May my thoughts and actions
Spread love in every place.

Help me to remember
The debt you paid for me.
May I always honor you
For the gift of Calvary.

Before you now I humbly bow,
With all my heart of praise.
I pledge my life into your hands
To love you all my days!"

Dear Lord, eternity isn't long enough to thank You for Jesus, our Savior. We thank You today with all that is within us. In His beautiful name. Amen.

November 9 Read Psalm 103:1-4

THE CROWN OF LIFE

Bible Thought: "Henceforth there is laid up for me a crown of righteousness, which the Lord, the righteous judge, shall give me at that day: and not to me only, but unto all them also that love his appearing" (2 Timothy 4:8).

The crowning of my beautiful granddaughter as Homecoming Queen brought tears to my eyes. To say I am proud of my granddaughter is putting it mildly, yet I am filled with even more pride because of her Christian witness to her schoolmates. She stands firm in her convictions.

In ancient times and today "doing what is right in their own eyes" seems to prevail. (Judges 21:15). Yet sin is not an island and always affects others.

In contrast, the Christian is crowned with joy, righteousness and life. Obedience to God's commandments bring peace in our commitment, physically and spiritually. Jesus was crowned with thorns for our salvation. We owe our all to Jesus. He has crowned us with so many good things and yet there is another crown for those who love Him, the "Crown of Life."

What a wonderful "Coronation Day" that will be.

You come too!

Thank You Lord

Thank You Lord, for the crown You wore to transform me,

For the stripes You bore to heal me,

For the blood You shed to save me.

The pain and shame, I was to blame

I love You Lord, with all my strength.

Dear Precious Lord, thank You for Jesus who bore a "crown of thorns" that we might have a "crown of life." We give You praise and glory now and forever. In Jesus' name. Amen.

November 10 Read Mark 8:5-9

HAVE A COMPASSIONATE HEART

Bible Thought: "Great *are* thy tender mercies, O LORD: quicken me according to thy judgments" (Psalm 119:156).

"I'll work mam, for anything to eat. I've been walking several miles and I am hungry." These words were spoken many times during the depression. My grandmother lived by the highway and shared food with lots of people. She shared without requirements.

Today many charities offer food for hurting people. Yes, people have compassion and the ultimate compassion belongs to our Lord. He met the needs of three thousand who needed food. Even so, the Pharisees complained.

Doubts and anxiety reminds me of the Pharisees today. Do you ever wonder if God will meet your needs? Do you feel you have been forgotten? Do you think you are just a tiny speck on planet earth and God doesn't know where you live? Not so!

In this time of economic hardships worries seem to reign but God knows your address. He looks down at you with great compassion. Nothing is impossible with Him. He knows your needs and He is faithful in His Word.

His compassion reaches out to you today. Thank the One who sacrificed for you and be compassionate in your heart too!

Dear God, we thank You for Your Word. Empower us to spread Your love and compassion to others. In the name above all names. His name is Jesus. Amen.

November 11 Read Matthew 18:1-5

THE FAITH OF CHILDREN

Bible Thought: "But Jesus said, 'Suffer little children, and forbid them not, to come unto me: for of such is the kingdom of heaven'" (Matthew 19:14).

My students became my teacher. Those little people taught me many things about life. I shall always be grateful for the lessons they gave me, interwoven with love, faith, hope, courage and forgiveness.

"It's what on the inside that counts. To stay out of trouble, follow the rules. When you smile it 'rains' sunshine. Everyone gets a turn. Being mad at someone will make you sick. Make it right before night. If you do something wrong somebody will always find out. Look through someone else's glasses. It changes how you see things. You can't listen and talk at the same time. Holding hands with someone keeps you from getting lost. Listening is better than talking."

I share just a few of these thoughts from little people but aren't these applications of life? Children may be little but their attitudes are amazing. All of us could benefit from their "out of the mouths of babes" principles.

Children keep life in perspective. Their innocence brings hope for the future. At the beginning of school each year I wonder where they are and how they are, and yes, I claim them for the Kingdom in my prayers.

We can learn a lot from children.

Dear Lord, thank You for children. May we become as a little child in our faith. May we trust You in all our ways. We praise You today for Jesus, our Savior. In His mighty name. Amen.

November 12 Read Joshua 6:12-16

A LAST TRUMPET SOUND

Bible Thought: "In a moment, in the twinkling of an eye, at the last trump: for the trumpet shall sound, and the dead shall be raised incorruptible, and we shall be changed"(1Corinthians 15:52).

One of our fondest memories is that of our youngest son playing his trumpet with the High School marching band.

At our wedding of our grandson Cody, the trumpet was blown before the "Here comes the Bride" rendition on the organ.

In Bible times rams' horns were mostly used as trumpets although special trumpets were made from beaten silver. Many references in the Bible refer to trumpets. Trumpets were blown when kings were proclaimed and on other important biblical events. Trumpet blasts in ancient times reminded Israel of God's protection.

The trumpet has been a favorite instrument in our family and I think God must like trumpets too. So many scriptures are mentioned many times in the Bible. "And he shall send his angels with a great sound of a trumpet, and they shall gather together his elect from the four winds, from one end of heaven to the other" (Matthew 24:31).

Another scripture among others is Revelation 1:10, "I was in the Spirit on the Lord's day, and heard behind me a great voice, as of a trumpet."

One day a trumpet will sound, announcing the arrival of Jesus, our King. Those in Him will be caught up into the heavenlies where we will live with Him forever.

Oh happy day. Let's listen for the trumpet!

Dear wonderful Lord, thank You for beautiful clouds and trumpets that remind us of Jesus coming back for us. In His name. Amen.

November 13 Read Matthew 28:18-20

GO TELL IT EVERYWHERE

Bible Thought: "And I, if be lifted up from the earth, will draw all *men* unto me" (John 12:32).

Many special days are noted on our calendars. However, everyday is a day to recognize, appreciate and honor our Lord. I wonder if we realize the depth of His sacrifice. The agony, pain and stress had to be more than the mind can understand. Yet Jesus paid it all for you and me. He died for us for us to live for Him.

We are ambassadors for Jesus on earth. In a way we are aliens in this temporary journey of life.

Let us ask ourselves, "Will someone go to heaven because of me or will someone miss heaven because of me?

Because of Jesus mankind can be reconciled with God. It's the greatest news of the ages.

Tell someone today of Jesus 'great sacrifice.

"I will serve Jesus all my days,

With every joyful sound,

For the sacrifice He made,

Such great love I've found!"

Dear precious Lord, thank You for the sacrificial gift of Your Son. We will tell the "Good News" everywhere. In Jesus' name. Amen.

November 14 Read Psalm 21:21

LIVE A BLESSED LIFE

Bible Thought: "He that followeth after righteousness and mercy findeth life, righteousness, and honour" (Proverbs 21:21).

Time is too precious to waste. Do we make the moments count? Time spent worrying about tomorrow or regretting yesterday drains our life of the "now." The gift of life is squandered and wasted by dwelling on the past and worrying about the future.

Let's not lose a minute of life by being angry with anyone. Forgive offenses. Make things right before night. Be grateful for being alive. Open your heart to the Holy Spirit and allow God's love to flow.

Without repentance there is no forgiveness.

Without a cross there is no crown.

Without death there is no resurrection.

Without Jesus there is no salvation.

Without salvation there is no heaven.

Without heaven our lives our meaningless.

Begin to live today. Jesus paid the price for you and me. We should be happy as Kings. Let's live a blessed life.

Dear God, who is like unto You O God? You are everything. You are our all in all. Without You we are just a blob of clay. We arise today with exceeding joy and thanksgiving that You are our God, the One and only true God. In Jesus' most beautiful name. Amen.

November 15 Read Isaiah 41:10-13

YEA! WE WIN!

Bible Thought: "I press toward the mark for the prize of the high calling of God in Christ Jesus" (Philippians 3:14).

Does life ever seem to be one battle after another? Do you manage to survive one hurdle only to be confronted by another one? Well, I have "Good News!"

An airplane takes off against the wind and lands against the wind. With Jesus we "take off" and "land" in the storms of life.

Eagles spread their wings while the wind and storms carry them above the conflict. You and I can do that too. Let Jesus have your burden.

The bumblebee does not know his big body and tiny little wings are supposed to make it impossible for him to fly. Guess what? He flies anyway! His secret? "With God all things are possible." (Luke 1:37). That's why it is always too soon to quit in this race of life.

We have a God that planned your life and He wants the highest good for you. Trust in Him. Cancel all negatives. A stubborn faith in the midst of hard circumstances bring you to victory.

Be encouraged today. Set your face like a flint and say, "Life, here I come and I'm a winner."

How do I know all of this? I've read the last page!

Dear God thank You for the victory in Jesus. Thank You for Your everlasting love. Thank You for the celestial home to be with You forever. In Jesus' beautiful name. Amen.

November 16 Read Psalm 65:11-13

EVERY LIFE HAS A HARVEST

Bible Thought: *"Then* shall the earth yield her increase; *and* God, *even* our own God, shall bless us" (Psalm 67:6).

I love fall with its crisp air. It makes look everything so pretty. Golden grain decorates Gods' exquisite landscape and the chorus of "America the Beautiful" echoes in my mind.

Each day you and I are planting seeds. Those seeds eventually bring a harvest. Someone has said, "Bad seeds turn into weeds." To me, the application can be physical and spiritual. Bad seeds can plant on people.

If I am to reflect a godly lifestyle it means that every day I must be on guard for those subtle, sabotaging sins. "Little things" can be glossed over and overlooked. BeforeI know it they are giant weeds.

The Bible warns me about the "little foxes that spoil the vines" (Song of Solomon 2:15). I need to be careful about what I hear or see. If I let my guard down my harvest does not go well. I must guard my words because long before my harvest comes the seeds are growing.

The Bible is my blueprint for a successful harvest. I have a responsibility, not only to my children and husband but also to the world. My life is a book many people will read.

Sow godly seeds in your life to reap great dividends in a bountiful harvest.

Dear Lord, thank You for Your Word. Through Your Words we plant seeds of righteousness, hope, love and peace. Thank You for the beautiful Prince of Peace. His name is Jesus. Amen.

November 17 Read 2 Timothy:1:6

A PRAYER FOR OUR MILITARY AND VETERANS

Bible Thought: "And he increased his people greatly; and made them stronger than their enemies" (Psalm 105:24).

"Dear God,
Please keep our soldiers safe. Keep their loved ones and families in Your loving care. May our love and prayers surround them with firm affirmations of strength and strong faith. May all of us be quick to express our gratitude to every military member and soldier. May we never take them for granted.

Bless them in every facet of their lives. Help them to hide beneath Your wings. Grant them the peace that passes all understanding. Give them wisdom and guard each step they take. May their feet be as hinds' feet, to walk upon the high places of the earth.

Please bestow peace on those loved ones at home. Send comfort and assurance for the many sacrifices their families make. Remind all of us to remember the high price of freedom.

May the power of our prayers follow and pursue our service men and women In that name above all names…His name is Jesus. Amen."

Dear precious Lord, thank You for Your ever-abiding presence. You will never leave nor forsake us. We acknowledge our daily dependence upon You. Thank You for Your gracious mercy. Most of all, thank You for Jesus, the hope of all mankind. Amen.

November 18 Revelation 21:23-27

YOU CHOOSE YOUR DESTINY

Bible Thought: "For he looked for a city which hath foundations, whose builder and maker *is* God: (Hebrews: 11:10).

Each one of us have been given a chance to live…a time frame…a span of living…a destiny. My great grandmother was one of those. She had eleven children. She cooked on a wood burning stove. She had to haul water and use a rub board to do laundry. Despite many hardships, she was happy, loving and God-fearing. Knowing her Lord and Savior she knew without a doubt she had chosen her destiny. She kept her eyes on Jesus every day of her life. How do I know this? I have her Bible, her book of poetry and some journals.

None of us take a trip without having a destination in mind. We make many plans and preparations along the way. We study the map, tune up our car and on we go.

Our journey in this life is similar by comparison. If we choose heaven as our goal, then we study our road map, the Bible. We follow the guidelines and instructions for victorious living. We maintain and guard our temples. We travel cautiously, avoiding pitfalls and potholes.

It is sobering indeed to know we alone determine our course and final habitation of eternity.

You can know where you are going.

Choose the right destiny today.

Dear Lord, how we thank You for making a way to save us through Jesus. We will praise You throughout endless ages. In that mighty name of Your Son. Amen.

November 19 Read 2 Corinthians 4:15-18

ALL OUR CONFLICTS PAST

Bible Thought: "And God shall wipe away all tears from their eyes, and there shall be no more death, neither sorrow, nor crying, neither shall there be any more pain: for the former things are passed away" (Revelation 21:4).

Do your ever experience conflict? Does life seem to be one long battle after another? Do you grow weary in always trying to be a peacemaker? Do you wonder if things will ever change? The answer is a resounding "Yes!" When Jesus comes upon the scene, situations change and people change.

With Jesus you can walk through any battle and be victorious. He is the cutting edge in any circumstance. Nothing is impossible to you with Jesus by your side. He is the "Light" in a dark world of sin. He is the hope in the midst of despair. He is healer to the broken-hearted. He is the Balm of Gilead to life's wounds.

We are in a battle in this temporary journey on the earth. It is a fight to the finish. It is wonderful news to know Jesus is in the midst of the battle with you, and because of that, you come out a winner!

On that great day when we meet Him face to face, all our conflicts will be past. Meanwhile down here we win. I've read the last page of the book.

"With Jesus there is hope.
Hope beyond in the grave.
Life is short at best,
There are souls to save.
So let us work together,
Numbering our days
Making every moment count
While giving Him the praise!"

Dear Lord, how we praise You today for Your faithfulness.

November 20 Read Judges 6:14-16

INSIGNIFICANT PEOPLE

Bible Thought: "And Moses said unto the LORD, O my Lord, I am not eloquent, neither heretofore nor since thou hast spoken unto thy servant but I *am* slow of speech, and of a slow tongue" (Exodus 4:10).

God uses insignificant people to do great things. Gideon tried to tell God he wasn't much. So did Moses, but God takes our willing hearts and enables us to accomplish His purposes.

Time after time, the Israelites wanted to leave God's way and pursue their own way. The results were disastrous, but God in His mercy listens to the repentant heart.

Gideon's army was only 300 but 120,000 of the enemy's swordsmen had fallen.

When you have God on your side, that is all you need. With God's help the weakness becomes strong. In God there is nothing that cannot be accomplished. There is no any place for fear in God's Army. God's soldiers are alert and full of faith.

Numbers and size are insignificant. Faith in God is what is significant.

Do you sometimes feel insignificant for God to use? Every deed, every kind word and every thought of others makes you very "significant!"

Dear Lord, thank You for rising up strong in us. Thank You our weakness is Your strength. We praise and love You today and every day. In Jesus' wonderful name. Amen.

November 21 Read John 4:10-14

PARCHED DRY LAND

Bible Thought: "For I will pour water upon him that is thirsty, and floods upon the dry ground: I will pour my spirit upon thy seed, and my blessing upon thine offspring" (Isaiah 44:3).

My husband tied his windmills off. He wanted his tanks to dry out so he could clean them. The metal tanks had an overflow hose which made a little pond. The tanks dried up and so did the pond. We were already in a drought. The pond had been an oasis, a refreshing spot for wildlife. Now they suffered and when crows started their nest in the silenced windmill…that was the last straw.

"Forget it!" my husband exclaimed. "I'd rather see life than this dead barren land."

Instantly I felt in my heart this very thing could happen to people too. Neglecting God's Word can leave a dry parched land in the lives of people. Our souls thirst for the "Living Water." That water brings life, peace and refreshment.

Emmitt turned on his windmill and in our windy country it didn't take long to have a lovely, thriving pond again.

It's a real joy to see the quail come for water in the cool of the evening. Deer and antelope tracks tell us "Thank you."

Now it is an oasis of living water not a dry parched land.

Studying your Bible gives you "Living Water" and you won't be dry.

"Thank You Father, for the Living Water that satisfies our bodies and souls. In Jesus' wonderful name. Amen.

November 22 Read 2 Chronicles 32:19-21

SEE WITH EYES OF FAITH

Bible Thought: "Now faith is the substance of things hope for, the evidence of things not seen" (Hebrews 11:1).

Sennacherib made a fatal mistake. He spoke against, even insulted the Lord and His servants. Sennacherib's men outnumbered Hezekiah and his forces. He blocked the stream and threatened to make war. He had not thought about Hezekiah seeing with eyes of faith.

Numbers meant nothing to Hezekiah as long as he had God on his side. Hezekiah did what he could in preparing for the battle and then he left the rest to God.

As a result, the Lord delivered Hezekiah and the people.

The same example applies to us today. We do what we can and then leave the rest to God. That is "seeing with eyes of faith."

This principle applies in any area of our lives, at home, work, in a crisis, an emergency or anything else that comes against us. We need this principle working in our lives. Seeing with eyes of faith enables the runner to break the tape at the finish line. Believers have the "cutting edge."

God is moved by faith.

See with eyes of faith today!

Dear Lord, may we have ever increasing faith. Empower us to stand strong in You, knowing that we only have to stand still. In that name above all names, Jesus. Amen.

November 23 Read Joshua 14:10-12

REAL BEAUTY

Bible Thought: "They shall still bring forth fruit in old age; they shall be fat and flourishing" (Psalm 92:14).

A prevailing concept exists in our society. It is the belief the very young and very old are expendable. It is called "pro-choice" and "euthanasia." I disagree! Only God decides the time of death. ("Thou shalt not kill.").

Who can measure the value of that unborn what some call a "fetus?" It's a baby. Think about an innocent little baby and think about how horrible it is to be aborted.

How about older people? Who can measure the wealth of wisdom and judgment of an older person? If you want to see real beauty, look into the faces of babies and older saints who have lived their lives in Jesus. The real secret is their beauty of the heart.

Those who want abortion I wonder if they are glad their mother didn't abort.

The older are never too old, to love, laugh or to pray.

We need them...little ones and older ones. There is something valuable about every person.

"And whosoever shall offend one of *these* little ones that believe in me, it is better for him that a millstone were hanged about his neck, and he were cast into the sea" (Mark 9:42).

"Hearken unto thy father that begat thee, and despise not thy mother when she is old" (Proverbs 23:22).

Dear precious Lord, thank You for the time we have had to live and the strength You impart to us. May we go forward each day with a renewed zest for living to share Your marvelous love. In that beautiful name of Jesus. Amen.

November 24 Read Psalm 139:1-6

THE GOD WHO SEES

I grow a little weary of hearing what consensual adults do is their own business. It is as if no one else knows, but there is One who does. There is One who sees.

Instead of trusting God to work things out, Sarah took matters in her own hands and then blamed Hagar. She had Hagar sent away. Yet God saw Hagar's condition and sent an angel to minister to her.

In Hebrews, "El Roi," means ""The God who sees. Whatever pain, sorrow and suffering we have God is always there. God sees those with a hurting repentant heart.

God is all powerful. Earth is not too big for Him. No one gets by. God sees everything. What a great comfort for His children.

The good news of all time is Jesus' precious blood removes sins from those who turn to Him. He removes them "as far as the east is from the west."

God sees. God helps. God delivers.

The God who sees is on our side.

That makes us a winner.

Dear wonderful Lord, thank You for seeing us. Thank You for engraving us in the palm of Your hand. You are mindful of us. Teach us how to love You. You are beautiful. In Jesus' name. Amen.

November 25 Read The Song Of Solomon 8:6-7

REQUIRE AS A NECESSITY

Bible Thought: "But if from thence thou shalt seek the LORD thy God, thou shalt find him, if thou seek him with all thy heart and with all thy soul" (Deuteronomy 4:29).

My husband has taught me a lot about God's love. Emmitt loves me with all his being. In fact, he wrote in a card on our anniversary: "I need you as I need food and water to sustain me."

If a man can feel that passionately about a woman, how much more do we need God for daily survival. He is our spiritual food and "Living Water." Including Him in every area is an absolute necessity. This means He is our constant companion, our forever friend. He is our wisdom and counsel. We read, study and meditate upon His Word. We are totally dependent upon Him. Our lives revolve around Him. In Him, we live, move and have our being. He gives purpose and fills our days with gladness. He is our hope and stay, the glory and the lifter of our head.

He is a necessity for our lives and without Him our lives are worthless.

Require as a necessity the Lord in Your life.

"The name of the Lord is a strong tower. I run to it and I am safe.

Though the mountains crumble and fall into the sea, I will not be alarmed.

I dwell in the secret place of the Most High and I dwell under His shadow.

I will rejoice in my Savior for He has made me glad. Let the winds blow.

Let the storms rage. They don't bother me for I'm safe within His love.

That love keeps me and guides me safely home
I will praise My Lord for evermore."

Dear wonderful God, we humbly come before You, seeking You with every fiber of our being. Thank You for revealing Your great love. May we return that love every second of our lives. In Jesus' beautiful name. Amen.

November 26 Read 2 Kings 16:1-4

NO REGRETS

Bible Thought: ""The fear of the wicked, it shall come upon him: but the desire of the righteous shall be granted" (Proverbs 10:24).

The Bible contains many stories of people whose lives ended with many regrets. King Ahaz was so evil he even sacrificed his own son to pagan gods. Jezebel, the most wicked woman ever, had influence upon Athaliah and Jehoram, leading to Judah's downfall. Jehoram died a painful death to no one's regret.

I read a statement by a famous heart surgeon: "Unbelievers fear death and with good reason, while the Christian looks forward to eternal life."

This leaves a choice. You can have peace or your fear. You can live your life with a hope and a future or you can live a life of sin to eternal destruction.

Living a God-fearing and God-honoring life reaps great benefits in this life and in the life to come.

Ask Jesus to be the Lord of your life today. Repent of all sin. Be a new creature. Serve Him all of your days. When you breathe your last breath your will have no regrets!

Dear Lord, thank You for the power to live victoriously in this life. Thank You for Jesus, who conquered death for us. Thank You for the Comforter who guides us. Thank You for our heavenly home where we will sing Your praises forever. In Jesus' marvelous name. Amen.

November 27 Read Numbers 11:4-10

THANKFULNESS: A WAY OF LIFE

Bible Thought: "Rejoice evermore" (1 Thessalonians 5:16).

The Israelites could only remember the Egyptian food when they complained about "manna." They forgot about what they had to endure physically to eat "leeks and garlic." Somehow the miracles and blessings God had given obliterated from their minds.

How could they have forgotten the Red Sea parting, the "cloud by day" or "the pillar of fire by night?"

Every day let us realize how really blessed we are. Thankfulness and faith moves us into action. Gratitude enables us to keep on keeping on.

Thankfulness is shown by the way we live our lives. Witnessing and sharing God's glory shines light in a dark world.

A life of thankfulness never takes God's loving care for granted.

"Thank You Lord, for enduring pain, every shame, ever stain, for cleansing me, healing me, loving me.

Blessed be your name!"

Dear precious Lord, we praise and thank You today for Your many blessings. For the gift of life, we thank You. For family and friends, for food and shelter. Lord we thank You. For Jesus, we especially thank You. May we thank You with every breath and every heartbeat. In Jesus' mighty name, that name above all names. Amen.

November 28 Read Colossians 1:12-16

AREN'T YOU GLAD YOU'RE ALIVE?

Bible Thought: "We give thanks to God and the Father of our Lord Jesus Christ, praying always for you" (Colossians 1:3).

Aren't you glad you are alive? Can you hardly contain the joy of knowing your birth was planned by God? He has a special plan for your life. Isn't it just too wonderful knowing He will never leave or forsake His children?

The promise of spending eternity with Him makes every day living an exciting adventure.

Give thanks for the freedom to live in the greatest land on earth. This freedom has been bought with love and sacrifice.

I'm thankful God has given each one of us a measure of faith. Faith believes in the ultimate goodness of life. Faith forges straight ahead, knowing with God "all things are possible."

Most of all, I'm thankful God sent Jesus. Life after death would be eternal torment in a place separated from God. God is love and that's where I want to be.

Love is the twinkle in my husband's eye when he holds my hand. Love is hugging my sons as far as I can reach. Love is holding my grandchildren.

Love is saying "I love you" to the special people in my life.

Think of all the things you are thankful for and be blessed.

Dear Lord, our hearts overflow with gratitude for Your great love and blessings, so new every morning. Teach us how to love You more. You are our God and we will ever praise You. Amen.

November 29 Read Song of Solomon 8:6-7

LOVE, A PRICELESS GIFT

Bible Thought: "He brought me to the banqueting house, and his banner over me was love" (Song of Solomon 2:4).

I heard a touching story. The dear couple's long time friends were dying all around them. They realized their days were numbered too. They didn't have much in the way of worldly possessions, but they wanted what they had to go to their children. They shared this thought with one of their sons one day.

"Mom, Dad, you have already given me everything I have ever needed and it will last me a lifetime."

What a legacy. Would that all children could say the same about their parents. True love is a lasting value. All the money in the world can never buy it.

This kind of love makes the blood of Jesus so precious. He voluntarily died on a cross for you and me. He had us in mind and heart when He went to Calvary. Can you imagine a love so great it would endure pain and agony for the sins of the world?

Jesus' love paid the price for us to live with Him forever and ever. Will you accept so great a love?

It is His great love…a priceless gift!

Dear precious Lord, how we praise and thank You today for Jesus, a gift so priceless we could never ever thank You enough. It is the gift of life, physically and eternally. In Jesus' wonderful name. Amen.

November 30 Read Deuteronomy 28:1-6

CHOOSE TO BE A WINNER

Bible Thought: "Order my steps in thy word: and let not an iniquity have dominion over me: (Psalm 119:133).

One of the greatest revelations of my life occurred the day I realized God created me to be a winner. He doesn't create anyone to be a loser. Those caught up in the trap of rejection, self-pity, condemnation, peer pressure or any other destructive thing, can be set free by Jesus! The truth will set you free." (John 8:32).

Jesus reigns mightily in His children. They are not wimps but strong, courageous and victorious.

Plow right through that situation or problem. Be encouraged. The Almighty is on your side. The enemy would love for you and I to think, talk, and walk in defeat, failure and misery. I have a secret to share: "The enemy is no match for our God."

When shadows try to dim my view, the Light of my Redeemer overtakes the darkness, illuminating my soul with joy. God is in control of my every circumstance. He gives His angels charge over me. A thousand may fall at my side and ten thousand at my right hand but it shall not come nigh me. Greater is He!

These earthly cares and trials are very short at best. For all our days let's sing His praise and God will do the rest.

Rise up boldly today with me and declare,

"I'M A WINNER!"

Dear wonderful God, thank You for being our strength as we walk with You victoriously.

May we stand undaunted in our faith and straining forward, press on toward the mark.

In Jesus' name above all names. Amen.

DECEMBER

December 1 Read Isaiah 12:1-5

A GIFT FOR ALL GENERATIONS: THE BIBLE

Bible Thought: "The grass withereth, the flower fadeth: but the word of our God shall stand for ever" (Isaiah 40:8).

I have inherited many Bibles from loved ones who have gone. My grandfather's Bible appears almost threadbare but I cherish those tattered pages. Memories return when I think of the guiding force of his life. Early dawn found him in his favorite chair with the "Good Book" opened on his lap.

"This Book of Wisdom has answers to life's problems," my grandfather used to say and he proved it by living a long blessed life of those principles.

God's Word has been a blueprint of life for all generations. This Book has inspired thousands of men and women down through the ages. In every walk of life countless numbers have turned to the Bible for strength, comfort and guidance.

This "Book" proclaims the dignity of the individual and teaches that we are created in the image of God. It displays promises of well being with standards to live by to find peace and happiness.

The Bible, a precious gift for all generations.

Read it and be blessed.

Dear precious Lord, thank You for Your Word. It is a" lamp unto our feet and a light unto our feet," a light unto our pathway. May we hide that "Light" it in our hearts forever. In Jesus' beautiful name. Amen.

December 2 Read Psalm 48:11-14

A FATHER'S LOVE FOR HIS CHILDREN

Bible Thought: "That which we have seen and heard declare we unto you, that ye also may have fellowship with us: and truly our fellowship is with the Father, and with his Son Jesus Christ" (I John 1:3).

Our middle son lives seven hours away so we don't get to see him as often as we would like. Yet every few days he phones us. We visit a long time. We love to hear our loved one's voice. Lance loves to hear our voices too. Finally he ends his calls with "Goodnight. I love you," and that brings special memories of his childhood to me. In my mind I see a little boy being tucked into bed with the same loving words.

If I find myself saying the same thing to my "Father." I think of all of God's children as being tucked into bed with love. If our children feel that much about us, how much more does God feel about us, yet God loves even more than we love our children.

Lance's loving words to us thrill us to our very core. Our loving words to God must surely do the same.

Like Lance, I want to visit a long time with my heavenly Father before I say, "Goodnight. I love you." I am His child. I will always be God's child.

Talk a long time with your Father tonight before you say, "Goodnight. I love you."

Dear Lord, You are so beautiful and we lift our hearts to You today. May our love overflow in returning love to You. Thank You for the greatest gift of love. In Jesus' wonderful name. Amen.

December 3 Read Psalm 127:1-5

A GODLY HERITAGE

Bible Thought: "And the LORD passed by before him, and proclaimed, The LORD, The LORD God, merciful and gracious, longsuffering, and abundant in goodness and truth" (Exodus 34:6).

One of my unforgettable childhood memories is that of my grandmother's elderberry bushes. They made tall white flowers with little balls of purple. From the window the aroma from those flowers lulled me to sleep on Granny's goose feather bed.

Granny took bouquets of her lovely elderberry blooms every Sunday to sit on the vestibule table at church.

Granny gave me a start of these memorable bushes and I have grown them ever since. Although Granny has been in her heavenly home for many years, I can still look out my window and see her bushes in full bloom. What a loving memory she left upon her granddaughter in flowers and in faith. Her perseverance in hard times and her great love for God has shaped my life.

The way we live our lives today will leave a monumental impression on our descendants. I want to leave a loving memory and a faith to live by. I will pass this great heritage on to my grandchildren.

I will give them a start of elderberry bushes and faith too.

Dear God, thank You for godly grandmothers who nurture their grandchildren in Your love. In Jesus' wonderful name. Amen.

December 4 Read Psalm 62

LIVE TO WIN THIS GAME OF LIFE

Bible Thought: These things have I spoken unto you, that my joy might remain in you, and *that* your joy might be full" (John 15:11).

Do you remember playing "Hide and Seek" as a child? The object of the game was to outmaneuver the opponent, to hide and touch base before being tagged. Then we could say. "Home Free!"

I am reminded of this game when I face difficulties as I run this race of life. It is at these times I must stand in faith regardless of what I see with natural eyes. I am not alone and my weakness is made strong in God's strength.

In life's battle, hope is still there. When felt alone, Jesus is still there. When the last breath ends, love is still there. God never abandons His children He makes a way where there is no way. Our responsibility is to trust Him and to give Him praise with all of our hearts.

When problems seem overwhelming I hide "under the shelter of His wings." This life isn't over until God says it's over. He is the hope, the refuge and the everlasting love.

Let's win this game of life. At life's end we will arrive saying "Home Free!"

I just love to win don't you?

Dear Lord, may we walk in victory each day of our lies because of Jesus. In His wonderful name. Amen.

December 5 Read 1 Corinthians13:11-13

ACT ON THE WORD TODAY

Bible Thought: "Jesus said unto him, Thou shall love the Lord thy God with all thy heart, and with all thy soul, and with all thy mind" (Matthew 22: 37).

The enemy's master plan is to destroy the human race. God has told us in His Word to resist the enemy. Resist is an active verb. It is ongoing. It is now…this very minute.

The Kingdom of God is unconditional love. Let's share God's love on this earth. God's Word is for the now of our lives…this very moment.

The gift of life is wasted by dwelling on the past and worrying about the future.

A friendly ninety-six years young lady was asked, "What was the best day of your life?" To which she relied, "Today. Right now. This very moment. It is the very best day of my life."

Laugh…live…love…and forgive!

Act on the Word today.

He us there in the sunshine. He is there in the rain.

He is there when I'm weary and in the midst of pain.

He is there in the trials when the shadows block my view.

He gives me daily blessings with a day that's always new.

He is there when clouds of sadness try to dim my life.

He is there to remind me to refrain from any strife.

He is there to provide for everything I need.

He is there to protect me and on His Word I feed.

He is there to receive me as I reach my end of days.

He is there throughout forever and I'll give Him all my praise.

Dear precious Lord, thank You for Your great love. In Jesus' beautiful name. Amen.

December 6 Read Psalm 98-102

WISE TEACHER

Bible Thought: "Give *instruction* to a wise *man* and he will be yet wiser: teach a just *man,* and he will increase in learning" (Proverbs 9:9).

Do you know there is an answer in the Bible to every problem you will ever have in life? Being a teacher today's Bible thought is especially dear to my heart. Children learn so much easier and faster in a joyful setting.

You don't have to be a teacher though to apply the today's scripture. We are all teachers in one way or the other. Whether we realize it or not our lives and actions are influencing every person we meet.

It is a sobering thought to know you and I have influence on others. What we do or say determines eternal destiny.

In this "school of life," we need to be "wise" teachers. Are we teaching holiness and godliness by the way we live? How does the "book" of our lives read? Do we show Jesus to others by conversation, actions and speech?

A wise teacher is one who points others to Jesus.

Be a wise teacher today. As you enter life's "classroom" make learning a joy for someone.

"On the last day of life what would you do?
Keep taking for granted those around you?
Or would you be thankful for a life filled with love
With untold blessings from God up above?"

Dear Lord, thank You for sending Jesus, the "Master Teacher." May the joy in knowing Jesus spread to others. In Jesus' wonderful name. Amen.

December 7 Read 1 Corinthians 15:55-58

AN EMPTY SHELL

Bible Thought: "For what man knoweth the things of a man, save the spirit of man which is in him? even so the things of God knoweth no man, but the Spirit of God" (1 Corinthian 2:11).

Have you ever found an empty insect shell? Just a large empty shell with nothing inside, a cover which a body used to live.

The apostle Paul tells us our bodies grow weak and old and embarrass us, but oh the inside. The spirit is the reality of man.

If we know Jesus, even though our outward "shell" grows older and eventually stops to rest, our spirit man is developing and growing. One day maturity will blossom. For the Christian our spirit man will never have to say goodbye.

Have you ever noticed a beautiful godly, older person? Their bodies are obviously wearing out. Their spirits are gorgeous, blooming and prospering, anxiously awaiting the Lord's return.

I once read of a man who became so excited about seeing Jesus he kept getting healed. The doctor said if he ever died he would have to keep it a secret.

One day our "shell" will be empty. Our spirits, the reality of our being, will return to the Lord. So shall we ever be with the Lord.

Hallelujah!

Dear precious Lord, thank You for the hope of eternal life. Thank You for Jesus who made it all possible. In His mighty name. Amen.

December 8 Read John 14:1-4

THE BEST IS YET TO BE

Bible Thought: "As thou hast given him power over all flesh, that he should give eternal life to as many as thou hast given him" (John 17:2).

Those who have gone on before us are alive in one form of life and we in another. When we cross over that barrier, it won't be into death. It will be into life made possible through the incredible love of Jesus.

Jesus is our Champion. His crucifixion for you and me demonstrates the depths of His love. I cannot fathom such love but my heart is filled with praise and thanksgiving. This man at Calvary was willing to be nailed to a cross for the sins of mankind.

We are simply travelers in a journey of life. Because of Jesus, we can be citizens of another world, a land where no one is ever sick and never dies. It is a world where peace and joy reign forever. Resurrection makes a new world possible. How joyful we shall be.

It is more than a historic event. It is demonstrated every day in the lives of hungry hearts. Receive that life today and resurrect from the deadness of just an ordinary existence.

We are on our way to glory.

The best is yet to be.

How beautiful heaven must be.

Dear Lord, how thankful we are to be Your children. Thank You for Jesus and our eternal home. In Jesus' precious name. Amen.

December 9 Read Isaiah 11:1-5

CLING TO THE ROOTS

Bible Thought: "That Christ may dwell in your hearts by faith; that ye, being rooted and grounded in love" (Ephesians 3:17).

We made a hill of sand in our front yard and planted a tree in it thinking it would look pretty in our landscape. Little did we know the roots would not sustain in a sandy high place. It grew taller but it toppled with the first windy storm and the roots went with it.

So it is with our lives. We must plant our faith in good soil. The roots of our faith will keep us strong in every situation. I tell myself daily, *I must cling and rely on Jesus.*

Daily we hear bad reports. It seems everything is negative. We must remind ourselves we are only travelers in this world. It is not our permanent home.

Today's thought is about trusting in Jesus. Reading and meditating in His Word makes our roots grow deeper. When difficulties arise we have a fortress as we "dwell in the secret place of the Most High."

Cling to His roots today and every day.

He will keep us strong!

"He is my lighthouse in a stormy sea.

He is my anchor in deep waters.

He is my light in a world of darkness.

He is my guide in a troubled wasteland.

He is welcome rain in the desert of my life.

He is sunshine in the garden of my heart.

He is "Living Water to my thirsty soul."

Dear Lord, send us down roots than can never be uprooted. In Jesus' name. Amen.

December 10 Read Nehemiah 12:27-30

BE THANKFUL

Bible Thought: "Enter into his gates with thanksgiving, *and* into his courts with praise: be thankful unto him *and* bless his name" (Psalm 100:4).

Have you ever helped someone and not receive a "thank you?" Taking something for granted is a thankless wound. Jesus healed ten lepers but only one returned to thank Him. (Luke 17:15).

Contrary to the world's belief system of, "He who has the most toys wins," only joy comes from knowing Jesus. "Godliness with contentment is great gain" (1 Timothy 6:6). Giving thanks changes attitudes and creates peaceful relationships.

A simple "thank you" makes everything better for the giver and for the recipient. An attitude of gratitude displays humility and appreciation. It's all about being thankful today and every day. That makes a happy person.

Our founding fathers realized the importance of thanking God for His many blessings. Being thankful in their day of uncertainty reminded them of God's providential care.

The apostle Paul wrote from a prison cell, "I give thanks to my Lord and Savior Jesus Christ."

Throughout history God never left His people. He will not leave us today, tomorrow or forever. That is a reason to be eternally thankful.

Dear precious Lord, our hearts are filled to running over for Your many blessings. We are ever mindful of Your infinite love and mercy. Blessed be Your name, now and forevermore. In Jesus' beautiful name. That name is above all names. Amen.

December 11 Read Proverbs 10:1-4

ARE YOU SPIRITUALLY BANKRUPT?

Bible Thought: "But lay up for yourselves treasures in heaven, where neither moth nor rust doth corrupt, and where thieves do not break through nor steal" (Matthew 6:20).

The world's financial system is composed of assets and liabilities. Wise investments and planning ensure a solvent business. Checks and balances are monitored closely.

When income going in is exceeded by income going out financial failure occurs and bankruptcy is declared. Unless there is intervention the business is closed.

This same principle applies to our spiritual lives. Our prayer life, Bible study, and church attendance are our greatest assets. Neglect in any of these areas increase liabilities. The void shows slowly at first, but surely. The backslidden condition mounts and spiritual "bankruptcy" ensues.

Yet the business does not have to be closed dear reader. We have someone to intervene in our spiritual "business." His name is Jesus. He can change those liabilities into assets. He has a wonderful bookkeeping system. He has an eternal "ledger."

If you don't know Him, give Him your life today. Arise a new creature. If you have become bankrupt, repent and renew your commitment to Him.

Jesus shed His blood for you.

The receipt reads "PAID IN FULL!"

Dear wonderful Lord, grant us the wisdom and knowledge to daily increase the reserves in our spiritual bank account. May we truly realize that our "treasures" are stored in heaven. Thank You for Jesus and in His name. Amen.

December 12 Read Exodus 15: 1-6

CELEBRATE JESUS

Bible Thought: "But I have trusted in thy mercy; my heart shall rejoice in thy salvation" (Psalm 13:5).

Our calendar year has many holidays and stores that display merchandise well in advance of the season. Yet there is something more special than any other. It's the celebration of Jesus, not just at Christmas or Easter but every day of the year.

What is more wonderful than having the joy, assurance and hope in our everyday living? We have been redeemed. We have been forgiven. It is truly joy unspeakable and full of glory. Jesus is with us every second of our lives.

It seems to me the world wants to celebrate everything else except Jesus. Thankfully, some turn to Him before it is too late. They find what they were looking for all of their lives. They become free from bondage and sin and have a life of joy and peace. Is that not cause for the most wonderful celebration of all?

So let's make every day a celebration of Jesus. Let's celebrate the One who gave His life for us. Let's celebrate the fact that we are going to live with Him forever because we have been redeemed from the enemy's snare.

An eternity would not be long enough to praise and thank the One who died for us.

Hallelujah!

Celebrate Jesus!

Dear precious Lord, we celebrate the risen Savior every day of the year. We praise and thank You for His sacrificial love. He is King of kings and Lord of lords. In His beautiful name. That name is Jesus Amen.

December 13 Read Mark 15:20

BE A WITNESS FOR JESUS

Bible Thought: "Then they that feared the LORD spake often one to another: and the LORD hearkened, and heard *it*, and a book of remembrance was written before him for them that feared the LORD, and that thought upon his name" (Malachi 3:16).

The floral shop radiated with beautiful Christmas decorations. The owner's gracious spirit added to the joyful spirit of the season. I found myself sharing the joy of Jesus' birth and it came so natural. We talked at length about what this world would be like if Jesus had not been born.

The next day I received a lovely poinsettia with a card that read: "Thank you for sharing Jesus."

I have found that people become receptive to the things of the Lord, once I initiate the concept. Taking advantage of the opportunity is so easy. Make it a habit to witness. It is a life changing thing to do. You may never know the impact of your witness upon a life for eternity.

Pray for boldness to witness. God will provide the opportunity.

I love today's "Bible Thought." Every time you talk about Jesus, the angels write it down in your Book of Remembrance.

"What can you do for Jesus today
Traveling down life's road?
Those weighted down with earthly cares
Need help to carry the load."

Dear Lord, grant us the boldness to witness for You today and every day. In Jesus' mighty name. Amen.

December 14 Read Psalm 27:4

HOPE OR HOPELESSNESS?

Bible Thought: "The hope of the righteous *shall be* gladness: but the expectation of the wicked shall perish" (Proverbs 10:28).

Without God, life is a hopeless end. With Him, it's an endless hope. Without hope for the future, there is no hope for the present. A life without hope is a life without living and a prisoner of worry. Hopelessness comes from emptiness, a void, a restlessness, a weariness from life. There is a need that cannot be met until Jesus is met.

I have wonderful news! Hope was born many years ago in a lonely stable and mankind has never been the same. He brought hope to the hopeless and meaning to the lives of insignificant existence.

Jesus is the risen Savior. He died on a rugged cross to give you a hope and a future. A personal daily relationship with Jesus is an abundant life here and an eternal one hereafter.

He is truly "Joy to the World." He turns sorrow into joy. He is endless "Light" for a sighing, dying, crying world of darkness.

Will you choose hope or hopelessness?

Choose hope!

"He will not leave or forsake me.

He is my Lord and Guide.

He keeps me in His loving care,

Because He is on my side."

Dear precious Lord, how we praise and thank You today for Jesus. In His name. Amen.

December 15 Read Matthew 1:21-25

RECEIVE GOD'S GIFT

Bible Thought: "For unto you is born this day in the city of David a Saviour, which is Christ the Lord" (Luke 2:11).

Imagine how Jesus must have felt knowing the suffering and the pain awaiting Him. Imagine how God felt knowing He would have to turn His back on His only Son. His Son had to die alone for you and me. Still Jesus came. His love is more the world will ever know.

Jesus is the Prince of Peace, Lamb of God, Bread of Life, Chief Cornerstone, High Priest, Bridegroom, King of king and Lord of lords.

Jesus came to earth in the form of a little baby wrapped in love as a gift for mankind. He walked this earth only thirty-three years but changed the world forever.

Long before we were born Jesus knew me and you. He placed us on this earth for a reason…a purpose.

Have you received your gift? It is straight to you from the heart of God.

Receive God's precious gift today. Ask Jesus to come in your heart.

Your life will never be the same.

Dear God, thank You for Jesus. In the depths of our being gratitude reigns. Without You we would be hopelessly lost with no purpose. May our every breath honor and glorify You. In the night watches we long for You. We awaken with songs of praise. Who is like unto You O Lord? The joy we feel spills and runs over. In the deepest part of us we belong to You. We are not our own. You will never leave nor forsake us. You are our beautiful bridegroom. In the wonderful name of Jesus. Amen.

December 16 Read Luke 2:75-80

LOVE LASTS FOREVER

Bible Thought: "For the mountains shall depart, and the hills be removed; but my kindness shall not depart from thee, neither shall the covenant of my peace be removed, saith the LORD that hath mercy on thee" (Isaiah 54:10).

Just imagine for a moment, if you can, that Jesus had never been born, or that King Herod had succeeded. The thought makes me shudder.

If Jesus had never been born the blessed hope is gone. Without Jesus, there is no respect for life nor is there regard for man's welfare. Yet God reached down to man.

Jesus had no earthly possessions. He brought love, healing, peace and hope. For that He was ridiculed, mocked, persecuted, scourged, beaten and killed.

The Babe of Bethlehem truly brought" Joy to the World." He forever changed the course of humanity bringing salvation for sin sick souls. No other single event in all of history has affected the world as this one man called "Jesus."

Years and years have come and gone but He still reigns. He lifts the hearts of the downtrodden and heals the brokenhearted.

Let His love fill you today. It is the only thing that lasts forever!

"On that Christmas morn so very long ago,
A Babe in Bethlehem was born that all the world might know
That we have been redeemed from mankind's ugly sin,
The blessed Christ Child's birth brings hope and we can win.
Such joy our hearts contain, His love, it cannot end.
Oh the joy and peace from that Babe of Bethlehem!"

Dear Lord, may every breath we take say, "thank You" for the priceless gift of Your Son. Let heaven and earth rejoice in His beautiful name. Amen.

December 17 Read 116:8-15

ONE DAY CLOSE TO HEAVEN

Bible Thought: "He shall enter into peace: they shall rest in their beds, *each one* walking *in* his uprightness (Isaiah 57:2).

I am standing by my window looking at the "winter wonderland." The ice storm has made the landscape breathtaking with sparkling dazzling beauty. However, the sun has begun to shine through the frosty clouds and the diamond rays are quickly melting. Soon I will see bare branches and beige grass as if the wondrous scene had never happened. Even though my yard looks dead I know beyond the season spring will arrive with new life.

When a loved one is laid to rest the pain is indescribable and one wonders if life will ever be the same. The memories are bittersweet, especially on Christmas or birthdays. Yet God in His wonderful grace and mercy gives strength and comfort. As a seed planted in the ground dies to give life so does our temporary vessels of clay. Because of the resurrection we will see loved ones again.

I shall never forget what a man said before he prayed over Communion. "This is the best day of my life…because I am one day closer to heaven."

If you have lost a loved one dear reader be comforted today, "And I heard a voice from heaven saying unto me, Write, Blessed *are* the dead which die in the LORD from henceforth: Yea, saith the Spirit, that they may rest from their labours; and their works do follow them" (Revelation 14:13).

Dear Lord, thank You for life's purpose. Thank You for everlasting life where we will be with You forever. In our Savior's name…that name above all. Amen.

December 18 Read Psalm 27:1-4

THE JOY OF SALVATION

Bible Thought: "Wait on the LORD: be of good, courage, and he shall strengthen thine heart: wait, I say, on the LORD" (Psalm 27:14).

The greatest miracle in this world is salvation. Oh, the joy and gladness the "Good News" brings. Jesus is coming back and we will live with Him throughout endless ages. It's the most wonderful news of all time. If we ask Jesus to come into our hearts and serve Him, obey Him and follow Him, we are on our way to glory! People, that is something to shout about. Shouldn't we be happy as kings?

Remember that first love when you asked Jesus into your heart? Remember the joy of it?

It reminds me of my wedding day waiting on the arm of my Dad to walk down the aisle. I wanted to be married to my tall dark handsome bridegroom. I remember the tremendous joy of that day. I wanted to be with my beloved for all of my life.

I want to be that way with Jesus. He is my spiritual bridegroom and He is coming back for me. I will see Him with joy and gladness. I am loved. I am forgiven.

I will rejoice.

I will sing and praise Him.

I will be thankful with joy of salvation!

Dear Lord, thank You for being our soon coming Bridegroom. May we always rejoice and give You eternal praises for our salvation. In Jesus" wonderful name. Amen.

December 19 Read Ecclesiastes 11:6-9

BE OF GOOD CHEER

Bible Thought: "These things I have spoken unto you, that in me ye might have peace. In the world ye shall have tribulation: but be of good cheer; I have overcome the world" (John 16:33).

Jesus is our peace in the midst of the storm. He is our anchor...our rock...our refuge. We have God's Word in us and we are full of faith. So let us boldly proclaim it. Let's not let fear dominate or intimidate.

Have you ever noticed the whole armor of God does not include protection for our backs? This means we do not retreat but boldly face our enemy with confidence in our Lord. We stand our ground in Christ Jesus who will never fail us. In Him we have everything. Now that is "Good News." That is reason to be of good cheer.

The apostle Paul still believed God in spite of his shipwreck. Your life may be close to shipwrecking but take heart today and be of good cheer anyway. Believe God. Believe that He is able.

Paul spoke with extreme confidence when he told his fellow travelers in Acts 27:25, "Wherefore sirs, be of good cheer: for I believe God, that it shall be even as it was told me."

We could say the same. We have a Savior who has redeemed us, saved us and is coming back for us.

Be of good cheer!

Dear precious Lord, thank You for Jesus and the wonderful good news. Amen.

December 20 Read John 3:15-19

HE LOVES ME ANYWAY

Bible Thought: "Fear thou not; for I *am* with thee; be not dismayed; for I *am* thy God: I will strengthen thee; yea, I will help thee; yea, I will uphold thee with the right hand of my righteousness"(Isaiah 41:10).

My God knows every hair on my head. He knows every breath I take. He knows my every step. He knows my faults, my sins, my weaknesses, and He loves me anyway.

My Lord knows the inner recesses of my being. He formed me and planned for me to be born on earth. He knew I might stumble and fall but He loves me anyway.

My God delights in me. He joys over me with singing. I am precious in His sight. I am unique. He made me special because He loves me like I am.

I don't have to be someone else. I don't have to keep up a false front. I don't have to try to be impressive. I'm just me because my God loves me just as I am.

My God will never leave me. He will never allow my feet to stumble. I soar with Him in heavenly places. I live in that secret place and dwell under the shadow of the Almighty.

My God is my refuge and my fortress. He gave His only Son to die for me when I was lost forever, when I was lost and stained with sin. His precious blood covers me and makes me whole.

My God loves you that way too!

Dear God, how can we ever thank You for Your love and blessings? May we praise You with every breath for Your unspeakable love and kindness. In Jesus' beautiful name. Amen.

December 21 Read Psalm 67:3-5

BLESSINGS SURROUND EVERY DAY

Bible Thought: "Blessed *is* every one that feareth the LORD; that walketh in his ways" (Psalm 128:1).

Walking in God's ways brings a multitude of blessings. It's the only way to live. "The fool hath said in his heart, *There is* no God…" (Psalm 53:1) He or she who doesn't believe has no hope in this life or in the life hereafter.

On the contrary, the Christian has a hope and that hope comes true. Jesus sacrificed His life for those who accept Him. I am so thankful for His love.

I love God's beauty in nature. New Mexico has sunrises and sunsets that are masterpieces from God's paintbrush.

I have friends and family who are glistening diamonds in my life. I let them know how much they mean to me.

I believe we are surrounded by blessings every single day. Let's celebrate life with a deeper appreciation of what Jesus did for us.

Be happy today.

It's a wonderful life.

I wouldn't have missed it for the world.

Dear precious Lord, thank You for Your love. It makes us happy and joyful to know that we are going to live with You forever. It's all because of Jesus…that beautiful name. Amen.

December 22 Read Psalm 18:46-50

LET'S BE HAPPY

Bible Thought: "But my God shall supply all your need according to his riches in glory by Christ Jesus" (Philippians 4:19).

I hear a lot of cynicism these days. "The country is going to the dogs." The future is bleak. Dark clouds are swirling. People get unhappy, miserable or angry. That makes me sad. Life can be wonderful. Yes, we all have calamites, adversities and rough times but we always have more blessings than problems.

I like to be happy and I have a lot to be happy for. In Christ Jesus, there is every reason to be joyful. Not anywhere in the Bible have I read about God abandoning His children. If that isn't cause for getting fired up with optimism I agree with a preacher I heard say, "Then your wood is wet!"

The world tries to drag us down. "Good News" of Jesus Christ cancels out the bad news we are daily bombarded with. What could be more positive or optimistic than God's Word?

Happiness is being grateful for being alive. Life is all around us. Let's count our many blessings and be content with what we have. Look in the mirror and say,

"God loves me!"

Dear Lord, thank You for Your steadfast love and Your mercies that never cease. We give You our hearts and every fiber of our being. In that wonderful name of Jesus. Amen.

December 23 Read Psalm 37:4-8

ENJOY THE PRESENCE OF THE LORD

Bible Thought: "Let us come before his presence with thanksgiving, and make a joyful noise unto him with psalms" (Psalm 95:2).

Don't you love to be in the presence of loved ones? There is such joy in sharing and enjoying the company.

Although our children are grown and gone, how we relish the times we get to visit with them. It's being together. It's love. It's family. We enjoy each other.

Enjoying God is like that too. Enjoying God is an attitude of gratitude. Enjoying God puts zest in living.

The God of this universe will never leave nor forsake us. His Son has given His sacrificial life. Now that will put a spring in your step and a song in your heart. God walks daily with us in every circumstance. It thrills our soul and gives us peace.

Take time to enjoy God today. Delight to be in His presence. You will be greatly rewarded. Your day will be better and you will have a song in the night.

Enjoy the Lord!

In The Stillness of the Night

I find Him waiting in my secret place.

He receives me with gladness.

I am precious in His sight. I hear His gentle voice.

"I will always be there…in the sunshine, in the rain."

in the storms and in the pain."

The breaking of dawn finds me in His embrace.

I hear Him whisper,

"I will never leave you."

Dear Lord, early we seek You and all through the day our thoughts turn to You. In Jesus wonderful name. Amen.

December 24 Read 1 Timothy 6:12-15

I WILL NOT QUIT!

Bible Thought: "Nay, in all these things we are more than conquerors through him that loved us" (Romans 8:37).

Some of us reach the weary point where giving up would be so easy. That's the coward's way out. It takes real faith and perseverance to stay in the race. The one who keeps the faith and finishes the race is the real winner. Quitters never win and winners never quit. Winners know who they are in Jesus.

The enemy tempted Jesus for forty days. He did not quit. We are not giving up either. We will not quit. We press on to the prize. We are stubborn in our faith. We stay in the fight because we are anchored to the Rock, our Savior. We will finish the race with determination.

Rise up today dear reader. Take the armor of God and go forth in His might. Praise the Lord on your way. Sing and be joyful. Keep a victorious attitude. "The mountains in my life I cast into the sea." I walk in victory.

Boldly declare with me, "I will not quit. I will not give up. Look out. Here I come! Here I come in the mighty name of Jesus. I have the God of glory with me. With Him on my side the enemy is helpless and doomed."

I WILL NOT QUIT!

Dear Lord, help us to realize with You on our side nothing is impossible to us. Thank You for our armor. We go forth today conquering every foe. In that mighty name of Jesus. Amen.

December 25 Read Luke 2:7-11

THE GREATEST GIFT

Bible Thought: "And she shall bring forth a son, and thou shall call his name JESUS: for he shall save his people from their sins" (Matthew 1:21).

The Bible doesn't give a specific date when Jesus was born, but at least with the season the world hears a message of hope.

No other single event has affected history as much as this man called Jesus. No other religion offers hope. None other brings peace like the "Prince of Peace."

Many people are wrapped up in pretty ribbons and shiny paper on the outside. Yet on the inside they are just empty boxes without Jesus. Without Him there is no purpose in life. There is only emptiness loneliness and despair.

Allow the star that led the wise men to the cradle lead you to the One who shines.

Jesus makes a pretty package, inside and out. He is the gift of love. He is the gift that keeps on giving.

Sharing His love is the greatest gift you can give this Christmas.

Each day is a treasure box of gifts from God,
Just waiting to be opened.
Open your gifts with excitement.
You will find forgiveness attached to ribbons of joy.
You will find love wrapped in sparkling gems.
Steadfastness, faithfulness and hope will be in your gifts.
Begin to rejoice.
Such an abundance of good things...
Enough to share with everyone you meet today!

Dear precious Lord, thank You for the greatest gift ever known to mankind. A Savior is born. His name is JESUS. In His beautiful name...JESUS. Amen.

December 26 Read 1 John: 5:1-4

LOVE HAS A LANGUAGE

Bible Thought: "And we have known and believed the love that God hath to us. God is love; and he that dwelleth in love dwelleth in God, and God in him" (1John 4:16).

I had many students who spoke in a language other than English. I only heard their native tongue when the parents came to visit. My students became excited showing their parents work they had done. The children always talked to them in their native "family language." While I couldn't understand the language, the love came through loud and clear. It was a language of love.

How special was Jesus' love for Mary, His earthly mother. Amidst severe anguish and excruciating pain Jesus looked down from the cross at His mother. Then in terrible pain told John to take care of His mother. Every time I think of that I can hardly keep back the tears.

On the cross Jesus also spoke to His Father and said, "Eli, Eli, la-ma sabach-th-n."

Jesus is the "language of love."

Talk to Him in your language today!

Dear precious Lord, thank You for Your great love. Thank You for Jesus, who understands love in any language. In His wonderful name. Amen.

December 27 Read Ruth 1:16-18

THE POWER OF FAMILY

Bible Thought: "Of whom the whole family in heaven and earth is named" (Ephesians 3:15).

Holidays are special times for my husband and me. I love the sights and sounds...the decorations, the aroma from the kitchen...the anticipation of family being reunited. It all warms my heart.

Our sons come home again with their families. They look at the white paint on the brick wall. They laugh now about the paint fight they had as children. (They weren't laughing then.) They measure grandchildren heights again to see the one who has grown the most.

It's family. It's love. It's about a mother and dad who love every one. It's the power of family.

God has a family. He cares about each and every one of us.

One day all the family members will be reunited. We will all be home. What a glad day that will be...and it will be forever.

"This life is just a vapor,
Chasing in the wind.
Its charm is quickly gone
When coming to life's end."

Dear precious Lord, thank You for family, love and home. Thank You for the greatest homecoming of all. In Jesus' wonderful name. Amen.

December 28 Read Colossians 3:13-15

MEMORIES

Bible Thought: "Blessed *are* they that do his commandments, that they may have right to the tree of life, and may enter through the gates into the city" (Revelation 22:14).

Life gives us treasured moments. Embrace those moments. Savor them. Cherish them. Tuck them away in your mental file.

Among my many cherished moments is one of our youngest son on his wedding day. He called my husband and me aside, held us in his big strong arms and said, "I want you to know what you mean to me. How can I thank you for giving me such a happy childhood, guiding me when I was a teenager, and being my best friends now. You will always be in a special place in my heart!"

The wonderful moment with our son crossing the threshold from boyhood to manhood was a moment I embraced to have forever.

Little children, neighbors and friends have lots of memories. The world is full of friendship. Take time to find them. Life is such a great adventure. Look for a memory today. Tell someone how much you admire them. Visit a rest home. Volunteer meals on wheels.

Memories will always be in your heart.

"Special moments come from God
A glimpse He does bestow.
He shows us little secrets
While we're on earth below."

Dear Lord, thank You for the gift of life! In Jesus' name. Amen.

December 29 Read Jeremiah 31:1-4

GOD'S GREAT LOVE

Bible Thought: "As the Father hath loved me, so have I loved you" continue ye in my love" (John 15:9).

I wonder if we can ever understand how great God's love is for each one of us. In Psalm 139:17-18 we are told, "How precious also are thy thoughts unto me, O God! how great is the sum of them! *If I should count them, they are more in number than the sand: when I awake, I am still with thee."*

God's thoughts are always on you and me. While we were yet sinners His love died for us. God longs for us. He yearns for us.

The prodigal son's father spent countless hours looking for his wayward son. This is a picture of God's attitude toward us when we walk away from Him.

God's love is gracious love. We cannot earn it yet His love is focused on us continually. Who would not want to be the recipient of His incredible love?

Invite Jesus to make His home in your heart. Repent of all sin. Live for Him all the days of your life. Keep Him in your thoughts today. Focus on Him. Tell Him of your love and thank Him too.

It's all about God's great love for you.

Dear precious Lord, we are overwhelmed today by Your great love for us. May we always send love back to You. May we awaken each morning saying, I love you Lord. What can I do for You today? In the name of Jesus. Amen.

December 30 Read Psalm 39:4-8

SQUEEZE LIFE WITH LOVE

Bible: "A merry heart doeth good *like* a medicine: but a broken spirit drieth the bones" (Proverbs 17:22).

Making the most of each day is what I call "squeezing life." Sunrise and sunsets are "squeezeable" times for me. Sunrise proclaims God's glory and He paints the sunsets with spectacular strokes of magnificence. Even the birds awaken with a zest for life. The glorious rays of dawn's light illuminates the horizon welcoming another day of God's wonder.

I squeeze life when my husband comes home and says, "What's cooking?" I squeeze life when a dear friend moves back to my town and I get to see her often. I believe friends are angels sent by God to remind us to squeeze and "hug life." I squeeze life when it rains. I squeeze when I hear mockingbirds. I think I squeeze everything because it makes me happy.

Live today. Love your loved ones. Seize the moment. It's a great day all the time.

"Life is delicious!" Please don't waste a single day of it. Squeeze it. Love it. Be grateful for it. Each day is a gift attached with ribbons of joy just waiting to be opened with gladness.

Squeeze life with love!

Dear precious Lord thank You for life that's all around us. May we join nature's chorus and sing our praises to You every day. In Jesus' beautiful name. Amen.

December 31 Read Psalm 150:1-6

A SERVANT'S PRAYER

Bible Thought: "Bless the LORD, O my soul: and all that is within me, *bless* his holy name" (Psalm 103:1).

"Help us to live just for today.
Yesterday is gone and tomorrow we cannot see.
May we be quick to express our love to others.
Guide us to find happiness in simple pleasures…
the soft sound of snow crunching underneath our feet,
the cooing of a dove, the welcome dripping of rain
against our window pane.
Help us to number our days. May we make each
moment count, for time is fleeting.
Grant us deeper truths of our heavenly kingdom.
When the midnight hour of our lives have ended,
May we have run the race with patience.
Having fought a good fight, may we greet the dawn of glory
with singing and thanksgiving to You, beholding
Your beauty…our King, our Redeemer
Our Savior, our Lord!
Amen."

Would you like to see your manuscript become a book?

If you are interested in becoming a PublishAmerica author, please submit your manuscript for possible publication to us at:

acquisitions@publishamerica.com

You may also mail in your manuscript to:

**PublishAmerica
PO Box 151
Frederick, MD 21705**

We also offer free graphics for Children's Picture Books!

---

www.publishamerica.com

CPSIA information can be obtained at www.ICGtesting.com
Printed in the USA
LVOW13s2310170813

348301LV00001B/5/P

9 781630 007881